100 American Independent Films

100 AMERICAN INDEPENDENT FILMS

2ND EDITION

BFI SCREEN GUIDES

Jason Wood

A BFI book published by Palgrave Macmillan

1st Edition published by the British Film Institute 2004
Reprinted 2005

2nd Edition published in 2009 by
PALGRAVE MACMILLAN

on behalf of the

BRITISH FILM INSTITUTE
21 Stephen Street, London W1T 1LN
www.bfi.org.uk

There's more to discover about film and television through the BFI. Our world-renowned archive, cinemas, festivals, films, publications and learning resources are here to inspire you.

Palgrave Macmillan in the UK is an imprint of Macmillan Publishers Limited, registered in England, company number 785998, of Houndmills, Basingstoke, Hampshire RG21 6XS. Palgrave Macmillan in the US is a division of St Martin's Press LLC, 175 Fifth Avenue, New York, NY 10010. Palgrave Macmillan is the global academic imprint of the above companies and has companies and representatives throughout the world. Palgrave® and Macmillan® are registered trademarks in the United States, the United Kingdom, Europe and other countries.

Series cover design: Paul Wright
Cover image: *Junebug* (Phil Morrison, 2005, © Junebug Movie LLC)
Series design: Ketchup/couch
Set by Cambrian Typesetters, Camberley, Surrey
Printed in China

This book is printed on paper suitable for recycling and made from fully managed and sustained forest sources. Logging, pulping and manufacturing processes are expected to conform to the environmental regulations of the country of origin.

British Library Cataloguing-in-Publication Data
A catalogue record for this book is available from the British Library

ISBN 978–1–84457–289–2 (pbk)
ISBN 978–1–84457–290–8 (hbk)

Contents

Acknowledgments

Numerous people generously assisted with the completion of both the first and second editions of *100 American Independent Films*. Those who I wish to thank for their help and inspiration include: Nigel Algar, Geoff Andrew, Eileen Anipare, Nicky Beaumont, Clare Binns, Sophia Contento, Douglas Cummins, Andi Engel (in memoriam), Jane Giles, Daniel Graham, Philippa Hudson, Steve Jenkins, Michael Jones Leake, Asif Kapadia, Andrew Lockett (the editor of the first edition), Ben Luxford, D. A. Pennebaker, Salvatore Raimato, B. Ruby Rich, Howard A. Rodman, Jonathan Romney, Dave Shear and Gavin Whitfield.

My special thanks are extended to Scott McGehee, David Siegel and Tom Kalin for their extremely generous and spirited involvement and support. I'd particularly like to thank my editor Rebecca Barden, not only for commissioning this volume but for her valuable insights and general good humour.

Preface to the 2009 Edition

'The sky is falling! The sky is falling!' So said Chicken Little. And maybe that damn chicken was right; maybe it wasn't just an acorn after all. In a bracingly grim keynote address in Los Angeles this June, film executive Mark Gill agreed with the proverbial bird. He cited massive staff cuts and shutdowns at New Line, Picture House and other companies, the evaporation of 'hedge fund' Wall Street money, a marketplace glutted with films and the diminishing returns of independent distribution. And that was just the prologue, before the curtains pulled back to reveal act one of global recession.

In this atmosphere of gloom and uncertainty – brightened by the fall of George W. Bush and the rise of Barack Obama – it's easy to lose perspective. Since I can't even tell you exactly what we mean by 'independent film' anymore, I'll leave it to others to predict how changes in technology, financing, distribution and audience taste will impact on what we make and watch in years to come. But I do know this: if you ask most film-makers, they'll tell you their careers have been defined by a series of 'sky-is-falling' moments. When you're drawn to the nail-biting high-wire act peculiar to low-budget film, you learn to court happy accidents (which are really just disasters in disguise or what my producer Katie Roumel calls a 'shit storm'). Long before the crisis in 'Indiewood' (yipes! what a word), iconoclasts as diverse as Sam Fuller, John Cassavetes, John Waters or Charles Burnett found ways to beg, borrow or steal the shots their stories demanded. Recent directors including Kelly Reichardt, Ramin Bahrani and Eric Mendelsohn have made astonishing, original movies on shoestring budgets. A smart approach: put your money where your mouth is.

Like many of the film-makers you'll read about in this book, my unsentimental education began at home (in my case, suburban Chicago). Born youngest of eleven in a middle-class Catholic family, I learned from my family everything I would later need to know about the art of navigating difficult personalities, improvising within chaos, or the strategies of pleading, silent coercion and nimble debate required to get things done. Like a latter-day low-rent Mitford family across the pond, we're a tribe of autodidacts rich with strong characters and complex intrigues (tenant organiser, corporate executive, Transcendental Meditation teacher, 'born-again' Christians, medical professionals, college professors, troubled loners – you name it, we got it).

My interest in crime springs from family roots too: my father had a long career in social work and criminal justice. (Just beneath lurks the dramatic irony: he studied at seminary and nearly became a priest. After he married my mother, he rarely went back to church.) He was the director of a reformatory school called the Saint Charles School for Boys and worked for the National Council on Crime and Delinquency. He spent the end of his career at the State of Illinois Parole Department, which includes Stateville Penitentiary where Leopold and Loeb were imprisoned. Since my parents were children in the early 1920s, the 'Crime of the Century' depicted in *Swoon* loomed large as family folklore. My mother and I went out to Stateville on several occasions to visit a prison pen pal we met through a Catholic charity. It took years for me to really appreciate my relatively unique teenage life.

I discovered the fast-paced, hard-boiled world of Warner Bros. on late-night television and developed an abiding affection for genre movies and actors like James Cagney (Irish Catholic American antihero) and Barbara Stanwyck, world-weary but wise. Later I'd put this love of genre to good use and discovered the potential to fly below the radar within these deceptively familiar forms. Like a number of my contemporaries (including Todd Haynes, Mary Harron, Gregg Araki or Christopher Münch), I've been drawn to material such as the 'biopic', the crime story or the domestic melodrama. I'm inspired by the reinvention and subversion of these genres by trailblazers such as Joseph Lewis, Nicholas Ray, Douglas Sirk, Max Ophüls, Robert Bresson, Jean-Luc Godard, Rainer Werner Fassbinder and Arthur Penn.

When I moved to New York City from Chicago during the blazing hot summer of 1987, I only knew one person who had died from AIDS. Leslie Harvell. It wasn't easy growing up in 1950s America as a black gay boy named Leslie, but his disarming, sly humour paved the way. He got sick and died with cruel and breathtaking speed. Shortly after, I came to attend the Whitney Museum's post-graduate studio art programme. Thinking I would be here for a year, I packed light. (A good thing too, since for the next five years my bedrooms never measured more than eight by twelve feet, barely large enough for a bed. This city quickly redefines public and private space.) I was in blind unconscious flight from Leslie's death. Now, in retrospect, it's easy to see irony and humour in the fact that I escaped AIDS by moving to the world's epicentre.

Within months I found my way into a meeting of ACT UP (the AIDS Coalition to Unleash Power) held in a crowded room at the Gay and Lesbian Community Center, where I first met Todd Haynes and Christine Vachon. It's nearly impossible now to conjure the urgency, possibility and electricity in that room. Through Todd, Christine and others, I discovered the legendary Collective for Living Cinema, Anthology Film Archives and Millennium: mainstays of the downtown film world. I came too late for the fertile scene at the Mudd Club and watched from afar the first features of Lizzie Borden, Spike Lee or Jim Jarmusch. In the 1980s, most of my friends made short films – not 'calling card' auditions for future studio careers but rather shorts as a destination, a vital form to be explored. One of my watershed moments was seeing the low-fi masterpiece *Superstar: The Karen Carpenter Story* (1987). Who else but Todd Haynes could make emaciated Barbie dolls so utterly heart-rending? A handmade cinematic tour de force (it's emotional tone both 'in quotes' and stirringly, not), *Superstar* unspools a riveting story while heightening our awareness of storytelling itself.

Through ACT UP, I met Mark Simpson, another close friend who later died of AIDS. (More layers of connection: we were both members of Gran Fury, an artist/activist collective that included Todd Haynes, Marlene McCarty and Donald Moffett – Don and Marlene designed *Swoon*'s distinctive titles.) Mark and I became room-mates in a decrepit tenant-owned building rescued from collapse in the 1970s. The East Village was another planet then; homeless people camped in Tompkins Square Park in a sprawling shanty town. On my way to work, I used to watch a man shave himself in front of a broken mirror nailed to a tree. (The confusion, again, of public and private space.) Junky squatters lived in the building behind us. They stayed up late nodding by candlelight, and in the morning climbed down the fire escape carrying business suits, on their way, presumably, to respectable jobs. I always wondered where they showered.

In 1988, the police descended on a group protesting recent curfew rules in Tompkins Square and began to drive the homeless people from the park. They attacked with nightsticks and chased us up the trees. Video footage shot by demonstrators showed cops with concealed badge numbers swinging clubs. This early moment of local media activism – which became overnight national news through the release of the amateur video footage – provided another spark to the collective imagination. Despite limited means, the whole world was watching.

New York in the 1980s has been mythologised aplenty, given a romantic gloss in the hit play *Rent*. Well, it *was* a romantic time – but an awful one too, full of exhilaration and despair. But too much nostalgia leads you down a blind alley. The world of film production a mere twenty years ago now looks like a dusty curiosity shop crammed with Steenbecks, Moviolas and enormous optical printers, with a white cotton-gloved negative-cutter hunched over a bench in the corner. Yes, the tools continue to evolve but a story well told will always quicken the pulse.

When I made *Swoon*, I barely understood continuity or the 180-degree rule; much of my 'bold camera placement' came from art-school ignorance. When cinematographer Ellen Kuras and I watched the first screening at Sundance, the print practically still wet from the lab, we were horrified to see the harsh, grainy blow-up from 16mm. Three days later, Ellen won the first of her three Best Cinematography awards at the festival. What did we know? Like any business, after some years you learn about spin and damage control – instead of forgetting to shoot coverage, you intended a long take; can't show an expensive prop so you 'activate off-screen space' with the framing.

Savage Grace gave me another chance to explore the tension between documentary fact and dramatic truth. It also completely shifted my perception of what it means to be an American independent film-maker. We shot entirely on location in and around Barcelona, and I quickly learned that the standard shooting day in Spain is shorter than I was used to and that six-day weeks are rare. I also learned some new things about moving fast while looking good from my superb Spanish crew. Nearly everyone spoke a mixture of Spanish and Catalan and put me to shame with their fluent English. Though I eventually picked up some slang and learned to fumble around with my meagre vocabulary, I could never follow the intricate dance of language on set. This linguistic bubble was both crippling and useful – it encouraged a heightened awareness.

One particular shoot day included three scenes set at two different locations: Brooks and Blanca's rustic villa in Mallorca and Tony and Jake's hash-infused Cadaqués lair. Finding something that worked for both proved difficult. We finally settled on a remote house in the mountains and the art department went to work transforming the interior – walls covered with hippy drawings, the room resplendent in velvet and fur. Two days before shooting, they returned to find every scrap of set dressing scattered by the dirt road in front of the house. After some prodding, the owners tersely informed us that they sensed the hand of Satan. So we lost that location on suspicion of witchcraft. Scurrying to fix the crisis, we found and re-dressed an even better replacement.

Sometimes what film-makers need creatively is *more* chaos, not less, to fly without a net. In the words of the great Robert Bresson, 'My movie is born first in my head, dies on paper; is resuscitated by the living persons and real objects I use, which are killed on film but, placed in a certain order and projected on to a screen, come to life again like flowers in water.'

Tom Kalin, New York, 2009

From short experimental videos to feature-length narrative films, Tom Kalin's critically acclaimed work has been screened throughout the world. His debut feature, *Swoon*, was awarded Best Cinematography at Sundance, the Caligari Prize at Berlin, the Open Palm at the Gotham Awards and the FIPRESCI Prize in Stockholm. His work is in the permanent collection of the Centre Georges Pompidou and MoMA. His recent film, *Savage Grace*, premiered at the 2007 Quinzaine des Realisateurs in Cannes. As a producer, his films include *I Shot Andy Warhol* and *Go Fish*. He has been a faculty member of Columbia University's Film Program since 1996.

Preface to the 2004 Edition

Scott McGehee and David Siegel

For the record, we only agreed to write this preface thinking we would have some sway over the content of the book itself, and might be able to insist on the inclusion of *Billy Jack*, which was.for both of us a first and formative experience with American indie film-making. But as it turns out, we've had no impact whatsoever on the author's choices, and you will find that *Billy Jack* is not, in fact, included, and as far as we know, isn't even mentioned within these pages except right here. That being said, there are 100 other films listed, all of them somehow American and apparently 'independent' in some meaning of the word.

It's an interesting phenomenon that even the lowliest of social groups (in this case 'independent film-makers') manages to figure out a way to instil some sense of snob exclusivity to their meagre social or cultural identity. How often have we been with our fellow independent film-makers and their few remaining friends (if you can really call them that) and been party to conversations about whether or why a particular film or film-maker is not actually 'independent', as if having no money, respect or financial prospects to carry on making films were somehow a highly prized social privilege or badge of honour.

Because the American independent film movement is a more or less ad-hoc affair, lacking a charismatic leader or a Vow of Independence (or any kind of vow, for that matter) to give it shape or discipline, one finds that there tend to be almost as many opinions about what qualifies a film as 'independent' as there have been entries to the Sundance Film Festival recently. Luckily, over the years, we've culled our own list of ten or so indisputable ground rules that we thought might be helpful to the reader in the context of this list of 100 films:

- Rule no. 1: No one in the entire film industry ever helped the independent film-maker make his or her film. In fact, every gainfully employed industry person the film-maker ever spoke to about the film said it was a lame, derivative, unintelligible – or at least a financially unviable – idea.
- Rule no. 2: If someone in the film industry did help somehow, the help was not substantial or financial, and/or the 'brave' film industry helper was in danger of losing his or her job by providing help. (Since everyone in the film industry seems always in danger of losing his or her job, this rule can often be brought into play.)
- Rule no. 3: The film was made for no money. The meagre goods and services involved in production were stolen or borrowed or bartered, or charged on credit cards that were already past their limit.
- Rule no. 4: If there was money involved, it wasn't nearly enough, and most importantly, it was less than lots of other films that claim to be independent that aren't as good. If the film in question had a budget larger than the budget of one's own independent film, however, the film in question is especially questionable.
- Rule no. 5: No film industry money was involved. Any real money came from investment by non-film industry dentists, or from something called a 'German Tax Fund' that (it will one day be proven) is actually a code name for non-film industry German dentists, and is wholly unreliable. If film industry money was involved, it was from an 'independent' company, such as Fine Line or Miramax or Fox Searchlight, which are by unspoken agreement somehow considered 'independent' from AOL Time Warner or Disney or the Fox News Corp despite considerable evidence to the contrary.
- Rule no. 6: The film was poorly distributed, if at all. If it found success it was against common wisdom, and by luck, fluke and

happenstance, or because the film-maker personally telephoned everyone who ever attended.

- Rule no. 7: The film as an enterprise was pure financial folly. Even though it was made for no money, it miraculously stands to lose more money than it would have been made for had it been made for money. Occasionally certain distributors might profit from an American independent film due to shady accounting practices, but under no circumstances can the dentists or German dentists profit, and certainly not the film-makers.

- Rule no. 8: The film has no proper stars. If it does have stars, they have somehow fallen out of favour due to evidence of low morals, or worse, the poor box-office performance of a recent film. They worked for no money and wore no make-up except what they put on themselves.

- Rule no. 9: The film has no special effects. If it does have effects, they are not special.

- Rule no. 10: No animals were harmed in the making of the film.

We believe *Billy Jack* qualifies under this or any other reasonable set of criteria, and why it is not included here is a question to be put to the author of the book. Indeed, lots of films qualify that aren't here. (Our last film, in fact.) No doubt the author has some slap-dash criteria of his own. As Billy Jack's girlfriend Jean said in explaining the founding principle of the Freedom School, 'Each man has the right to follow his own centre, follow his own conscience, do his own thing …'.

Which brings us to one final rule, which we call the 'Independent Spirit' rule:

- Rule no. 11: In the spirit of independence, the above rules should be ignored when it is found helpful to ignore them. If a film is good, no matter how it was produced and financed, it can be found to have an 'independent spirit' that distinguishes it from its studio-developed brethren. (And of course, if a film is bad, its relative dependence or independence will rarely be an issue.)

A writer friend of ours describes studio development as the process whereby a script that could only possibly have been written by one person is transformed into a script that could possibly have been written by anyone. We suspect that one reason we tend to like independent films is that they have usually been spared this process (for better or worse), and it shows. (They've usually been spared all sorts of other really useful things that studio films have loads of, but enough complaining.) Or perhaps the entrepreneurial spirit that is a necessary component of the independent film-maker's character does, mysteriously, have some sort of aesthetic analogue that leads to some fresh, surprising, worthwhile and entertaining movies. Or perhaps it's a simple matter of probabilities, that given enough struggling American film-makers, enough typewriters and cameras, and not quite enough film, sooner or later there will inevitably be movies made to fill a book called *100 American Independent Films*.

Strip yourself of your greed and ego trips and let the spirit enter you.

Billy Jack

Scott McGehee and David Siegel are the writer-producers-directors of *Suture*, 1994 (Official Selection at the Cannes Film Festival and Jury Prize at the Toronto Film Festival), and *The Deep End*, 2001 (selected for Director's Fortnight at the Cannes Film Festival). Both films won the Best Cinematography prize at the Sundance Film Festival. *Bee Season*, McGehee's and Siegel's third collaboration, was released in 2005. The pair recently completed *Uncertainty*, the story of a young couple whose decision to flip a coin at the film's opening sets in motion two wildly different stories that unfold simultaneously.

Introduction

So what is an American independent film? What is meant by this elusive, contradictory and complex term, independent film-making? Jim Hillier, in his introduction to *American Independent Cinema: A Sight and Sound Reader* (2001), suggests that it has always meant something different from the mainstream, be that the economic mainstream (production and distribution) or 'in aesthetic or stylistic terms' (p. ix). I have followed these basic criteria in the selection that follows. Films are selected according to this twofold understanding – economic and aesthetic. Of course, as with any selection process, personal preference cannot be entirely discounted and this may ultimately be the reason why some films you would expect to see in a volume of this nature are here, while others quite simply are not.

As many of the entries and the film-makers focused upon here show, economic independence and aesthetic independence can, but need not necessarily be, mutually exclusive. As a term, 'independence' is open to multiple reinterpretations. In Chris Rodley and Paul Joyce's excellent documentary *Made in the USA* (1994), Hal Hartley, who claims to take his inspiration from small businesses, declares that he has 'never understood what people mean by independent. I know what they mean by low budget.' It is worth remembering, too, that Hollywood was initially formed by independent figures who migrated west during the 1908–13 period in response to the formation of the Motion Picture Patents Company, the first attempt at a monopoly in US cinema. Similar circumstances precipitated the forming of United Artists in 1919 by Charlie Chaplin, Mary Pickford, Douglas Fairbanks and D. W. Griffith. Independent cinema could be said to be a series of 'moments' that change according to the perspective of the beholder.

In the illuminating preface that opened the first edition of this book (and which has been retained in this second edition because a) many of its points remain relevant and b) it's very entertaining), Scott McGehee and David Siegel, whose *Suture* (1993) is represented in these pages, lament the omission of Tom Laughlin's *Billy Jack* (1971). This has been rectified, with McGehee and Siegel themselves undertaking the task of providing the entry to a film they clearly feel a close personal affinity with. Other readers will no doubt raise an eyebrow when ruminating on other absences and may question why figures such as Roger Corman, Ed Wood, Christine Vachon, Nick Wechsler, Edward Lachman, Oscar Micheaux, Ira Deutchman, Frederick Elmes and Jeff Lipsky to name but a handful are only given passing mention. Selecting 100 films – the 'hot 100' as one colleague originally termed it – was and remains an intimidating task, largely because it both seems to tantalisingly suggest the comprehensive nature of this project while actually undermining that comprehensiveness; choices had to be made at the expense of countless others. Therefore, the selections provide an overview of the leading films and film-making figures (concentrating on directors and actors opposed to, say, producers and cinematographers) while also attempting to reflect some of the historical developments encapsulated under the broad umbrella of American independent film. A truly comprehensive analysis of American independent cinema is beyond the scope of this introduction. There is here no mention of the politically inspired Leftist film-making of the 1930s or the numerous works that evolved during the anti-communist, post-war period in Hollywood. Similarly, Russ Meyer aside, the consideration of pornography, its vast profitability versus its low production cost and basic aesthetic values has also been left unexplored. Suffice to say that there are distinct parallels with the way in which a film such as *Deep Throat* (1972) penetrated the mainstream and the various 'indie' titles that were economically successful enough to encourage the studios to form alliances with independent figures. Mainstream Hollywood always reacts to success in the same way: it attempts to exert ownership. And I should add that while the intention of this selection was to suggest the broad sweep of American independent cinema, the primary aim was to be contemporary, and so most of the films here date from the mid-1980s onwards.

For practical purposes, it was decided that all the inclusions should be of feature length – at 56 minutes Michael Almereyda's *Another Girl, Another Planet* (1992) just sneaked under the wire. Hence the unfortunate but largely unavoidable deflecting of focus from those figures working within the American avant-garde and underground cinema of the 40s, 50s and 60s. Figures such as Maya Deren, Kenneth Anger, Jack Smith and Stan Brakhage irrefutably exerted a major influence on the American independent sector. And this influence can be viewed not only in terms of how these film-makers funded their projects (through arts organisations and public-funding bodies or out of their own pockets), but also in how they established a network of venues where such work could be enjoyed. Of equal import, the work of these directors expressed a desire to explore new approaches to the language of film, opening up the medium to new ways of communicating meaning by deviating from dominant cinema's reliance upon narrative, character and genre. The influence of these film-makers is traced through the inclusion of works such as Shirley Clarke's *Portrait of Jason* (1967) and Andy Warhol's *Lonesome Cowboys* (1968), and later pictures, including David Lynch's *Eraserhead* (1976) and Jem Cohen's *Chain* (2004). Any readers interested in further analysis of the bleeding between the avant-garde, conceptual art and cinema are directed to Aaron Rose and Joshua Leonard's documentary *Beautiful Losers* (2008).

A film like Anger's *Fireworks* (1947) audaciously highlights issues of gender, expressing a sensibility and viewpoint previously denied by mainstream cinema. In doing so, it and films like it were instrumental in laying the groundwork for the subsequent New Queer Cinema cycle of films that emerged during the 90s. A similar movement occurred with the gradual emergence of films from African-American film-makers. When surveying what American independent cinema has contributed to film worldwide, the 'transformed representations of ethnic minorities –

particularly African-Americans (but also Hispanics and Chinese Americans) – and of gays and lesbians' (ibid., p. ix) register as prominent. So by extension, therefore, the term independent has also been taken to embrace those films and film-makers whose work expresses a sensibility that contrasts with prevailing political, sexual and racial ideologies.

Take for instance Spike Lee. Few directors have done more to foreground issues of race. John Pierson, himself a major figure as a rep for American indie product from the early 80s onwards, cites Lee's *She's Gotta Have It* (1986) as a pivotal moment in both contemporary American independent and African-American cinema. In my original introduction, I cited Lee as a contradictory figure in terms of his 'independent' status, but now I am less sure. Much like Steven Soderbergh, Lee frequently alternates between personal, lower-budget fare (his *When the Levees Broke: A Requiem in Four Acts*, 2006, is one of the benchmarks of contemporary documentary and a damning indictment of the Bush administration) and more visible studio assignments such as *The Inside Man* (2006), his first bona-fide box-office hit. Lee and Soderbergh personify the 'one for them and one for us' breed of contemporary directors who seem suited to both studio and non-studio environments. True, there is the danger in that by blurring the boundaries the 'one' becomes indistinguishable from the 'other' but arguably both Soderbergh and Lee are able to imbue even cursory assignments, recent entries to the *Ocean's Eleven* franchise excepted, with some authorial flare.

Whichever side of the Spike Lee fence you sit on, it is difficult to argue that he has not provided an authentic expression and celluloid representation of African-American hopes, aspirations and desires. Lee's style is fresh, inventive and cine-literate, showing the influence of the French New Wave, Italian neo-realism and the New German Cinema of the 70s and, in his later films, echoes of Martin Scorsese (e.g. *The 25th Hour*, 2003). Though Lee has retained relative autonomy over his work through his 40 Acres and a Mule production outfit and fought to retain final cut, his post-1986 output has been financed, produced and distributed by studio companies. Courted by the majors after *She's Gotta Have It* had caused a sizeable critical splash and alerted studio executives to an income sector more or less ignored since the blaxploitation heyday, Lee has made no apologies for his desire to work regularly with the major resources a studio can provide.

Other African-American directors such as Julie Dash and Charles Burnett consciously resisted assimilation into the mainstream, fearing that their methods and their message would be diluted. This refusal to assimilate is typical of numerous other directors who consciously choose to operate outside of the Hollywood system. Jon Jost, for example, has continued to plough his own resolutely independent furrow, frequently expressing his criticism of the system and an independent sector he sees as increasingly susceptible to its overtures. Jost's militancy has drawn admiration and censure in equal measure. Gregg Araki appropriated both Jost's low-budget mindset and his raw and highly individual aesthetic, but others within the industry, Pierson among them, have dismissed Jost as a 'politically cranky, experimental film-maker' (Pierson, 1996, p. 235), turning out films on minuscule budgets that very few people ever actually see. Jost may be able to claim freedom of expression and economic autonomy, but at what cost?

Lee was one of six directors in the first edition of *100 American Independent Films* to have more than one entry. One of the others was John Cassavetes. Regarded as the pioneering forefather of American independent cinema, Cassavetes' *Shadows* (1959) is very much a benchmark work. The reasons for this film's mighty reputation and importance relate both to economics (it was arduously self-funded and promoted) and aesthetics (an experimental European-influenced 'learn as we shoot' policy). Cassavetes, who was to set up his own distribution company, had a radical effect on alternative approaches to production, exhibition and distribution in the US. Subsequently courted, seduced and then, as Pierson puts it, 'screwed' (ibid., p. 8) by the studios on *Too Late Blues* (1961) and *A Child Is Waiting* (1962), Cassavetes thereafter severed all involvement with the system, save for acting in studio projects as a means of raising finance for his own uncompromised productions. John Sayles (as a writer for hire and sometime actor), Steven Soderbergh and Steve Buscemi are just three recent figures who have used studio and other acting fees as collateral for more personal ventures in the same way. Cassavetes himself retained rights to the negatives of his work and was able to exert control over subsequent exploitation, exercising a rare privilege that only Jim Jarmusch and a handful of others have also enjoyed. For Cassavetes, paradoxically, this sometimes hindered audience accessibility to his films in subsequent years, but his methods and spirit continue to provide inspiration to a legion of American independent film-makers.

One of the first directors to openly acknowledge the liberating power of Cassavetes' autonomy was Martin Scorsese, one of the new breed of directors accorded creative liberty in the auteur-friendly studio climate of the late 60s and early 70s initiated by Arthur Penn's *Bonnie and Clyde* (1967). This period brought to prominence other cult favourite directors, including Bob Rafelson, Francis Ford Coppola, Robert Altman, Peter Bogdanovich and Sam Peckinpah. Altman, the leader of the so-called 'sons of Hollywood', remained a maverick dignitary; abandoned by the studios with the advent of event movies and saturation releases, he adapted by turning to independent financing and television. In an industry founded on creativity and frequently in need of fresh ideas, Altman remained perceptive on the subject of the awkward relationship between Hollywood and independent film-making. 'The biggest assets the studios have are the independents that are fighting them' (Rodley, 1994).

The period led to the forming of classics divisions within the studios, establishing a continuing parasitical and symbiotic marriage of convenience. On an aesthetic level, this provision for innovative work within the confines of the mainstream remains very much in evidence today. One need only look at the work of Steven Soderbergh and other figures like Wes Anderson, Paul Thomas Anderson (whose digressive, multi-character dramas owe much to Altman), David O. Russell and David

Fincher, all of whom enjoy studio subsidisation allied with a degree of creative freedom. The notion of independence continues to be something of an oxymoron: how can films and film-makers be considered to stand apart from the system when they have been so comprehensively integrated by it? Many of the pioneers of independent cinema of the last twenty years are now very much part of the Hollywood establishment. Tom Bernard, the co-president of Sony Pictures Classics, has been quoted as saying that 'The "independent" should be taken out of "independent cinema"; commerce and capitalism have pretty much taken over' (Winter, 2006, p. 26). The recent economic climate has led to a process of consolidation in Hollywood, with production being been scaled down and the activities of specialist divisions frozen or closed. What this means for American independent cinema will be discussed later (and the outlook may be sunnier than you think) but first let me flag up three titles and dates that have become synonymous with American independent cinema as we know it today.

Former Fine Line president Ira Deutchman and director Whit Stillman are just two figures who have argued that modern (i.e. post Cassavetes) American independent cinema began with John Sayles' *Return of the Secaucus Seven* (1979). This film was one of the first independent features to announce, as part of its marketing campaign, that it was entirely self-financed and made on a very low budget. Completed for $125,000 and subsequently sold by Sayles to Specialty Films (with Libra handling sub-distribution), the $60,000 needed to cover the direct production costs came from Sayles himself. Interestingly, he saw the film as an audition piece. 'I wanted to direct, and the only way you get to direct in Hollywood is to have a film to show' (Rosen with Hamilton, 1990, p. 182). Released in October 1980, the film immediately benefited from the contrast with the studio calamity that was Michael Cimino's *Heaven's Gate*. Its co-distributors were able to instil in an American press already sympathetic to the film's fine script, naturalistic performances and political insight an acute awareness of its meagre budget in comparison to Cimino's $44 million monster. With Sayles personally attending screenings across the country (a tactic he maintains today, even arranging for a band to appear to play the music from his latest feature, *Honeydripper*, 2007), the film also demonstrated that a grass-roots approach to promotion and outreach could work, with *Return of the Secaucus Seven* going on to achieve an impressive estimated box-office gross of $2 million.

Citing 1984 as heralding what he terms 'the first golden age', John Pierson places Jarmusch's minimalist *Stranger Than Paradise* as modern American independent cinema's point of origin. Detailing the film's bargain-basement budget of $110,000 and its own organic and original aesthetic – 'identifiably European and quintessentially American at the same time' (Pierson, 1996, p. 25) – Pierson makes the case that the film represents a new departure identifiably distinct from earlier US indie fare such as Susan Seidelman's *Smithereens* (1982), in that it managed to be 'both brilliant and attainable' (ibid., p. 27). Moreover, *Stranger Than Paradise*, with its subsequently much-imitated deadpan performances, introverted characters, sparse, ironic dialogue and static camera (which reduced the cost of filming and fascinated an impressionable Kevin Smith), grabbed attention on a truly international scale, with Jarmusch becoming the first American to win the Cannes Camera d'Or for Best First Feature. The film was then acquired by the Samuel Goldwyn Company, proving a commercial success both domestically and in key foreign markets including France and Japan. *Stranger Than Paradise* acted as a reminder to the industry that the lower the budget, the higher the potential profit margin. Other notable films released during Pierson's golden period included Sayles' *The Brother from Another Planet* (distributed by Cinecom, 1984), the Coen brothers' *Blood Simple* (Circle Releasing, 1983) and Alan Rudolph's *Choose Me* (Island/Alive, 1984).

Nineteen eighty-nine was another year when 'it all changed' (ibid., p. 126), with the release of Soderbergh's *sex, lies and videotape*, which had a truly global impact. Soderbergh's debut – completed at the age of just twenty-six – encourages parallels with Hopper's *Easy Rider* (1969), in terms of sheer impact, and similarly precipitated the studios to rush to associate themselves with young directors whose work, though formally audacious and apt to appeal to the counterculture, could be modestly acquired and then advantageously marketed. A $1.2 million production that offered an intelligent and adult delineation of sexual impotence, infidelity and relationship trauma in an age made weary of promiscuous coupling by the devastation of AIDS, *sex, lies and videotape* slipped relatively unnoticed into the Sundance Film Festival and thereafter indelibly altered – for better and for worse – the festival's profile for ever.

Sundance was founded in 1981 as a response to the Reaganite administration's hostility towards the arts, and was dedicated to the support and development of emerging screenwriters and directors of vision. Though the festival had assumed increasing importance among the independent sector and carried critical kudos, it did not figure highly on the itinerary of studio executives until a series of feverishly received screenings of Soderbergh's film. In anticipation, major film industry figures from the East and West coasts descended upon Park City, Utah. They have returned ever since, causing many insiders to suggest that Sundance has become a rather large and picturesque shop window for Hollywood. Though undeniably true, and in recent years the festival has been derisively tagged 'Indiewood' (a term that equally applies to films and film-makers dining at the studio table), it would be unfair to deny the positive role Sundance has played in bringing to wider attention the work of American directors such as David Gordon Green, Karyn Kusama, Alexander Payne, Darren Aronofsky, Mary Harron and Jonathan Dayton and Valerie Faris.

sex, lies and videotape was also the film to put the fledgling, independent outfit Miramax on the map, a company once regarded as the corporate Goliath of American independent/arthouse production and distribution. Disney subsequently acquired Miramax (a deal that quickly soured and saw the departure of Bob and Harvey Weinstein to form the Weinstein company), just as the once independent New Line, whose Fine Line boutique division fostered kitsch auteur John Waters, was subsequently gobbled up by Time Warner. Bob and Harvey Weinstein's bold approach to positioning *sex, lies and videotape* began in Cannes with Harvey's insistence that the film should appear in the main competition. The cajoling paid off, with Soderbergh becoming the youngest ever winner of the Palme d'Or. On awarding a somewhat bemused Soderbergh his prize (the director commented sardonically, 'I guess it's all downhill from here', and for many years for Soderbergh it was), jury president Wim Wenders pronounced him the future of cinema. The prize could equally have gone to Spike Lee's *Do the Right Thing* – Lee was furious that it didn't – and Wenders could still have made the same remark. Arguably, neither Soderbergh nor Lee became the future of cinema (observers like to appoint a new prophet every few years or so, just ask Jonathan Caouette) but they have continued to work both within and outside the Hollywood system and consistently produced interesting and also frequently commercial pictures.

After launching the film and Soderbergh internationally, Miramax adopted an equally audacious approach in the US where they eschewed the niche, limited-release pattern traditionally associated with independent titles and instead put out the film widely on multiple prints. Both in the US and the UK, a multiple-release platform is now the norm, with titles earmarked as having crossover potential opening in both arthouse and multiplex cinemas on anything up to 150 prints. The advent of digital has made this pattern even more sustainable, with the expense of a wider release diminished through access to digital copies as opposed to costly 35mm.

The 'sex' aspect of the title undoubtedly helped and became a part of the indie 'package'. Likewise, the violent aspect of American indie pictures would be foregrounded after the success of Quentin Tarantino's *Reservoir Dogs* two years later. Miramax's gamble again brought dividends, with Soderbergh's debut eventually going on to achieve a seismic worldwide gross of over $100 million. This success was accountable for establishing an unrealistic financial benchmark for an American independent film and presented many emerging film-makers with a daunting objective. The ratio of budget to box office remained a focus of attention. Both film-makers and distributors would often actively stress the meagre means for which their project was made, with both *El Mariachi* (1992) and *Clerks* (1993) making much of their respective and approximate $7,000 and $27,000 completion costs.

With hindsight, there is much validity in Hillier's suggestion that *sex, lies and videotape* represents the total assimilation of American independent cinema. This feeling intensifies when surveying a number of releases over the past ten or so years that replicate this pattern of assimilation. *Girlfight* (1999), a gritty, medium-budget picture that tackles both ethnicity and feminism through the domain of the boxing movie, was produced and distributed by Sony Classics, a division of Sony Pictures. *Boys Don't Cry* (1999), Kimberly Peirce's compelling account of the life and murder of Brandon Teena, a young woman who for most of her adult life passed as male, was produced and distributed by Fox Searchlight. In fact, of all the boutique divisions of major studio companies, Fox Searchlight have been the most active in the production and distribution of 'independent' pictures, releasing *Little Miss Sunshine* (2006), *Juno* (2007) and *Waitress* (2007), the final film from the tragically murdered Adrienne Shelly. Paramount Vantage has also produced a steady stream of notable titles, bringing us *I'm Not There* (2007), *Into the Wild* (2007) and *No Country for Old Men* (2008).

Immediately post-*sex, lies and videotape*, figures including Hal Hartley, Richard Linklater and Michael Almereyda, all directors who have subsequently embraced advances in digital production as a means of reducing budgets and all directors operating at the more esoteric, less commercial end of the independent spectrum, had projects backed and released by the specialist divisions of studio companies. After winning a Special Jury Prize at Sundance, David Gordon Green decided that he didn't want his growing-pains love story *All the Real Girls* (2003) playing only to arthouse audiences and entrusted Sony Pictures Classics with the task of broadening the demographic. Green, a man of genuine integrity who seems torn by the compromises necessary to reach a wider audience while continuing to work by his own organic methods, recently directed the genial stoner comedy *Pineapple Express* (2008), written by Evan Goldberg and Seth Rogen. *There Will Be Blood*, one of the standout pictures of 2008, and also one of the most formally and thematically rigorous, was undeniably the work of an auteur with a singular and independent vision. In economic terms, however, Paul Thomas Anderson's bracing adaptation of Upton Sinclair's novel was produced by Paramount Vantage and Miramax and released worldwide by Buena Vista. To remind us of the factors by which we consider a film independent, a quote from John Sloss, executive producer of films by Linklater, Todd Haynes, Peter Hedges and Errol Morris, seems pertinent here:

> I define independent film as the product of a singular vision. I'm in the financing business, and financing can come from a million different places. To define it by financing is completely irrelevant. To me, independent films are not the product of a committee but the product of a person. We're talking about auteurism; otherwise it's a slippery slope. (Winter, 2006, p. 26)

If you look closely enough, you are likely to find some studio involvement, either through production or distribution, in the majority of titles that may commonly be considered as independent. There is still, of course, a handful of marginal directors such as Bruce LaBruce who continue to avoid both aesthetic and economic dependency on Hollywood and maintain a relatively prolific output. Maintaining a higher visibility, Gus Van Sant could be considered another example. A film-maker of genuine vision and integrity, he tried his fortune within the studio system, before for whatever reason, returning to his low-budget, independent roots, utilising European financing as he set out to become the closest thing America has to Bela Tarr. Presented by Focus Features, Van Sant's *Milk* (2008), a humanistic and moving portrait of Harvey Milk, the first openly gay man to be voted into American public office, is obviously a far cry from *Gerry* (2002) and *Paranoid Park* (2007) in terms of production costs, but it absolutely retains the same spirit.

Each year also sees a number of breakout titles that bypass the studios entirely and become critical and commercial successes almost of their own volition. A perfect example is *In Search of a Midnight Kiss* (2007), which was released in the US by IFC, alongside ThinkFilm, one of the most reputable and successful independent American distributors. Somewhat ironically, the film only came about after its director moved to LA and grew tired of waiting for his phone to ring bearing the offer of lucrative assignments. The truly independent status of films such as Alex Holdridge's charming tale of a fledgling relationship was for a prolonged period very much the exception rather than the norm, but at the time of writing, the aforementioned recession is really beginning to bite. Paramount Vantage has had its production slate slashed from twelve to six movies per year. Time Warner seems to have dispensed with Warner Independent entirely. By necessity, film-makers and independent producers have to be canny when it comes to securing financing for their movies, and with the studio well seemingly running dry, or at least access to it restricted, explore new avenues and funding possibilities. We may be about to witness a new era of financial independence in American independent cinema.

As well as Europe and organisations such as the Independent Film Channel providing much needed financial sustenance, digital-video enterprises like Independent Digital Entertainment (InDigEnt) have assumed increasing prominence. Digital became both a means to an end and an important aesthetic in its own right. It is important, however, to note that shooting a film on digital video is not the liberating medium that many first thought. Admittedly much cheaper to shoot and edit, and privy to regular advances in both editing software and camera technology, a film shot on digital video will still cost a not inconsiderable $60,000 to generate a print. However, the installation of digital projection facilities in many cinemas may soon eradicate this cost, or at least significantly reduce it. Digital technology has also arguably led to proliferation and by extension saturation. In 2008, Sundance received in excess of 3,000 submissions, from which only 125 features could be selected. Of the 125, fifty-five were American fiction films. That leaves an awful lot of films that will perhaps never be seen.

The advent of digital cinema has also redefined how films are actually seen and consumed by an audience. In a climate where films struggle to secure distribution, both due to market saturation and economic recession, this marks a move back to the self-distribution methods practised by John Cassavetes and others. With many cinemas now increasingly equipped for digital projection, it may not be too long before a film-maker will be able to deal directly with the cinema operator about showing his or her movie. In this way, the middleman distributor, studio or otherwise, is effectively removed. Moreover, in this manner, windows (the traditional period after which a film can appear on a home movie format after its theatrical run) are also being shattered with the increasing exploration of simultaneous format releases. Leading the way was Steven Soderbergh, whose *Bubble* (2005), a semi-improvised love triangle that otherwise attracted little interest, being one of the first films in the US to appear in cinemas, on DVD and on the digital cable channel HDNet Movies. There has been a proliferation of this practice, both in the US and the UK, though the results have so far been limited and inconclusive. However, the day is surely not too far away when films bypass cinemas altogether and are downloaded to home computer screens, iPlayers and mobile phones. The landscape for American independent cinema, and indeed cinema in general, is rapidly changing and in a current atmosphere where far too many films of genuine originality (but limited commercial appeal) fail to secure any kind of significant release after impressing at festivals, this can be no bad thing. We may need to adjust our viewing habits and how and even where we view a film, but if we are able to make this transition, then there is no reason why the American independent film should not enjoy a healthy, sustained and vital future.

This relatively sunny outlook is of course partly reliant on the continued commitment to the cause from more established figures such as David Lynch, whose *Inland Empire* (2006) led Michael Atkinson to describe Lynch as being representative of a select group of film-makers for whom 'independence is a principle still worthy of sacrifice' (Atkinson, 2007, p. 22). It is also dependent upon the continued emergence of new and interesting voices in what we now recognise as the broad spectrum of American independent film-making. One of the purposes of this second edition of *100 American Independent Films* was to look at some of these voices, and any particular 'movements' and reactions to funding and technology they may represent. I would argue that Kelly Reichardt, Ramin Bahrani, Andrew Bujalski (who I have taken to be representative of the 'mumblecore' trend) and Phil Morrison all provide evidence of this positive forecast. Lance Hammer's *Ballast*, Azazel Jacobs' *Momma's Man* and Courtney Hunt's *Frozen River* (which all emerged at the end of 2008 and so too late to have anything more than a ghostly presence here) further contribute to the notion that there may be good times ahead.

This second edition features twenty-five new entries, a brand new preface from Tom Kalin and has undergone a general overhaul. As well as including new titles, I also decided to make a number of historical additions, adding films that for various reasons have come to assume historical, cultural or even personal significance, or which it has been pointed out to me have in some way impacted on American independent cinema. Perhaps the clearest example of this is *On the Bowery* (1957), a key text for John Cassavetes and a film that has become increasingly significant in an era in which film-makers such as Lynn Hershman-Leeson are blurring the boundaries between fiction and documentary.

To maintain a balance between variety and importance, the first edition had a two films per one director rule and resultantly Spike Lee, John Sayles, John Cassavetes, Jim Jarmusch and Hal Hartley (a personal favourite) were afforded multiple titles while contemporaries such as Todd Haynes and Richard Linklater had to console themselves with just one. In order to include new films and figures, a certain amount of culling has been necessary, and so as well as extricating certain titles that have perhaps stood the test of time less well or that were included because of a close personal affinity I can no longer defend, I have decided to include just one film per director. This is not to detract from the achievements of any one figure but hopefully to broaden the scope of this book and bring it up to date. Thus, this new edition no longer includes essays on *Do the Right Thing* (1989), *Matewan* (1987), *Down by Law* (1986), *Schizopolis* (1996), *The Killing of a Chinese Bookie* (1975) and *Simple Men* (1992). Where pertinent, the films by these directors that are retained have been significantly updated.

Angel City
US, 1977 – 70 mins
Jon Jost

Jean-Luc Godard has claimed that Jon Jost 'is not a traitor to the movies, like almost all American directors. He makes them move' (quoted in Pym, 1977, p. 4). As Godard suggests, Jost is indeed one of the most truly independent and politicised of American film-makers. Existing at the very outer edges of radical, no-budget film-making and operating at 'the interface of the politics of form and the politics of production' (ibid.), Jost's work offers a sustained critique of the illusionist, capitalist nature of Hollywood feature films and the economic forces they serve. That said, the polemic (like Godard's) is one of a true cineaste's and wrestles with all the traits of popular genre film-making styles and structures in the process.

Directed, written, produced, photographed and edited by Jost on a budget of $6,000, *Angel City* adopts the framework conventions of the thriller genre as it tracks down-at-heel private detective Frank Goya (Glaudini) as he attempts to solve the murder of aspiring LA actress Gloria Franklin (Golden). Goya has been hired by Franklin's husband Pierce Del Rue (Del Rue), a respected businessman and president of the powerful Rexon Corporation. Goya's investigations reveal that after Franklin's first movie, *Death on the Installment Plan*, failed, Del Rue had his wife murdered, fearing that she would prove an obstruction to his own financial interests in the industry.

Self-consciously signposting the motifs and prescribed characteristics of the genre (e.g. Goya's direct-to-audience narration that later gives way to lectures on the redistribution of wealth), Jost alerts the spectator to *Angel City*'s artificiality and by extension to that of fictional film in general. Moreover, the glamour of Hollywood is deconstructed with an aerial shot of the mythical Los Angeles, accompanied by prolonged voiceover statistics about the city. The film reveals the raw materials of cinema through various reflexive, structuralist devices – it is organised into sections '12' to '1' – and through clumsily executed camera movements and optical effects. Most notable is a sequence in which Goya reassembles the screen in the form of a jigsaw puzzle and another in which he escapes from the clutches of Del Rue while exiting the film frame. Jost's technical imperfections are themselves intrinsic parts of *Angel City*'s ideological make-up, serving to further puncture the seductive, flawless surface of the commercial feature with its seamless illusion of reality.

Jost connects crime with capitalism, a subject, along with the dominance of multinational corporations, that is especially close to his heart. Shot like a commercial, a sequence shows Del Rue strolling along a beach extolling the virtues of Rexon and the social benefits of large companies. The image is followed with an animated logo of a dinosaur embracing a globe featuring the words 'One world'.

Angel City is a visionary, highly original work that marries the Brechtian distanciation of *Alphaville* (1965) with the political commitment of *Vent D'est* (1970). Jost himself expanded on the artist analogy of the central character by describing his film as having the subtlety of Vermeer in contrast to Hollywood films, which have the fleshy magnitude of Rubens. However, Jost's standing in the hierarchy of American independent film-makers has been diminished by the limited distribution of his films and by his own criticisms of an independent sector that he increasingly views as duplicating Hollywood's financial and economic imperatives.

Dir: Jon Jost; **Prod**: Jon Jost; **Scr**: Jon Jost; **DOP**: Jon Jost; **Editor**: Jon Jost; **Score**: Uncredited; **Main Cast**: Robert Glaudini, Winifred Golden, Pierce Del Rue, Kathleen Kramer.

Another Girl, Another Planet
US, 1992 – 56 mins
Michael Almereyda

A partly autobiographical love letter to Almereyda's native East Village, *Another Girl, Another Planet* takes its title from the seminal single by punk outfit the Only Ones. It may weigh in at just 56 minutes, but as a follow-up to the writer-director's engagingly spaced-out *Twister* (1990), this film packs a heavyweight artistic punch through its formal daring and endearingly romantic pessimism, as well as its effective, idiosyncratic use of a discontinued camera produced for children.

The simple, admittedly slight but nonetheless deftly crafted story concerns the relationship between two East Village apartment block neighbours: Nic (Nic Ratner, Almereyda's real-life neighbour playing

Another Girl, Another Planet: director Michael Almereyda's love letter to the East Village filmed on the Fisher-Price PXL 2000, a discontinued toy camera produced for children

himself), anxious and married, and bohemian Bill (Sherman), whose life appears to be a constant stream of rich encounters with strange, beguiling and capricious females. The film examines the reluctance of each man to surrender to the expectations and responsibilities of adulthood, and also observes (via male eyes) a kind of feminine pursuit of answers to the unanswerable. *Another Girl* was produced by Hartley associate Bob Gosse (an alumni of Hartley's 1984 graduation film *Kid*), and among the excellently cast ensemble lie further connections with the Long Island-born director, with *Another Girl* introducing the audience to the iconic talents of the Romanian actress Elina Löwensohn, later to be seen in *Simple Men* (1992) and *Amateur* (1994).

Influenced by the experimental, highly personal shorts of Sadie Benning, Almereyda and cinematographer Jim Denault (later to work on Hartley's similarly mesmerising and technically audacious digital exercise *The Book of Life*, 1998) imbue the monochrome material with an ethereal, otherworldly quality that manages to be extremely seductive while seemingly resembling the inside of somebody's head. The grainy, hazy, soft-focus look of the film is due to the use of the Fisher-Price PXL 2000, a high-speed instrument whose format came to be called 'Pixel vision'. Originally retailing at $45, and benefiting from the wonders of digital video production, the PXL 2000 proved to be a wholly viable economic alternative to 16mm and 35mm for a select number of low-budget/independent directors.

Almereyda was one of the relatively few independent directors at the time attempting to break new ground in terms of exploring how technology can shape an overriding visual aesthetic. He was to continue to experiment with the Pixel vision format, most notably on his subsequent picture, *Nadja* (1994), executive produced by David Lynch and Mary Sweeney.

Dir: Michael Almereyda; **Prod**: Michael Almereyda; **Scr**: Michael Almereyda; **DOP**: Jim Denault; **Editor**: David Leonard; **Score**: Uncredited; **Main Cast**: Nic Ratner, Barry Sherman, Elina Löwensohn, Mary Ward.

Bad Lieutenant
US, 1992 – 96 mins
Abel Ferrara

Ferrara made his bona-fide feature debut with the ultra low-budget 'video-nasty' *Driller Killer* (1979), following various amateur productions, excursions into Super-8 and even a pornographic movie. Ferrara has consistently dealt with themes of religion, salvation and redemption and a consideration of abject existential confusion in a morally bankrupt universe. Flawed, repellent and self-destructive characters provide the focus of this examination. Ferrara's provocative and erratic output is also marked by its unsettling visceral extremity. It comes as little surprise to also hear Ferrara pay homage to Godard, Pasolini and Fassbinder, the similarly 'serious' pre-eminent directors of post-war European art cinema. Today the prodigious director is reckoned to be, on the one hand, the most impassioned and 'driven American film-maker in American cinema' (Smith, 2001a, p. 182) and, on the other, a film-maker of 'little artistic merit' (Andrew, 1998, p. 6).

Bad Lieutenant marked a return to a more determinedly realist mode following the glossier *King of New York* (1990), and is an especially profane and sustained howl of anguish from the depths of despair. Perhaps the director's most powerfully realised work, it's certainly his bleakest. Set amid New York's violent, multicultural, urban squalor, the film features a shockingly raw and courageous performance from Keitel as the self-destructive NYPD bad Lieutenant of the title. The Lieutenant is addicted to a diet of drugs and alcohol, and his escalating gambling debts are a source of constant frustration, which he vents by sexually haranguing female members of the public. While investigating the rape and torture of a local nun, the Lieutenant is proffered redemption after seeing a vision of Christ.

Reflecting Ferrara's origins as an underground film-maker, *Bad Lieutenant* is almost entirely shorn of artifice. The credits are crude and the use of music is minimal. It offers few concessions to the conventions of mainstream cinema. At times the film resembles a particularly disturbing documentary, with Ferrara adopting a frills-free vérité approach to the self-consciously raw material; hand-held camera and jagged, abrasive editing dominate. The film is resolutely amoral in tone, to the extent that it frustratingly denies narrative closure and any restoration of moral order by allowing the rapists to go unpunished for their crimes.

Described by Martin Scorsese as being all he had hoped *The Last Temptation of Christ* (1988) would be, *Bad Lieutenant* offers Ferrara's most earnest consideration of the potentially redemptive powers of Catholicism, beneath the film's apparent blasphemy. This aspect is particularly evident in the scenes in which an increasingly wretched and contrite Lieutenant weepingly remonstrates with God for forgiveness. But on-screen depravity and moments of shuddering intensity (Keitel's masturbating while mouthing obscenities after questioning two female motorists is especially unrestrained) ensured that the film received a rocky reception upon release and radically polarised critics. It also managed to attract the scrutiny of the British Board of Film Classification, which eventually passed it uncut for theatrical exhibition. The film was penned by the director in collaboration with Zoe Lund, the star of Ferrara's rape revenge satire *Ms.45/Angel of Vengeance* (1980).

Dir: Abel Ferrara; **Prod**: Edward R. Pressman; **Scr**: Zoe Lund, Abel Ferrara; **DOP**: Ken Kelsch; **Editor**: Anthony Redman; **Score**: Joe Delia; **Main Cast**: Harvey Keitel, Victor Argo, Anthony Ruggiero, Robin Burrows.

Badlands
US, 1973 – 94 mins
Terrence Malick

Arguably the most lyrical and artistic directors of the auteur-friendly US cinema of the 70s, Malick's exquisite self-written and produced debut was compared by David Thomson with *Citizen Kane* (1941) in terms of its originality and enduring influence. Ostensibly a rural lovers-on-the-run gangster film in the tradition of Ray's *They Live by Night* (1948), the independently made *Badlands* is distinguished by the oblique approach Malick takes to his familiar material. This is perhaps most evident in the enigmatic attitude towards the psychological motivations of its characters, a pair of murderous juveniles in search of release from the banality of their existence in the American Midwest of the late 50s.

Loosely based on the true story of nineteen-year-old Charles Starkweather who murdered the family of his thirteen-year-old lover Caril Ann Fugate before embarking with her on a killing spree through Nebraska and Wyoming, *Badlands* relocates events to Fort Dupre, South Dakota. Garbage-man and James Dean lookalike Kit (Sheen) begins courting Holly (Spacek), a fifteen-year-old immersed in trashy, celebrity-fixated magazines. Holly's father (Oates) forbids the relationship and kills his daughter's dog as punishment when she disobeys him. As Holly impassively stands by, Kit shoots her father dead. Pursued by the law, the couple rob and kill their way across the Dakota badlands, but Holly's affections for Kit wither and she turns herself in. Kit, however, is seduced by the celebrity status the media bestows upon him and is arrested only after stopping to build a monument to himself during a high-speed chase. Having played no part in the killings, Holly receives a lengthy prison term; Kit is sentenced to execution.

Presenting the narrative elements from contrasting perspectives, Malick offers an at times mysterious and yet eloquent dissection of disaffection and the role the media plays in offering unsustainable alternatives to the commonplace. Self-obsessive and self-mythologising,

Kit regards himself as a heroic non-conformist whose good looks and affability will mark him out as worthy of remembrance. This conviction blinds him to the gravity of his actions (and indeed to Holly's growing disinterest in him) but is in effect fulfilled by the esteem in which his pursuers hold him. Contrastingly, the film is narrated in the dispassionate, listless voice of Holly whose description of mundane events is nonetheless littered with vocabulary from the romantic magazines in which she is constantly immersed. The disparity is furthered by the sensory perfection of the film and Malick's evocative combining of Carl Orff's ethereal music and Tak Fujimoto's painterly cinematography. Organically merging psychological and physical landscapes, *Badlands* has a mythic, iconic quality that recurs throughout Malick's hermitic career, as does the director's interest in man's capacity for destruction and the interaction of the characters, from whom we are purposefully distanced, with the natural world around them.

Acquired by Warner Bros. following its reception at the 1973 New York Film Festival, *Badlands* marked the emergence of a skilled perfectionist with little regard for the dictates of commercial film-making. The film is regularly cited as an inspiration by successive generations of American directors too numerous to mention, with David Gordon Green's *George Washington* (2000) being among the most notable recent works to bear Malick's indelible mark. In 2004, Malick would act as producer on Green's *Undertow*.

Dir: Terrence Malick; **Prod**: Terrence Malick; **Scr**: Terrence Malick; **DOP**: Tak Fujimoto; **Editor**: Robert Estrin; **Score**: Carl Orff; **Main Cast**: Martin Sheen, Sissy Spacek, Warren Oates, Ramon Bieri.

Being John Malkovich
US, 1999 – 113 mins
Spike Jonze

Being John Malkovich marked one of the most daring, entertaining and eccentric debuts in recent American cinema. The film was fashioned from a surreal, wildly imaginative script by Charlie Kaufman and directed with brio by pop-promo alchemist Spike Jonze. And it was produced by Michael Stipe's production company Single Cell Pictures. Though the project was enthusiastically greeted by Hollywood executives, it had been rejected as being impossible to bring to the screen.

Malkovich is about Craig Schwartz (Cusack), an out-of-work puppeteer who under duress from his animal-obsessed wife Lotte (an unrecognisably dowdy Diaz) takes a lowly filing job with LesterCorp, the occupiers of floor seven-and-a-half of a Manhattan office block. There he discovers a portal that leads directly into the head of John Malkovich. Entering the portal, Schwartz spends fifteen minutes within the star before being ejected on to the New Jersey Turnpike. In cahoots with voracious colleague Maxine (Keener playing against type as a cruel, scathing vamp), Schwartz begins charging people $200 to enjoy the experience. Unfortunately, the scam opens, as he neatly describes it, 'a metaphysical can of worms' when Lotte enters and falls in love with Maxine, who has since begun dating the actor. Craig uses his puppeteering skills to permanently enter Malkovich, who it transpires is the latest in a line of conduits used by a secret society to enjoy eternal life in new bodies. So far, so simple …

With a nod to Warhol's famous-for-fifteen-minutes maxim, this part-screwball, part-crackpot conspiracy theory comedy is an incisive parable about the cult of celebrity and the hollowness of fame. In one of its most amusing running gags, Malkovich is forever mistakenly associated for his turn as a jewel thief, a part he has never played. The film also takes great delight in monkeying around with notions of identity (Craig peddles his scheme with the pitch: 'Have you ever wanted to be someone else?'), offering an effective meditation on crises of sexuality and gender that even allows for a positive lesbian ending.

Given Jonze's MTV background and the material's whacky premise, the director largely adopts a surprisingly sober, low-key, almost naturalistic approach. Employing subtle lighting and a downbeat orchestral score from regular Coen composer Carter Burwell, Jonze impressively navigates the various shifts in tone, incorporating the more bravado, fantastical diversionary moments with quiet confidence. Such moments include a flashback sequence from the perspective of a recently captured chimp and an immaculately conceived 'training' film as dire as only training films can be.

John Malkovich acts as the film's foundation and proves to be an extremely game target for the far-from-gentle ribbing, offering a self-obsessed and repellent caricature of his perceived, narcissistic persona. The film was variously compared to works by Borges, Buñuel and Svankmajer. Though distributed by a major studio (Universal), it is included here by virtue of its independent spirit and irreverent sensibility.

Dir: Spike Jonze; **Prod**: Michael Stipe, Sandy Stern, Steve Golin, Vincent Landay; **Scr**: Charlie Kaufman; **DOP**: Lance Accord; **Editor**: Eric Zumbrunnen; **Score**: Carter Burwell; **Main Cast**: John Cusack, Cameron Diaz, Catherine Keener, John Malkovich.

Billy Jack
US, 1971 – 114 mins
Tom Laughlin

Writer-producer-director-actor Tom Laughlin says he wrote the script for *Billy Jack* in 1954 (aged twenty-three). At that point, he was just starting a career as an actor. In 1956, he will show up as 'regular guy' Ralph in Vincent Minnelli's male melodrama *Tea and Sympathy*. A year after that, he has the lead in Robert Altman's low-budget debut, *The Delinquents*. But it will take him sixteen years to get *Billy Jack* into production, because, as he says, 'No one was interested in making a picture about an Indian, half-breed or otherwise.' It's almost impossible to imagine what that 1954 version of *Billy Jack* might have looked like; the version Laughlin finally brought to the screen in 1971 couldn't be more indelibly imprinted with the character of its conflicted time.

After a magnificent title sequence of ranch hands driving wild mustangs across an Arizona high-desert landscape, *Billy Jack*'s real story begins as free-loving teen runaway Barbara (Webb) is delivered back into the unloving arms of her father, the small town's small-minded deputy sheriff. The beating he gives her sends her off again, this time into hiding at a local alternative shelter for wayward youth called the Freedom School. Set up on a pre-Casino-era Indian reservation by 100 per cent denim-clad Jean Roberts (winningly embodied by non-actress Delores Taylor, Laughlin's real-life wife and the film's producer), the Freedom School is a place with only three rules: 'No drugs, everyone has to carry his own load, and everyone has to get turned on by creating something.' In Barbara's case, that something is loads of trouble, as her father and his cronies come looking for her, only to find an unruly hoard of multi-ethnic, anti-authority folk-song-singing hippy youth.

The title character, a jeep-driving gunslinging hapkido-fighting half-breed Vietnam vet played by the director (with an irresistible stoic charm), first appeared on screen in Laughlin's *The Born Losers* (1967), but it wasn't until *Billy Jack* that he became legend. A resident of the Freedom

School's host Indian reservation, he is the unofficial guardian of the school, the kids and most particularly Jean, with whom he is silently in love. When he adds protecting Barbara to his list of chores, the escalation of townie antagonism and violence eventually leads to a shoot-out/stand-off between Billy and the law at (where else but) an abandoned church.

The main storyline is certainly engaging, but what really gives *Billy Jack* its life and spirit is an unlikely intermarriage of two very different breeds of theatrical set-piece. One is rooted in gentle, improvisation-based happenings that flesh out the life and values of the school and the reservation. Members of the San Francisco-based comedy improv group The Committee (including Howard Hesseman of TV's *WKRP in Cincinnati*) rule the school here: 'psychodrama and role-playing' demonstrations for visiting townspeople; street theatre to spread awareness about what's really going on at the school; a fully improvised 'City Council Meeting' where students and townspeople confront each other with their prejudices and fears; a folk-singing talent show on the school's stage. (Laughlin and Taylor's real-life young daughter wrote and performs the most memorable song.) There's an innocent, freewheeling, documentary-like naturalism to these scenes.

And then there is their counterpart: the highly choreo-stylised scenes of Billy Jack's barefoot-hapkido ass kicking. Whether he's saving the wild mustangs of the film's opening from an illegal slaughter, or rescuing a thirteen-year-old girl from the lechery (and bed) of the film's smarmiest villain, Bernard (Roya), Billy invariably happens upon a scene of injustice as though his kung-fu spirit guide has led him there. And then, in the most oft-quoted line of the film, he 'just goes berserk'.

The success of *Billy Jack's* pacifist-vigilante recipe sort of speaks for itself. Though it failed miserably when Warner Bros. originally dumped it in porno theatres in 1971, Laughlin managed to get it back on screens

---

(*Opposite page*) *Strip yourself of your greed and ego trips and let the spirit enter you.* Tom Laughlin, the star, writer, producer and director of *Billy Jack*

again in 1973, independently and under his supervision, and the film made more than $32 million. It was just the kind of anti-Establishment entrepreneurial success story to perfectly amplify the *Billy Jack* ethos, and it led to two less successful sequels. But no sequel (or the later re-released prequel, *Born Losers*, or Laughlin's occasional bids for the US Presidency) could ever again plug in so perfectly to the half-breed spirit of that time. The owl feathers, sacred corn and snake teeth of Billy's medicine bag kept this film 'inside the flow of life's forces' just long enough to make it an independent legend.

Scott McGehee and David Siegel

Dir: Tom Laughlin; **Prod**: Tom Laughlin; **Scr**: Tom Laughlin; **DOP**: Fred J. Koenekamp, John M. Stephens; **Editor**: Larry Heath, Marion Rothman; **Score**: Mundell Lowe; **Main Cast**: Tom Laughlin, Delores Taylor, Julie Webb, David Roya.

The Blair Witch Project
US, 1999 – 81 mins
Daniel Myrick, Eduardo Sanchez

The Blair Witch Project makes every effort to present itself as a factual document, opening with titles informing us that what we are about to see is the surviving footage shot by three student film-makers who mysteriously disappeared into the woods around Burkittsville, Maryland. With a nominal budget of just $25,000, Myrick and Sanchez understood that they would not be able to deliver a picture that corresponded to the contemporary approach to the horror genre – slick and expensive special effects and/or Hollywood stars – and so instead adopted an approach that has its precedent in the 70s' and early 80s' wave of mock-documentary movies of which Ruggero Deodato's *Cannibal Holocaust* (1980) is among the most notorious.

The factual feel of the film is largely achieved through the use of video and Super-8, formats made necessary by the low budget. Assigning their characters the names of their lead actors to further maintain the conceit, Myrick and Sanchez presented the trio with a camcorder on which they were to document the experiences of the seven-day shoot and sent them out into the woods, where their only interaction with the crew would be the receipt of written instructions concerning rudimentary directions. The cast was subjected to sleep deprivation and various disorientating provocations to ensure that the resulting film, edited in its entirety from the hand-held footage recorded by the actors, had the requisite elements of authenticity, spontaneity and abject terror.

Unable to physically reveal or even suggest the fabled witch due to budget constraints, the directors employ an inventive and wholly effective approach to sound design, filling the night air with rustles, shrieks and cries that come suffocatingly closer as the characters experience social and psychological breakdown. The breakdown is in part effected by the character Heather's determination to film everything (like the 'real' crew, the characters are all assigned technical duties) and to experience 'reality' through her camera lens.

Blair Witch caused an immediate Sundance sensation and was snapped up by independent distributor Artisan. It mirrored the deliberately 'artless' approach exhibited in pictures such as *Night of the Living Dead* (1968), offering a fresh alternative to the attractively packaged but ultimately tiresome teens-in-peril cycle. *Blair Witch* was also undoubtedly the first film to truly harness the phenomenal power of the Internet as a marketing tool – the directors created a website to

The Blair Witch Project: an unsettling, documentary-style horror that rapidly became a modern-day marketing phenomenon

perpetuate the impression that the film was a documentary. Even though costly prints and advertising spend pushed the completion budget way over the originally quoted $25,000, in terms of profit against production costs, the film has gone on to be one of the most commercially successful films ever, grossing over $100 million worldwide and triggering a host of inferior sequels and reproductions.

Dir: Daniel Myrick, Eduardo Sanchez; **Prod**: Gregg Hale, Robin Cowie; **Scr**: Daniel Myrick, Eduardo Sanchez; **DOP**: Neal Fredericks; **Editor**: Daniel Myrick, Eduardo Sanchez; **Score**: Tony Cora; **Main Cast**: Heather Donahue, Michael Williams, Joshua Leonard.

Blood Simple
US, 1983 – 99 mins
Joel Coen

A contemporary noir with acute awareness of the origins of the genre, *Blood Simple* owes a specific debt to James M. Cain's tales of duplicitous females and two-time male losers trapped in a net of betrayal, murder and double-cross. Opening with a suitably cynical voiceover monologue that observes 'the world is full of complainers. But the fact is, nothing comes with a guarantee', the tone is immediately set for the stagnant moral universe this stylish and confident debut sucks us into.

Solely credited to Joel, though brother Ethan shares key roles, *Blood Simple* concerns Marty (Hedaya), a cuckolded bar owner who hires Visser (who also provides the opening narration), a sleazy private detective, to kill his wife Abby (McDormand) and Ray (Getz), the bar employee she is having an affair with. A million miles from the customarily cool big-screen gumshoes, the constantly sweating, reptilian Visser (convincingly portrayed by rangy character actor Walsh) encapsulates the brothers' desire to put an mischievous but undoubtedly auteurist and entertaining spin on familiar genres. It's a trick they've continued to mine with success, establishing themselves as among the most consistent, idiosyncratic and entertaining artists currently at work in contemporary cinema.

Blood Simple makes virtuous use of its low-budget status (it originated from a 3-minute teaser trailer assembled to secure funding), relatively obscure cast and stark and unfamiliar rural Texas locations where, as the opening narration ominously informs us, 'you're on your own'. Beautifully shot by Barry Sonnenfeld (the first of his three cinematographic outings for the Coens before establishing his own directorial career), the film deploys an inventive use of *mise en scène* and an especially audacious attention to texture and high-contrast lighting effects. In the grand tradition of noir, a genre popular among American independent film-makers for its existential qualities, relatively minimal lighting requirements and B-movie origins, *Blood Simple* is almost endlessly dark. Reflective of the murky goings-on, surprisingly sexless furtive couplings and the pervading unhappiness and nihilism of its characters, colour in the film is used to sparing but startling effect. Hence the vulgar neon signs, the garish pool of blood accumulating under what appears to be Marty's corpse and the catch of silver-blue fish, slowly spoiling on his desk.

Leavening the brew and confounding expectations are blackly comic interludes and gruesome yet strangely silent visual set-pieces. Moments, such as the knife that skewers Visser's tarantula-like hand, borrow freely from the modern American horror movie, an unsurprising debt given Joel's association with Sam Raimi, for whom he edited *The Evil Dead* (1982). Similarly, the film delights in repeating aural motifs (The Four Tops' 'Same Old Song', later used in Lodge Kerrigan's *Keane*, 2004, recurs to resonant and disarming effect) and exaggerated and disquieting sound effects, including the perpetual hum of a fan and the wince-inducing sound of Marty's index finger being broken.

Cold-blooded and claustrophobic, the film was instantly acclaimed, not least by J. Hoberman, who cited it as the most influential film noir since *Chinatown* (1974). With a clutch of festival accolades, including Best Dramatic Feature at Sundance in 1985 and Best Director and Best Actor (Walsh) at the 1986 Independent Spirit Awards, *Blood Simple* went on to become a modest commercial success. Later re-released in a fifteenth-anniversary 'director's cut', which, with characteristic Coenesque perversity, runs slightly shorter than the original.

Dir: Joel Coen; **Prod**: Ethan Coen; **Scr**: Ethan Coen, Joel Coen; **DOP**: Barry Sonnenfeld; **Editor**: Roderick Jaynes, Don Wiegmann; **Score**: Carter Burwell; **Main Cast**: John Getz, Frances McDormand, Dan Hedaya, M. Emmet Walsh.

(*Next page*) Something wicked this way comes ... the cuckolded Marty (Dan Hedaya) hires Visser (M. Emmet Walsh) to kill his wife in neo-noir *Blood Simple*

Boogie Nights
US, 1997 – 156 mins
Paul Thomas Anderson

One of the most striking recent features of American independent cinema is the return to the formal risk-taking and elaborate, multi- or parallel narrative structures popularised by the leading post-studio-system maverick directors of the 70s and early 80s. With his second feature following the low-key *Hard Eight* (1996), Anderson, again working with the resources that major backing and sizeable funding can provide (*Boogie Nights* was produced by mini-major New Line), made explicit his debt to the work of three of the key directors of this earlier period: Altman, Demme and Scorsese.

Beginning with the title displayed in neon lights on a San Fernando Valley movie marquee circa 1977, *Boogie Nights* asserts its formal daring and stylistic exuberance in an opening 4-minute sequence that through a variety of impressively mounted cranes and Steadicam shots moves into a bustling nightclub to introduce several leading characters. There, with a little help from a roller-blade-wearing porn starlet (Graham), lowly busboy Eddie Adams' (Wahlberg) trouser talent is spotted by porn impresario Jack Horner (Reynolds), who exclaims: 'I've got a feeling in those jeans there's something wonderful waiting to get out.' Horner, with the help of kooky 'actress' Amber Waves (Moore), transforms Eddie, via moniker Dirk Diggler and on-screen persona Brock Landers, into the biggest porn superstar of his generation.

Evolving from *The Dirk Diggler Story* completed by Anderson when just seventeen, *Boogie Nights* is informed by the director's own private viewing habits and authorative knowledge of pornography as both industry – the film deals with the seismic repercussions of the emergence of the home video market – and art form. In part a loose, unofficial retelling of the life of John 'Johnny Wadd' Holmes, the film's almost uncanny reproduction of an authentic porno aesthetic (extended long takes, desperate storylines and cheesy formal flourishes) also owes much to the onset consultancy of porn legend Ron Jeremy. Anderson's intelligently and exhilaratingly deployed visual flair and distinctive eye for period detail (nostalgic fun is poked at garishly opulent interiors and ill-fated technological advances such as the 8-track) is more than matched by his ability to negotiate the tricky tonal shift between comedy/parody and drama. Anderson cites F. W. Murnau's *Sunrise* (1927) and Demme's *Something Wild* (1985) as inspiration in terms of 'gearshift movies' (interview with Gavin Smith, 'Night Fever', in Hillier, 2001). When the tight-knit, fun-loving surrogate family implodes amid Oedipal tensions and cocaine-fuelled arrogance and paranoia, Anderson makes impeccable use of soundtrack to steer the film into darker but still morally neutral waters. The feel-good soul and disco tracks slowly give way to a contemplative, melancholy score by Michael Penn that compounds the profound loneliness and longing underpinning the hedonism and excess.

A recurring feature of the US indie and the cherry on top of an ambitious, sprawling, exhibitionist epic are the performances of a well-marshalled ensemble cast. Anderson regulars John C. Reilly and Philip Baker Hall particularly excel, as do William H. Macy and Philip Seymour Hoffman as a cuckolded cameraman and a repressed gay crew member respectively. The latter movingly express the director's interest in the often fraying and tenuous threads that bind and connect people, a pervading theme to which he has subsequently clung, most recently in the multi-award-winning *There Will Be Blood* (2007).

Dir: Paul Thomas Anderson; **Prod**: Lloyd Levin, John Lyons, Paul Thomas Anderson, Joanne Sellar; **Scr**: Paul Thomas Anderson; **DOP**: Robert Elswit; **Editor**: Dylan Tichenor; **Score**: Michael Penn; **Main Cast**: Mark Wahlberg, Burt Reynolds, Julianne Moore, Heather Graham.

Born in Flames
US, 1983 – 80 mins
Lizzie Borden

Before taking up directing, Borden was a self-taught editor, who had worked on projects such as Murray Lerner's *From Mao to Mozart* (1980) and sculptor Richard Serra's *Stahlwerk*. *Born in Flames* was a largely self-financed $40,000 project that began in 1977, but this skilful and provocative blending of art and activism took six years to reach fruition. It quickly achieved recognition as a seminal chapter in both independent and feminist film-making. Borden's working conditions and lack of finance resigned her to a single shoot per month. Working without a script and with scant regard for continuity, the resulting footage was painstakingly self-assembled on a Steenbeck installed in Borden's home.

Born in Flames was inspired by former Detroit resident Borden's arrival in New York and her surprise at the degree to which the contemporary feminist movement suffered from divisions along race and class lines. The film is intended as a political discovery process and an attempt to show how a microcosm of black, white and Hispanic women could all come together to address issues of inequality. Highlighting the emerging feminist sensibility at the beginning of the Reagan administration, the film is an allegorical tale that inventively and resourcefully draws upon elements of the science-fiction genre.

It is set ten years after a peaceful social revolution has created all men as equal. The streets of New York City are murmuring with the discontent of the seemingly forgotten female populace. Most prominent among the dissenters are Adele (Satterfield), a member of the militant women's army; Honey (Honey), a black presenter on the all-black, pirate Radio Phoenix; and Isabel (Bertei), who performs on the anarchistic Radio Regazza. The women are closely monitored by the FBI for signs of revolt. The prison death of a fellow feminist campaigner finally unites the disparate factions, precipitating the sabotage of the party-controlled media and a unified battle for liberation and equality.

A project that is very much improvisational in terms of performances (director Kathryn Bigelow, incidentally, also features) and execution, the perennially topical *Born in Flames* employs its restricted resources with style and imagination. The vibrancy and danger of New York's streets and the dynamism of the pirate radio stations and simmering countercultures are impressively rendered through a combination of well-paced editing, authentic news reportage and quasi-surveillance techniques. A suitably revolutionary and disparate soundtrack, which fuses elements of rap, reggae and punk, further complements the film's revolutionary air and agitprop spirit. Moreover, Borden's stimulating approach makes generous

Revolutionary radio in *Born in Flames*

concessions towards both amusement and entertainment, allowing her to sustain an intelligently posited feminist discourse in what Susan Barrowclough describes as a 'rare example of political film-making that doesn't rule out pleasure in order to preserve its integrity' (Barrowclough, 1984, p. 42).

Dir: Lizzie Borden; **Prod**: Lizzie Borden; **Scr**: Lizzie Borden; **DOP**: Ed Bowes, Al Santana; **Editor**: Lizzie Borden; **Score**: The Bloods, The Red Crayolas, Ibis; **Main Cast**: Honey, Adele Bertei, Jeanne Satterfield, Flo Kennedy.

Boys Don't Cry
US, 1999 – 118 mins
Kimberly Peirce

Four and a half years in the making, and nearly abandoned when a leading actor appeared impossible to find, Peirce's compelling debut is an original and irrefutably haunting study of gender and sexual transgression. It started life as a Columbia Film School thesis project before evolving into a feature through the involvement of superlative producer Christine Vachon.

Boys Don't Cry tells the remarkable true story of Brandon Teena (Swank), a twenty-one-year-old petty criminal found raped and murdered in an abandoned farmhouse near Falls City, Nebraska. The perpetrators, ex-con John Lotter (Sarsgaard) and self-mutilator and arsonist Thomas Nissen (Sexton), were revealed as friends of Teena's girlfriend, Lana Tisdel (Sevigny). What elevated the crime above the usual grim, Midwestern fare, catapulting it onto the front pages of America's tabloids, was the revelation that Teena was actually Teena Brandon, a young woman from Lincoln, who had for her adult life passed herself off as male.

The film is in part an attempt to reclaim the story from the tabloids that treated it with salacious glee. Peirce, whose exhaustive research included interviewing pre-op transsexuals and butch lesbians, was keen to gain an understanding of both the motivations for Brandon's desire and a wider insight into why a girl would want to pass/dress as a boy. Explained Peirce: 'I've always been interested in women dressed as men, because that's how I grew up, as a tomboy swinging from trees' (Leigh, 2001, p. 110). Brandon was the subject of *The Brandon Teena Story*, a 1994 Susan Muska and Gréta Ólafsdóttir documentary that revealed her self-perception as a transgendered person and not a lesbian or a woman. In sharp contrast, Peirce consciously avoids a factual, biopic approach and reveals nothing of Teena's life pre-Brandon. And though in part inspired by the novelistic journalism of Norman Mailer's *The Executioner's Song* and the unsentimental approach to rural American nihilism and violence evidenced by Brooks' *In Cold Blood* (1967), Peirce also intercuts the semi-fictionalised and at times harrowing narrative (the rape sequence induced nausea in the actors) with a transcendent expressiveness reminiscent of Malick's *Badlands* (1973). Peirce was herself quick to cite the inspiration of neo-realist works such as Hunter's *River's Edge* (1986) and Van Sant's *My Own Private Idaho* (1991), and her cinematographer Jim Denault certainly imbues the otherwise unremarkable landscapes with a tender, lyrical sense that conveys Brandon's romantic yearning.

Former *Beverly Hills 90210* star Hilary Swank is faultless and utterly convincing, giving an Academy Award-winning performance of luminous intensity and poise. The supporting cast, particularly Sevigny, is similarly impeccable. The film's progress was initially dampened by a surprising and unsuccessful defamation of character lawsuit brought by the real-life Tisdel. But *Boys Don't Cry* then went on to enjoy both critical and commercial success, bagging Peirce the FIPRESCI (International Federation of Film Critics) award at the London Film Festival and numerous nominations at the Independent Spirit Awards. Gender confusion continued beyond the film frame, most publicly at the Toronto Film Festival premiere, where Lindsay Law, then head of Fox Searchlight, the film's North American distributor, commended Brandon for 'her bravery', only for Peirce to then thank Brandon for letting her tell 'his story'.

Dir: Kimberly Peirce; **Prod**: Jeffrey Sharp, John Hart, Eva Kolodner, Christine Vachon; **Scr**: Kimberly Peirce, Andy Bienen; **DOP**: Jim Denault; **Editor**: Lee Percy, Tracy Granger; **Score**: Nathan Larson; **Main Cast**: Hilary Swank, Chloë Sevigny, Peter Sarsgaard, Brendan Sexton III.

Boyz N the Hood
US, 1991 – 107 mins
John Singleton

Buoyed by the success of Lee's *Do The Right Thing* (1989) and in a climate of increasing cultural heterogeneity in which black artists had assumed diverse profiles, bridging the gap between black and white consumers, Hollywood opened the door wider to a new wave of young black directors. Though dealing specifically with the black American experience from an Afro-American perspective, these directors were eager to produce polished, marketable films with mass appeal. Singleton, a twenty-three-year-old USC graduate, was one of the first to emerge with his high-profile debut.

Opening with a *Stand by Me* (1986) reference – the quest to see a dead body pursued by three ten-year-old friends already inoculated against the consequences of bloodshed by their brutal South Central LA surroundings – *Boyz* jumps forward seven years to find Tre (Gooding Jr), stepbrothers Doughboy (Cube) and Ricky Baker (Chestnut) as teenagers in an even more violent present. A gifted athlete and young father, Ricky's life offers promise, while Doughboy, the family scapegoat, is already falling victim to the pervading culture of drugs and killing. Tre is kept on the straight and narrow by his disciplinarian father Furious Styles (Fishburne), a neighbourhood survivor who instils in Tre a sense of self-pride and respect. Circumstances conspire to break the trio's bond, but they remain on good terms until a tragic incident tears them apart.

Financed and distributed by Columbia, *Boyz* was fashioned from a Singleton script based on his experiences growing up in the South Central area. Dubbed an 'American film of enormous importance' by Roger Ebert of the *Chicago Sun-Times*, it's a sobering rites-of-passage drama that packs a powerful polemic about male black-on-black violence. Making its message abundantly clear, *Boyz* opens with the statistic that one in every twenty-one black males will be murdered at the hands of another, and ends with a title card imploring an increase in peace. Singleton spreads his targets wide but is rarely scattershot, offering intelligent, coherent and balanced observations on the Eurocentric nature of the college education system and the hard-won rewards of community. Perhaps most remarkable is the willingness to tackle the issue of paternal responsibility through its criticism of Ricky's irresponsibility and praising of Furious' tough-love approach.

The implication that the absence of a father is likely to result in antisocial behaviour or death and the general affirmation of the paternal over the maternal (a flashback sequence reveals Tre's mother, played by Angela Bassett, abdicating her parental duties) do, however, provoke questions concerning representations of gender.

Singleton's thematic confidence is matched by assured visual aesthetics. Though citing Lee as an influence, Singleton's approach is subtler and more restrained, ensuring that the unfolding drama and performances remain centre stage. The director is rewarded by the excellence of his principals; Gooding Jr is especially outstanding in an early role. Auguring what would become a familiar transition to acting for black musicians (and a key component of the marketing and success of any film boasting a hip-hop element), former NWA member and one of rap's highest-profile stars Ice Cube lends Doughboy a tragic nobility.

A commercial box-office success, grossing over $57 million in the US, *Boyz'* popularity among young black American males helped sustain the continued visibility of young black directors in Hollywood and precipitated an ensuing crop of ethnic ghetto violence movies, tagged 'New Jack Cinema'. Arguably the best of this crop was the following year's *Juice*, an impassioned Harlem-set thriller from noted cinematographer Ernest Dickerson.

Dir: John Singleton; **Prod**: Steve Nicolaides; **Scr**: John Singleton; **DOP**: Chuck Mills; **Editor**: Bruce Cannon; **Score**: Stanley Clarke; **Main Cast**: Larry Fishburne, Cuba Gooding Jr, Ice Cube, Morris Chestnut.

Brick
US, 2005 – 110 mins
Rian Johnson

The dynamic debut feature of writer/director Rian Johnson, *Brick* won the Sundance Film Festival's Special Jury Prize for Originality of Vision. Taking its cues and its verbal style from the novels of Dashiell Hammett, James Cain and Raymond Chandler, *Brick* also honours the rich cinematic tradition of the hard-boiled noir mystery, here wittily and bracingly immersed in fresh territory – a modern-day Southern California neighbourhood and high school.

Student Brendan Frye's (Gordon-Levitt) piercing intelligence spares no one. Brendan is not afraid to back up his words with actions, and knows all the angles; yet he prefers to stay an outsider, and does – until the day that his ex-girlfriend, Emily (Emilie de Ravin), reaches out to him unexpectedly and then vanishes. Brendan's feelings for her still run deep and he becomes consumed with finding her. To do so, he enlists the aid of his only true peer, The Brain (Matt O'Leary), while keeping the assistant vice-principal only occasionally informed of what quickly becomes a dangerous investigation. Brendan's single-minded unearthing of students' secrets thrusts him headlong into the colliding social orbits of rich-girl sophisticate Laura (Zehetner), intimidating Tugger (Fleiss), substance-abusing Dode (Noah Segan), seductive Kara (Meagan Good), jock Brad (Brian White), and – most ominously – non-student The Pin (Haas). It is only by gaining acceptance into The Pin's closely guarded inner circle of crime and punishment that Brendan will be able to uncover hard truths about himself, Emily and the suspects that he is edging perilously closer to.

Determinedly labyrinthine in plot and written when Johnson was fresh out of high school, the independently financed *Brick*'s synthesis of the detective and American college genres also draws heavily on the Coen brothers. Attentive to the tiniest detail and adopting a witty production design – for example, The Pin, who still lives with his mother, has an outlandishly large and somewhat incongruous lamp in his limousine – this extremely stylish and stylised film is particularly indebted to *Miller's Crossing* (1990). This is most evident in Johnson's invention of a new set of colourful words and phrases, with terms such as 'Bulls' (cops), 'Duck Soup' (easy pickings) and 'Gum' (to mess things up) peppering the rapid-fire dialogue. Initially alienating and not a little perplexing, this rich glossary of terms – which become less impenetrable as the ear becomes attuned to them – also helps to create the notion of an environment that is partly familiar and yet still strangely macabre, dangerous and disorientating. This very distinctive and rather unique atmosphere is one of Johnson's most impressive achievements.

The casting is also canny and similarly effective in its sense of disorientation. Lukas Haas, best remembered for his role as the young Amish boy in Peter Weir's *Witness* (1985), makes a refreshing club-footed, cloak-sporting heavy, and Zehetner is a suitably duplicitous femme fatale. Best of all, however, is Gordon-Levitt, cast, Johnson claims, in a nod towards Bogart for his surprising physicality, emotional intensity and line delivery.

Dir: Rian Johnson; **Prod**: Ram Bergman, Mark G. Mathis; **Scr**: Rian Johnson; **DOP**: Steve Yedlin; **Editor**: Uncredited; **Score**: Nathan Johnson; **Main Cast**: Joseph Gordon-Levitt, Lukas Haas, Nora Zehetner, Noah Fleiss.

Buffalo '66
Canada/US, 1997 – 110 mins
Vincent Gallo

Prior to *Buffalo '66*, Gallo was best known for the demonic intensity of his acting, and had previously enjoyed success as a model, painter and then a musician in the experimental and influential New York band Gray. His acting credits included a number of independent pictures, including Alan Taylor's *Palookaville* (1995) and Abel Ferrara's *The Funeral* (1996). Gallo has a restless, idiosyncratic talent, and *Buffalo '66* marked his vaguely autobiographical, definitely personal, even maverick debut.

Buffalo '66 is ostensibly a poignant yet provocative love story. It opens with Billy Brown (Gallo) being expelled from prison onto the wintry, suburban streets. Heading back to his home town of Buffalo, Billy kidnaps Layla, a blonde tap-dancer (Ricci), and forces her to pose as his adoring wife on a visit to the home of his indifferent, abusive but football-crazy parents (Gazzara and Huston). During a fraught, hostile dinner, Billy's insecurities and his parents' simmering resentments rise to the surface.

Gallo follows the trend of many previous actors-turned-directors – and especially Cassavetes – favouring performance over narrative. The film is constructed as a loosely connected series of intricately stylised set-pieces linked by surreal, esoteric and often musical vignettes. Each of the cast is allowed at least one show-boating and invariably show-stopping moment, most memorably, perhaps, Gazzara's Frank Sinatra mime. Similarly, Mickey Rourke (an actor enjoying something of a renaissance in independent productions, witness Buscemi's *The Animal Factory*, 2001) delivers an impressive, direct-to-camera monologue that reveals how Billy came to owe him money. In a role that appears to have been constructed to satisfy male viewers seeking an element of wish fulfilment, Ricci still just about shades the acting honours, cementing her burgeoning indie icon status in the process.

As a comment on parental abuse and the horrors of blue-collar suburbia, the film is surprisingly lucid and moving, with Gallo's adoption of a washed-out naturalism (the film was shot on vintage reverse stock, a result of the director's obsession with detail) proving highly effective. At times painfully funny (Billy's desperate search for somewhere to take a piss during the opening brings tears to the eyes), the film, however, will undoubtedly be best remembered for its stylised visual aesthetic, meticulous production design and formal daring. *Buffalo '66* employs inventive, unconventional editing techniques, perhaps most impressively in the form of the flashbacks to Billy's unhappy childhood that begin as small frames within frames before multiplying and enlarging to fill the screen. Gallo has a fondness for off-kilter tableaux, and his sense of framing is equally audacious, denoting both distance (the reverse-angle shots around the dinner table in Billy's home) and tentative intimacy (the shot from above of Billy and Layla on the motel bed).

Gallo's publicising of the film was exuberant. The director responded to questions about how he got his stars to appear in a micro-budget production with an incredulous, 'How do you think? I fucking paid them.' Backed by a stack of impressive nominations (including the Grand Jury prize at Sundance and a Best First Feature Independent Spirit Award), *Buffalo '66* wasted little time in achieving cult status.

Dir: Vincent Gallo; **Prod**: Chris Hanley; **Scr**: Vincent Gallo, Alison Bagnall; **DOP**: Lance Accord; **Editor**: Curtiss Clayton; **Score**: Vincent Gallo; **Main Cast**: Vincent Gallo, Christina Ricci, Ben Gazzara, Anjelica Huston.

Candy Mountain
France/Switzerland/Canada, 1987 – 92 mins
Robert Frank, Rudy Wurlitzer

A co-production that begins in New York before meandering cross-country and concluding in Canada, *Candy Mountain* is nonetheless described as a resolutely American film by its two well-matched collaborators. An acclaimed photographer whose 1958 book *The Americans* depicted American iconography and the mythic allure of the road in a more downbeat light, Robert Frank segued into film-making, establishing his reputation with the unscripted Beat classic *Pull My Daisy* (1959). Combining a passion for the road movie genre as evidenced by his work on Monte Hellman's *Two-Lane Blacktop* (1970), scriptwriter Rudy Wurlitzer similarly mined the tarnished mythology of America, notably in Peckinpah's *Pat Garrett and Billy the Kid* (1973).

Informed by Wenders' *Kings of the Road* (1976), *Candy Mountain* tracks the dispiriting personal odyssey of ambitious but untalented New York musician Julius (O'Connor), whose quest for glory leads him to feign an association with Elmore Silk (Yulin), the J. D. Salinger of guitar-making. Charged with luring the legendary craftsman from hiding and retirement, Julius initially contacts Elmore's brother Al (Waits). Financially lighter (he is repeatedly sold cars that he either trades or crashes), Julius heads for the Canadian border and the remote home of Silk's former French lover (Ogier) who redirects him to a barren seaboard town. There, Julius finally tracks Silk down, only to discover that in return for a lifetime of security and freedom he has signed an exclusive deal with a Japanese businesswoman (Kazuko Oshima). A helpless bystander as Silk destroys his remaining guitars, a tired and broke Julius attempts to hitch a ride home.

Wurlitzer draws upon Frank's background, specifically the dichotomy between art and commerce; the pressures of fame; journeys toward selfhood and the defining importance of music (Frank directed the seminal *Cocksucker Blues*, 1972) for the third celluloid collaboration between the pair. In part developing from the practical imperative of having to satisfy the demands of the various international financiers, Frank/Wurlitzer also tapped into Frank's desire to make a film about a journey from the centre of one culture to the margins of another. In turn, the pair also debunk the romantic notion of the open road as a symbol of freedom; *Candy Mountain* certainly strikes a sobering note and can perhaps be seen as providing the natural conclusion to the American road movie.

Pio Corradi's photography – redolent of Frank's own – imbues the shifting landscapes and their weird, cranky and frequently lonely populace with a timelessness and distinctly iconic quality. Corradi's absorbing attention to detail further heightens the pervading malaise. In a key moment, a toothless van driver warns the initially optimistic Julius that 'life ain't no candy mountain' before, like so many others, smartly ripping him off. Co-ordinated by Hal Wilner, the music, provided by luminaries such as Arto Lindsay and Marc Ribot, is essential, intelligently foregrounding both character and action. Endorsing the film's endearing, counterculture sensibility, the film-makers cast from an esoteric pool of musicians and are repaid with accomplished and entertaining turns from the likes of Tom Waits, Dr John, David Johansen and Joe Strummer. The 'regular' actors aren't bad either, especially O'Connor as the bowed but not quite beaten Kerouac-lite hero.

Dir: Robert Frank, Rudy Wurlitzer; **Prod**: Ruth Waldburger; **Scr**: Rudy Wurlitzer; **DOP**: Pio Corradi; **Editor**: Jennifer Auge; **Score Co-ordinator**: Hal Wilner; **Main Cast**: Kevin J. O'Connor, Harris Yulin, Tom Waits, Bulle Ogier.

Chain
US, 2004 – 99 mins
Jem Cohen

A New York-based film and video-maker who has also worked with musicians including REM, Benjamin Smoke, Elliott Smith and Sparklehorse, Jem Cohen's work offers a unique perspective on how images are found, created, assembled and circulated. Often shooting in hundreds of locations with little or no additional crew, Cohen collects street footage, portraits and sounds. The projects built from these archives defy categorisation, frequently moving fluidly between documentary, narrative film-making and more experimental approaches. Loosely structured as city portraits, Cohen's films combine a fascination for people, places and daily rituals with more ephemeral moments.

In *Chain*, Cohen explores the man-made landscape of the post-millennium world as seen through two very different sets of eyes. Tamiko (Hal Hartley regular Nikaido) is a woman in her early thirties who works for a Japanese steel-manufacturing firm. Studying 'entertainment real estate' as part of a major international research project, she spends her days exploring shopping centres, hotel complexes and theme parks, and reports back on what she discovers. Meanwhile, Amanda Timms (Billotte) is a teenage runaway from Middle America who, after exhausting her mother's credit card, is holed up in an abandoned building near a huge shopping mall. Amanda spends her days working odd jobs in the retail stores and fast-food joints near her 'home', and, in her spare time, videotapes her surroundings for the benefit of her sister on a lost camera that she happens across. Set against a backdrop of Amanda's stream-of-consciousness narration, the tapes are an attempt to legitimise her existence.

Dedicated to Chris Marker (whose 1962 masterpiece *La Jetée* is the closest point of visual reference) and Humphrey Jennings, and listing Walter Benjamin's Arcades Project and Barbara Ehrenreich's *Nickel and Dimed* in the end credits, Cohen's extraordinary feature offers a

One of the man-made landscapes in Jem Cohen's *Chain*

Ballardian meditation on the corporate and cultural homogenisation of the contemporary landscape. Shot over a ten-year period and unfolding almost exclusively in establishing shots, *Chain* presents a melancholy photo-collage of chain stores, malls and conglomerated concrete spaces. Presenting a desolate and dispiriting spiritual limbo that the film-maker suggests could be just about anywhere, *Chain*'s end credits reveal that the film was actually shot across eleven American states and also incorporates footage from France, Germany, Poland, Australia and Canada.

Set to an intoxicating ambient score by Canadian experimental music ensemble Godspeed You Black Emperor!, part of *Chain* originally appeared in Cohen's 40-minute three-channel installation work.

The success of this project, and the fact that Cohen remained fascinated by the questions and discomfort he was able to use his images to pose about capitalist culture and the impersonal nature of twenty-first-century living led him to introduce a narrative element to his inquisitions. Whatever the process and the means by which Cohen arrived at *Chain*, what is beyond doubt is that it offers a nightmarish and terrifying glimpse of the future, now.

Dir: Jem Cohen; **Prod**: Jem Cohen, Mary Jane Skalski; **Scr**: Jem Cohen; **DOP**: Jem Cohen; **Editor**: Jem Cohen, David Frankel; **Score**: Godspeed You Black Emperor!; **Main Cast**: Miho Nikaido, Mira Billotte, Tariq O'Regan, Rick Aquino.

Chan Is Missing
US, 1981 – 80 mins
Wayne Wang

Chan Is Missing was shot vérité style on raw, grainy black-and-white
16mm for $23,000, with a combination of grants from the American
Film Institute and completion funding from the National Endowment for
the Arts. It offers a witty, offbeat and quizzical take on the Chinese-
American experience and the collision between Eastern and Western
cultures. Such subjects were close to the heart of Hong Kong-born
writer-director Wayne Wang (named in homage to his father's favourite
American actor), who, following the success of 1985's *Dim Sum*, was
credited with patenting the Chinese-American movie. Moreover, the on-
screen discussion and representation of issues relating to ethnicity and
diaspora were to act as a profound influence on more politicised
emerging directors such as Spike Lee.

A sprawling, meandering travelogue, the film is set amid San
Francisco's Chinatown, with its contrasting communities of American-
born Chinese who have largely embraced US culture, and the freshly
arriving Taiwanese and Hong Kong immigrants striving to remain true to
their roots. *Chan* tracks the search of two taxi drivers, Jo (Moy) and his
nephew Steve (Hayashi), for Taiwanese immigrant Chan Hung.
It transpires that Hung has mysteriously disappeared with the $4,000 Jo
and Steve had given him to establish them as independent cab operators.
Their enquiries turn up a miasma of conflicting theories concerning
Chan's whereabouts, including his implication in the murder of a
supporter of the People's Republic. Told by a scholar that they must
'think Chinese' to solve the mystery, Jo and Steve recognise that the
more they analyse Chan's character, the more unknowable and
contradictory he becomes. Acknowledging that some things happen
without reason, they call off their search.

Wang's ensuing career both in and out of the mainstream has
revealed an uncompromising and chameleon-like approach to form and

structure. Indeed *Chan*, described by the director in an interview with Tony Rayns as 'almost totally abstract' (Rayns, 1985), is no exception. Displaying a playful propensity for allusion and a disregard for orthodoxy, Wang kicks things off with an entertaining Cantonese version of 'Rock around the Clock' by Hong Kong pop star Sam Hui before mixing seemingly disparate generic conventions. Beginning as a detective mystery with film noir overtones (suspenseful editing, off-kilter camera angles, Marlowesque voiceover), the film changes tack to adopt a more naturalistic, observational aesthetic for its philosophical and at times melancholic exploration of contradictory attitudes to identity and values. With filming often taking place on tight schedules with friends and acquaintants, this aesthetic also in part derives from the original film conception as a 30-minute, non-fiction piece about cabbies.

Edited over nine months, the film was eventually completed by Wang himself following a disagreement over the film's structure with original editor Geraldine Kataka. Part of the problem with the editing process was that Wang had originally set up shots to suggest that the point of view throughout was possibly from the perspective of an omniscient Chan. When it became clear that this technique was not sustainable, Wang was forced to make drastic editing reconstructions. Premiered on 16mm at the Pacific Film Archive and subsequently screened to great interest at the New Directors and Films Festival in New York, *Chan Is Missing* was subsequently acquired by New Yorker Films and blown up to 35mm for US theatrical distribution.

Dir: Wayne Wang; **Prod**: Wayne Wang; **Scr**: Wayne Wang, Isaac Cronin, Terrel Seltzer; **DOP**: Michael Chin; **Editor**: Wayne Wang; **Score**: Robert Kikuchi-Yngojo; **Main Cast**: Wood Moy, Marc Hayashi, Laureen Chew, Judi Nihei.

Clean, Shaven
US, 1993 – 80 mins
Lodge Kerrigan

Filmed over a two-year period because of its low budget, Kerrigan's debut feature is representative of the more radical end of the independent spectrum. As a director, Kerrigan's adoption of an independent sensibility is not purely a result of enforced economics, but more a reflection of his aesthetics and his desire to attack mainstream cinematic conventions.

As such, *Clean, Shaven* implements a determinedly non-linear approach, instead painting an impressionistic, fractured and ambiguous portrait of Peter Winter (Greene), a schizophrenic and self-mutilator who undertakes a cross-country search for the daughter from whom he is denied access by her adoptive parents. Winter's release from an institution coincides with the discovery of the mutilated body of a young girl, a crime for which he is suspected and trailed by a homicide detective. Kerrigan withholds and denies information concerning Winter's complicity, forcing the viewer to share his protagonist's mental fragility and twisted perception of the world. At the beginning of the film, Winter grows annoyed with a child for bouncing a ball against his windscreen. He gets out of the car and while the camera lingers on the vehicle, out of shot there is a terrible scream. The aftermath is never revealed, denying the spectator the comfort afforded by the usual generic conventions surrounding the roles of hunter and the hunted.

Set in a bleak, drab landscape, from which director of photography Teodoro Maniaci's camera picks out abstract, ugly structures of metal and concrete, the film also takes an extremely expressionistic and inventive approach to sound design. There is virtually no dialogue but instead a cacophony of discordant screeching, squawking sounds, much of which emanate from Winter's car radio and from the noises that emerge as a result of his belief that he has been fitted with a radio receiver allowing the authorities to monitor his whereabouts. In a nearly unwatchable moment, Winter, whose self-mutilation is a result of his intense self-loathing (hence his inability to use mirrors, which he smashes or tapes over), gouges out his nails with a knife in an attempt to find the device.

Kerrigan presents a non-sanitised picture of mental illness that exists in stark contrast to traditional Hollywood flicks such as *Forrest Gump* (1994) that depict 'the mentally damaged as founts of simple wisdom' (Kemp, 1995, p. 43). In this regard, the writer-director is greatly assisted by Greene, who gives an intense, courageous and intelligent performance to render Winter's troubled psyche. *Clean, Shaven* is an uncompromising and provocative work by a film-maker with an astute understanding of the medium and a desire to use it to question standard modes of representation.

Dir: Lodge Kerrigan; **Prod**: Lodge Kerrigan; **Scr**: Lodge Kerrigan; **DOP**: Teodoro Maniaci; **Editor**: Jay Rabinowitz; **Score**: Hahn Rowe; **Main Cast**: Peter Greene, Molly Castelloe, Megan Owen, Robert Albert.

Clerks
US, 1993 – 90 mins
Kevin Smith

Tagged as 'a hilarious look at over-the-counter culture' and pitched squarely at the slacker generation, *Clerks* takes an eventful day in the life of young convenience store clerk Dante (O'Halloran) and his friend and fellow wage slave at the neighbouring video store, Randal (Anderson). Rudely awoken at 6am to be told that he has to work his day off, the film reveals Dante's incident-packed shift involving the explicit sexual confessions of his girlfriend, the impending nuptials of a high-school ex and an impromptu hockey match staged on the store's roof. A fight with Randal and a constant stream of eccentric and offensive customers further ensured a day Dante, who in a moment of pathos exclaims 'the real tragedy is that I'm not even supposed to be here today', is unlikely to forget.

A multiplex 'movie-brat' with a particular penchant for Spielberg and Lucas, Smith's sensibilities were challenged by a double-bill of Linklater's

Over-the-counter culture as depicted in *Clerks*

Slacker (1991) and Hartley's *Trust* (1990) as a twenty-one-year-old during his single semester in film school. Citing *Slacker* as the formative influence on his decision to become a film-maker, Smith similarly drew inspiration from Hartley's ability to adapt to economic constraints by simply placing the emphasis on dialogue. Enthralled by Jarmusch's visual minimalism and Spike Lee's reduction of narrative to a single location and concentrated time frame, Smith went so far as to thank the aforementioned directors for 'leading the way' in his closing credits.

Financed on credit cards by twenty-three-year-old Smith and shot on black-and-white 16mm stock (an economic consideration, not an artistic one), *Clerks* was completed with impressive ingenuity on a micro-budget of $27,000. Filming took place at night in the Leonardo Quickstop convenience store where Smith worked on minimum wage. The fact that the shutters remain permanently closed throughout is neatly incorporated to become a recurring joke.

In terms of editing, cinematography and composition, *Clerks* is crudely executed, though it does employ an endearing and inventive structuring into mini-episodes. It is, however, on the 'talk is cheap to film' aesthetic that the film thrives, propelled by Smith's sharp, scabrous and profusely profane dialogue and scattershot observational riffs on issues relating to friendship, hygiene, job prospects and the fragile fabric of life. Captured in long, static takes, the characters display an adolescent if often hilarious fascination with sex, but thankfully Smith's writing and the impeccable performances of the young cast (who reveal a natural aptitude for delivery and timing) ensure that the effect is rarely boorish or immature. As was the vogue following the success and influence of Tarantino's first two features, *Clerks* also offers numerous witty asides and observations on popular culture, most memorably the ramifications concerning the conclusion of *Return of the Jedi* (1983).

Warmly received at Sundance and a highly visible Miramax triumph – the $3 million domestic gross ensured that it became an oft-quoted paradigm of low-budget success – *Clerks* also brought Smith generational spokesman status and a loyal, vaguely obsessive coterie of diehard fans. *Clerks II*, a disappointing sequel, emerged in 2006.

Dir: Kevin Smith; **Prod**: Kevin Smith, Scott Mosier; **Scr**: Kevin Smith; **DOP**: David Klein; **Editor**: Kevin Smith, Scott Mosier; **Score**: Scott Angley; **Main Cast**: Brian O'Halloran, Jeff Anderson, Marilyn Ghiglotti, Lisa Spoonauer.

Crumb
US, 1995 – 120 mins
Terry Zwigoff

An eclectic documentary-maker firmly rooted in underground comic-book culture, Zwigoff formed a lasting friendship with the artist Robert Crumb in the mid-60s. Bonded through a love of esoteric music, particularly ragtime blues and traditional jazz, the pair played together in Crumb's band, The Cheap Suit Serenaders. More pertinently, however, the relationship spawned this film, an affectionate, intimate and often complex document of Crumb's life and work, which deservedly won the Grand Jury Prize at the 1995 Sundance Film Festival.

The film was executive-produced by David Lynch and filmed without restriction over a six-year period. *Crumb* begins by tracing the origins of Crumb's talent as a sensitive child, hailing from relatively humble beginnings, who was encouraged to draw by an older brother in order to escape the bullying of high-school jocks. The film reveals some of the formative experiences that would exert an influence on his art and personality (the seventeen-year-old Crumb developed a sexual attraction to Bugs Bunny) and then details how with *Fritz the Cat*, *Mr Natural* and *Keep on Truckin'*, Crumb became the archetypal underground artist of 60s' counterculture. Accorded celebrity status, Crumb began to indulge both in print and in reality his myriad sexual peccadilloes, in particular his fetishistic fixation with domineering, big-bottomed women. He was increasingly inspired to graphically depict his darker side, and accusations of pornography and misogyny soon followed.

In this often unflattering but frequently humorous portrait of an undeniably fascinating artist, Zwigoff largely retains an impressive objectivity, soliciting the animated participation of supporters and detractors of Crumb's work, examples of which are beautifully represented on screen with lingering camera pans of comic strips and larger scale drawings. Art historian Robert Hughes passionately argues that Crumb's work is in the subversive, misanthropic Rabelaisian tradition,

Gun crazy: artist Robert Crumb in *Crumb*

while female commentators such as fellow cartoonist Trina Robbins describe his output as self-indulgent, racist, pornographic and deeply misogynistic. The jocular Crumb himself refuses to be drawn on the debate, preferring instead to shrug off the issue with a laid-back affability that at times causes frustration in others, most notably Kathy Goodell (one of several ex-girlfriends), who is moved to deliver a blow to the head of the now happily married Crumb.

Crumb also examines Robert's relationship with his two brothers, Charles and Maxon, who both appear in the film. Tellingly, the end credits reveal that sisters Sandra and Carol declined to be interviewed, indicating the warped maleness of the Crumb household. We also learn that the chronically depressed, housebound Charles committed suicide shortly after the film's completion. It is in the relentlessly voyeuristic presentation of Crumb's hugely dysfunctional family that the film perhaps falters, presenting Charles and Maxon as freakish curiosities, as well as examples of the fate that Robert's talent and ability to function within society allowed him to avoid. That said, *Crumb* remains a compelling, exhaustive work and is required viewing for admirers of documentaries or those whose interest was pricked by *Ghost World* (2001), Zwigoff's inspired fiction debut.

Dir: Terry Zwigoff; **Prod**: Lynn O'Donnell, Terry Zwigoff; **DOP**: Maryse Alberti; **Editor**: Victor Livingston; **Music Arrangements**: David Boeddinghaus; **Main Cast**: Robert Crumb, Aline Kominsky, Charles Crumb, Maxon Crumb.

Daughters of the Dust
US, 1991 – 112 mins
Julie Dash

The first film directed by an African-American female to gain national distribution, *Daughters of the Dust* established Dash as an original and independent voice and a seminal figure for black feminist critics. The film was originally intended as part of a planned series of films dealing with the experiences and forgotten histories of black women during the last century (Dash's 1982 American Film Institute graduation film *Illusions* being the first part). The fraught passage of *Daughters* through financing, production and distribution can in part be attributed to Dash's insistence on total artistic control. Other factors that presented difficulties were its uncompromising Afrocentric, female perspective and highly sophisticated aesthetic, qualities to which a largely white industry and critical cognoscenti were unaccustomed.

Meticulous in even the smallest detail, and informed by Dash's attention to historical fact (as reflected in the exquisite costume design and eye for playful subversion), *Daughters* is a visually ravishing and hugely sophisticated costume drama set in the islands off the South Carolina coast at the turn of the century. A far cry from the urban terrain explored by emerging male African-American film-makers of the time, the film tells the impressionistic tale of a Gullah family who meet for a last supper before the migration of its members to a new life on the mainland. Central to the film is the tension between matriarch Nana Peazant (Lee Day), who wants the family to remain together, and Haagar (Kaycee Moore), who leads the journey away from roots and ancestral African heritage towards a new future.

Dash is an avowed disciple of influential black writers such as Toni Cade Bambara, Toni Morrison and Alice Walker (fans of whom provided a ready audience for *Daughters* when it received its limited theatrical release), and she also followed their preference for non-linear structure, enabling the incorporation of voices past, present and future.

Though originally conceived as a silent, the film uses dual narration, contrasting Nana's commentary with that of an as yet unborn child. It's an audacious device that demonstrates an awareness of the importance of oral storytelling in West African culture and that helps provide a clear link between the experiences of multiple generations of African-American peoples.

Beautifully rendered (it won a cinematography award at Sundance), with an arresting depiction of landscapes, *Daughters of the Dust* visually emphasises the spiritual and organic relationship between a people and their land and culture. Often mythic in tone, the film also abounds in images that denote an intense symbolism, intelligently signifying both the scars of slavery (a flashback to an indigo-processing plant establishes that the Gullah people depicted in the film are the descendants of slaves) and the customs, practices and superstitions, largely religious, waiting in the new world.

Unfortunately, Dash subsequently suffered similar funding problems to those that beset her when making *Daughters*. At the time of writing, she has been forced to use television as the canvas on which to further extend her oeuvre.

Dir: Julie Dash; **Prod**: Julie Dash; **Scr**: Julie Dash; **DOP**: A. Jaffa Fielder; **Editor**: Amy Carey, Joseph Burton; **Score**: John Barnes; **Main Cast**: Cora Lee Day, Alva Rogers, Barbara-O, Trula Hoosier.

Detour
US, 1945 – 68 mins
Edgar G. Ulmer

Edgar G. Ulmer was one of the relatively few film-makers to carve out a distinctive and personal style while working with the most meagre of budgets. A set and production designer and co-director for the likes of Max Reinhardt, F. W. Murnau, Fritz Lang and Ernst Lubitsch in the 20s, Ulmer joined the parade of émigrés from the Viennese high-art community who came to America and helped change its artistic landscape. After making the Universal horror classic *The Black Cat* in 1934, Ulmer suffered a change in fortune and found himself toiling in the depths, knocking out bargain-basement B-movie Westerns. Subsequently hired by the unglamorous P.R.C, Inc, headed by Leon Fromkess, Ulmer's frustration at the lack of studio funds was tempered by his being accorded complete creative freedom. Ulmer produced several notable films for the second-string, Poverty Row studio, of which arguably the best is *Detour*.

Downtrodden New York pianist Al Roberts (Neal) decides to hitchhike to Los Angeles where his girlfriend, Sue (Drake), is a waitress. En route, Roberts accepts a ride from affable playboy Charles Haskell Jr (MacDonald), who after imbibing some pills asks Roberts to take over at the wheel. When Haskell suffers a fatal heart attack, Roberts, afraid that he'll be accused of murder, disposes of the body, takes the man's clothes and wallet, and begins driving the car himself. He picks up beautiful but embittered Vera (Savage, recently coaxed out of retirement for Guy Maddin's docu-fantasia *My Winnipeg*, 2007), who suddenly breaks the silence by asking, 'What did you do with the body?' It turns out that Vera had earlier accepted a ride from Haskell and has immediately spotted Roberts as a ringer. Holding the threat of summoning the police over his head, Vera forces Roberts to continue his pose so that he can collect a legacy from Haskell's millionaire father, who hasn't seen his son in years.

Shot in a mere six days and hampered by shoddy, minimalist sets and clumsy in-camera optical effects, *Detour* nonetheless offers ample proof that few film-makers were able to do more with less. Clocking in at an economical 68 minutes, it's a thrillingly nihilistic and tawdry tale in which Ulmer taps into a deep well of bitterness to combine road movie and film noir conventions (the femme fatale, greed, the road as a descent into peril and degradation, chance encounters) with bold compositional framings and a distinctive visual style. Utilising both flashback, extended voiceover, changes of identity and a cross-country trek, even for a film noir *Detour*'s plot is convoluted, and yet Ulmer drives the film along with an exhilarating, manic zeal. The performances act as further propellants, Savage excelling as the evil, self-interested 'dame with claws'.

A bleak and cynical view of post-war America that surveys the psychological wrecks that litter its highways, *Detour*'s bona-fide cult status among cinephiles appreciative of cinema on the margins rested initially on the grisly life-imitating-art dictum that saw Neal sentenced to prison for killing his third wife. In the intervening years, however, its reputation has transcended this curiosity status and it has come to be regarded not only as *the* Poverty Row picture but also as evidence of Ulmer's visual expressiveness and ability to overcome significant economic obstacles.

Dir: Edward G. Ulmer; **Prod**: Leon Fromkess; **Scr**: Martin Goldsmith; **DOP**: Benjamon Kline; **Editor**: George McGuire; **Score**: Leo Erdody; **Main Cast**: Tom Neal, Ann Savage, Claudia Drake, Edmund MacDonald.

Donnie Darko
US, 2001 – 122 mins
Richard Kelly

A startlingly original debut from a then twenty-six-year-old fresh out of film school, *Donnie Darko* is as consistently intelligent, esoteric, dreamlike and downright perplexing as anything in contemporary American cinema. A disparate generic cocktail that comprises elements common to science fiction, high-school satire, horror and tales of suburban dissatisfaction, it's similarly liberally sprinkled with a multiplicity of filmic allusions. Most prominent examples include: *Harvey* (1950), *It's a Wonderful Life* (1946), *Carrie* (1976) and *Back to the Future* (1985). *Ordinary People* (1980) and, perhaps inevitably, *American Beauty* (1999) also come to mind. Imbued with the general other-worldliness of David Lynch, that the finished product should still be so confident and tonally assured is remarkable.

The 80s-set film concerns troubled teen Donnie Darko (Gyllenhaal in a magnetic performance that subsequently brought him a series of interesting leading roles in films such as Ang Lee's *Brokeback Mountain*, 2005, and David Fincher's *Zodiac*, 2007), whose recent psychiatric treatment for what appears to be a form of paranoid schizophrenia has caused escalating degrees of conflict among his uptight parents. While sleepwalking, Donnie meets Frank, a menacing six-foot figure sporting a fake-fur suit and disturbing rabbit mask who informs him that the world will end in precisely 28 days, 6 hours, 42 minutes and 12 seconds. Donnie returns home from his reverie to see a jet engine being lifted from his bedroom; had he been there it would have killed him. Any hopes of normality following the forming of a relationship with Gretchen (Jena Malone), a new arrival at Donnie's conservative school, are crushed by further visitations from Frank, who compels Donnie to commit a series of rebellious crimes.

Initially for the most part concerned with making incisive comments about personal and familial dysfunction, teenage introspection, the moral

Right and the charlatanism of new-age self-help gurus (in the insightful US DVD commentary, Kelly describes Donnie as 'a spiritual superhero'), the blackly comic film then moves into darker, phantasmagoric territory as the central character's hallucinatory episodes increase and eventually take over. The previously dry and acutely observed, if off-kilter, depiction of suburban life gradually recedes to be replaced with a frequent and dizzying use of slow- and fast-motion photography and disjunctive use of sound and image to depict the wormholes in time and alternative realities with which Donnie becomes increasingly and portentously fascinated. It is during these latter stages that *Donnie Darko*, with its overtones of universal interconnectedness, arguably teeters on the brink of collapse, compelled by its astringent sense of ambition, twisted logic and desire to uncork myriad unexplainable enigmas and mysteries.

Executive-produced by Drew Barrymore, who lends acting support (a surprisingly credibly creepy Patrick Swayze also features, sacrificing Hollywood fees for independent kudos), *Donnie Darko*'s limited US release was hampered by the events of September 11 and a curmudgeonly critical reaction to a rapturous Sundance reception. Subsequently, however, the film has acquired a sizeable reputation (*The Village Voice*'s J. Hoberman described it as 'a most original and venturesome American indie') and achieved instant and no doubt enduring cult status. Kelly is currently looking to get his career back on track after the ambitious folly of *Southland Tales* (2006), a sobering tale of a director being afforded too much money and creative freedom by a studio for their sophomore picture.

Dir: Richard Kelly; **Prod**: Chris Ball, Adam Fields, Nancy Juvonen, Sean McKittrick; **Scr**: Richard Kelly; **DOP**: Steven Poster; **Editor**: Sam Bauer, Eric Strand; **Score**: Michael Andrews; **Main Cast**: Jake Gyllenhaal, Maggie Gyllenhaal, Patrick Swayze, Mary McDonnell.

Dont Look Back
US, 1967 – 96 mins
D. A. Pennebaker

A landmark documentary, *Dont Look Back* evolved from what William Rothman calls 'the first generation of cinéma vérité film-makers' (Rothman, 1997, p. xi), who expressed a passionate commitment to 'truth'. Jean Rouch and his contemporaries influenced an emerging group of American directors of the late 50s and 60s who sought in their own ways to reveal the reality of specific subjects and social conditions. Pennebaker and his peers of the Direct Cinema group (Richard Leacock, Robert Drew, and Albert and David Maysles) refuted the notion that the presence of the camera had any significance, believing that they were offering a purely objective depiction of reality.

Pennebaker's film accompanies a young Bob Dylan on his 1965 tour of Britain. It was filmed using a hand-held camera, and is distinguished by an absence of voiceover narration and the replacement of montage with extended long takes to offer an approximation of real time. It begins with Dylan's iconic performance of 'Subterranean Homesick Blues', with the aid of outsized cue cards, and culminates in a tumultuous concert at London's Royal Albert Hall. *Dont Look Back* here captures Dylan, accompanied by an entourage spearheaded by manager Albert Grossman, as he undergoes the uneasy transition from folk singer to rock star. Dylan is by turns bored, arrogant, affected and disaffected. The film examines the dichotomies in the singer's increasingly fractured persona (such as his awarenesss of the artificiality of his image and paradoxical obsession with it) and his often fraught and uneasy interactions with fans, journalists and British music contemporaries.

When considering the significance of the film, it is necessary to recall that following the expulsion of Direct Cinema films from prime-time American TV networks, *Dont Look Back* (shot in 1965 but not released until 1967) was from the very outset intended to be shown in theatres. This intention was made easier to realise by the ascension of Dylan as a 'star'. The film therefore represents the moment that the commitment to 'truth' became a cinematic concern as opposed to a purely televisual one. Rothman cites the independently made *Dont Look Back* as marking the true birth of cinéma vérité in America.

Dont Look Back also marked a moment when advances in 60s' film technology began to make an impact on screens. The film was shot on a twelve-volt, battery-operated, home-made, 16mm camera with an Auricon movement and a feedback loop DC motor drive. And it had improved, crystal-determining, sound-recording equipment with increased playing time per roll. *Dont Look Back* thus became a hugely influential cultural and indeed countercultural document that shaped future documentary techniques (the 'fly-on-the-wall' method is credited to the film), pop videos (the opening sequence is interminably replicated) and music concert features. Evidence of the influence of *Dont Look Back* is discernible in works as diverse as the Maysles' *Gimme Shelter* (1970) and Wim Wenders' *The Buena Vista Social Club* (1999). The film had its detractors, though. Reviewing *Dont Look Back* upon its release, Andrew Sarris in the *Village Voice* pointed out that Pennebaker's film was only as good as its subject (Thompson and Gutman, 1991, p. 88), while the *Monthly Film Bulletin* described the film as 'shapeless', 'embodying all the deficiencies of cinéma vérité', and detailed the extent to which the work was 'staged' (*Dont Look Back* review, 1969, p. 201). The claims to objective observation must be viewed sceptically, given that the urgent 'whip-pan and shifts in focus often meant that the viewer was more aware of the camera's presence than before' (Andrew, 1998, p. 170). Formal semantics aside, however, the film and its maker more than deserve their rightful place in cinema history.

Dir: D. A. Pennebaker; **Prod**: Albert Grossman, John Court; **Scr**: D. A. Pennebaker; **DOP**: Jones Alk, Howard Alk; **Editor**: D. A. Pennebaker; **Score**: Bob Dylan; **Main Cast**: Bob Dylan, Joan Baez, Donovan, Alan Price.

Drugstore Cowboy
US, 1989 – 101 mins
Gus Van Sant

Having won the LA Film Critics' award for best independent feature and
attracted intense festival attention, *Mala Noche* (1985) enabled Van Sant
to upgrade from a $25,000 budget to a $6 million one for this
subsequent Hollywood indie. Though similarly set in the director's home
town of Portland, Oregon, *Drugstore Cowboy* transposes the gay milieu
of his improvisatory black-and-white micro-budget debut for a more
linear, conventional and less associative tale involving a quartet of
junkies.

Led by the charismatic and paranoiacally superstitious Bob Hughes
(Dillon), the young, makeshift surrogate family (a defining theme that
recurs throughout Van Sant's work, as does an interest in alienation and
outsiderism) is completed by Bob's long-term girlfriend Dianne (Lynch)

Matt Dillon as junkie outlaw Bob Hughes receives some sobering advice from William
Burroughs' ex-priest in *Drugstore Cowboy*

and fellow couple Rich (LeGros) and Nadine (Graham). They support their habit by knocking off drugs and money from local pharmacies in a series of increasingly perilous raids. Events take a more sombre turn when Nadine overdoses, causing Bob to re-evaluate his life and check into a rehabilitation programme in an attempt to straighten out. Set during the early 70s (the authentic outfits and attentive production design are superb), the film is narrated in flashback by a fatally wounded Hughes, who we learn is the victim of a vicious attack by an amoral junkie.

The film was adapted by Van Sant and Daniel Yost from an unpublished autobiographical novel by convicted felon James Fogle. It offers further evidence of the director's ability to respond with empathy to both environment and the failings and foibles of his characters. Refreshingly, Van Sant resists adopting a judgmental and sanctimonious tone towards chemical addiction, and presents the activities of his protagonists as partly a reaction to the numbing boredom of lower-middle-class suburbia and the oppression of everyday existence. In such circumstances, drugs present a genuine allure, which Van Sant never shies away from depicting. Counterculture icon William Burroughs contributes a cameo as a junkie ex-priest (his *The Discipline of D. E.* formed the basis for one of Van Sant's earliest shorts).

Robert Yeoman's understated cinematography lends the film a gritty realism, but as in the more determinedly surreal *My Own Private Idaho* (1991), Van Sant also punctuates proceedings with a series of stylishly exuberant interludes to replicate Bob's superstitious paranoia (he harbours a fear of dogs and red hats) and descent into a chemical haze. Another of Van Sant's strengths as a director lies in his ability to coax intelligent performances of depth and subtlety from his cast. Van Sant here draws an articulate and surprisingly nuanced performance from former teen idol Dillon, resurrecting his faltering career in the process.

Dir: Gus Van Sant; **Prod**: Nick Wechsler, Karen Murphy; **Scr**: Gus Van Sant, Daniel Yost; **DOP**: Robert Yeoman; **Editor**: Curtiss Clayton, Mary Bauer; **Score**: Elliot Goldenthal; **Main Cast**: Matt Dillon, Kelly Lynch, James LeGros, Heather Graham.

Easy Rider
US, 1969 – 95 mins
Dennis Hopper

Originating from an idea by Peter Fonda expanded into a loose story outline by Fonda and Dennis Hopper, *Easy Rider* began life as *The Loners*. With Fonda producing and the livewire Hopper slated to direct, financing for the project was in a state of flux until a chance meeting with Bob Rafelson's and Bert Schneider's independent Raybert company provided the required $360,000 to make a picture Fonda promised would challenge the rules of film-making and traditional screen representations of contemporary American society.

Easy Rider tells the story of anti-authoritarian bikers Wyatt 'Captain America' Earp (Fonda) and Billy (Hopper) who, buoyed by the proceeds of a cocaine deal and with alcoholic, part-time lawyer George Hanson (a star-making turn from Nicholson) in tow, 'went looking for America and couldn't find it anywhere'. Dealing with male camaraderie, the quest for freedom and America's pioneering spirit, the film offered a rebellious riposte to Establishment ideologies. Laszlo Kovac's sweeping cinematography of iconic national landmarks such as Monument Valley lends the film a mythic symbolism, but this is undercut by both the indolence and drug dependency of the protagonists and the depiction of the country as populated by narrow-minded bigots. Admitting that they 'blew it', the film closes with Earp and Billy being slain by a group of vicious rednecks.

Though in places technically raw and riddled with imperfections (Hopper cited underground film-making and the immediacy of the French New Wave as inspirations), the film saw Hopper crowned Best New Director at the 1969 Cannes Film Festival. The subsequent critical and commercial reaction to both the film and its huge-selling rock-orientated soundtrack was phenomenal; *Easy Rider* grossed over $50 million during its initial release (according to Hopper in Peter Biskind's *Easy Riders, Raging Bulls*, the film made all its money back in one week and in one theatre), putting the film and its film-makers at the forefront of the industry and contemporary counterculture politics. The film is also retrospectively viewed as establishing the road movie as a key post-60s genre.

Perhaps most importantly, the film precipitated in Hollywood a move toward pictures dealing with this counterculture, revealing among studios and major companies (*Easy Rider* was distributed by an initially wary Columbia) an ever-evolving opportunistic hunger to cash in on the latest fad. By extension, the independent nature of the film and its refusal to adhere to presubscribed formulas was enough to grant independent producers and artists a new autonomy, ushering in a period of relative artistic freedom and experimentation. Described as the 'New Hollywood' directors, figures such as Peckinpah, Altman and Bogdanovich found themselves comfortably accommodated within the confines of the mainstream.

Moreover, this general move towards risk-taking and a looser, less consequential narrative structure led more by character than plot to be found in *Easy Rider* and its immediate progeny has much in common with what we today traditionally regard as key aesthetics of American independent films and film-making practices.

Dir: Dennis Hopper; **Prod**: Peter Fonda; **Scr**: Peter Fonda, Dennis Hopper, Terry Southern; **DOP**: Laszlo Kovacs; **Editor**: Donn Cambern; **Score**: Hoyt Axton, Mars Bonfire, Roger McGuinn; **Main Cast**: Peter Fonda, Dennis Hopper, Jack Nicholson, Antonio Mendoza.

(*Next page*) Billy (Dennis Hopper), Wyatt Earp (Peter Fonda) and George Hanson (Jack Nicholson) on the road in search of America in *Easy Rider*

Eating Raoul
US, 1982 – 83 mins
Paul Bartel

Bartel was working as an animator when spotted by Gene Corman, and was taken under the wing of Gene's mogul brother Roger with his first film project *The Secret Cinema* (1969). Like Corman's numerous other protégés, Bartel came to occupy the niche between independent films and cheaply made, subversive variants on traditional genre pictures. Invited to direct *Private Parts* (1972), quickie, low-budget *Rollerball* (1975) and remake *Death Race 2000* (1975), Bartel's work revealed a preoccupation with sex and violence, the main staples of the exploitation genre. Also prone to sating his bad-taste sensibilities and displaying a penchant for what was commonly considered outrageous, risqué humour, Bartel earned a reputation as a purveyor of the strange and unusual, inspiring comparisons with John Waters.

Eating Raoul is arguably the film for which Bartel is most fondly remembered and which most clearly encapsulates his maverick provocateur ethos. The film endured a traumatic genesis. Financed piecemeal by Bartel's parents over a five-year period and supported by a plethora of actors working on the cheap, the picture was predominantly shot on weekends when cast, cheap equipment and materials were available. The finished film attracted negligible distributor reaction, but it immediately acquired a mighty must-see reputation on the late-night, cult circuit following a series of sell-out shows.

Bartel and regular B-movie cohort, the formidable Mary Woronov, star as Paul and Mary Bland, an intellectual, highly cultured and moralistic married couple disgusted by the hedonism and perversity of their LA neighbours. Harbouring dreams of a rural restaurant retreat complete with a well-stocked wine cellar, but lacking the cash to achieve it, the pair fortuitously hit upon an ingenious scheme that involves Mary masquerading as a prostitute. Luring unsuspecting prospective johns to their doom, Paul and Mary make a killing selling the men's bodies to a local dog food plant. Things, however, hit a snag when Hispanic delivery boy Raoul (Beltran) threatens to blow the whistle on their ghoulish activities, and so the Blands are forced to concoct an elaborate plan to kill, cook and eat him.

Bartel serves up an ordinary tale of everyday cannibalism, a blackly comic, deliciously deadpan satire on covert racism and intolerance, moral conservatism and cultural snobbery. Avoiding the kitsch and often self-consciously unrestrained style of Waters, the more literary and often surprisingly refined *Eating Raoul* is informed by Bartel's previous experience as a playwright and jobbing writer. The film's mordant wit and observational prowess are accentuated by deft performances, with Bartel and company wisely, and somewhat against the grain, playing their roles relatively straight.

Up until his untimely death in 1999, Bartel continued to offer incisive if 'trashy' and knowingly absurd critiques of the more repellent aspects of bourgeois society. Like Corman before him, Bartel also became a useful resource for emerging independent directors. Jim Jarmusch was just one beneficiary of Bartel's support, in the form of completion funding for *Stranger Than Paradise* (1984).

Dir: Paul Bartel; **Prod**: Anne Kimmel; **Scr**: Richard Blackburn, Paul Bartel; **DOP**: Gary Thieltges; **Editor**: Alan Toomayan; **Score**: Arlon Ober; **Main Cast**: Paul Bartel, Mary Woronov, Robert Beltran, Susan Saiger.

El Mariachi
US, 1992 – 80 mins
Robert Rodriguez

Hispanic director Robert Rodriguez burst onto the scene with this
Mexican-set feature that was to become as exalted for its low budget as
for its routine if stylishly executed content. With the dextrous Rodriguez
handling the majority of key technical duties and casting through a
combination of family, friends and non-actors, the $7,000 cost of
shooting and editing soon made *El Mariachi* a touchstone for aspirant
film-makers. The immediate effect on the industry was an increase in the
number of films being independently shot on non-film stock (*El Mariachi*
was originally shot on video as a straight-to-video production for the
Spanish-speaking market). The film's success was also responsible for a
mistaken understanding of the costs involved in getting a film into
distribution. As it turned out, the film was acquired by Columbia after
motoring to the Audience Award at 1993's Sundance. The studio spent
significantly on post-production, including a 35mm blow-up and a
sizeable marketing campaign, to bring the completion and releasing costs
up to the $1 million mark. With that backing behind it, the $7,000
budget was subsequently called into question. John Pierson is
unequivocal: 'I don't call the Rodriguez budget "alleged"; he sold a
$7000 movie cut on video and didn't personally spend another cent on
it' (Pierson, 1996, p. 235).

Whatever its financial status, there can be no doubting the
constrictive economic origins of the film and the adversities a
determined, self-sufficient Rodriguez was forced to overcome to make it.
Having completed numerous prize-winning home movies in Austin,
Texas, Rodriguez raised the money for *El Mariachi* by accruing various
loans, working as a guinea pig for cholesterol medication while penning
the screenplay, and finally by selling his body to medical science.
The narrative and structure are conventional enough: a young, black-clad
mariachi (Gallardo, boyhood friend of Rodriguez and star of his home

movies) drifts into a small Mexican border town, and through a combination of mistaken identity (a similarly attired gun-toting killer has arrived the same day) and a simmering attraction to local barmaid Domino (Gomez) soon finds himself embroiled in a vengeful warlord's blood feud.

Well aware of the formal and generic sources from which the film freely draws (the Leone Western, the stunt-fixated Hollywood action flick, Hong Kong martial arts pictures, and the melodramatic and romantic conventions of silent cinema), Rodriguez gleefully adopts an exuberant visual style to parodic but undeniably thrilling and polished effect. Rodriguez whips the whole shebang along at an enjoyably breakneck and breathless pace, employing an at times dizzying array of zooms, wide-angle lenses, intricately edited set-piece shoot-outs and an inventive understanding of the possibilities of sound design. His ironic, often deliciously droll dialogue is another plus, and the casting of non-actors and the 'found' locations and props lend the film an atmospheric authenticity that belies both its modest design and its more excessive if thoroughly unpretentious cinematic trickery.

Unlike some other directors working in the independent sector (though few mined the action genre), Rodriguez made little secret of his aspirations to work within the Hollywood mainstream. *El Mariachi* provided instant gratification, becoming a respectable commercial success and the launch pad for a successful studio career for Rodriguez that began with *Desperado* (1995), a big-budget makeover of his debut.

Dir: Robert Rodriguez; **Prod**: Robert Rodriguez, Carlos Gallardo; **Scr**: Robert Rodriguez, Carlos Gallardo; **DOP**: Robert Rodriguez; **Editor**: Robert Rodriguez; **Score**: Marc Trujillo; **Main Cast**: Carlos Gallardo, Consuelo Gomez, Peter Marquardt, Jaime De Hoyos.

Eraserhead
US, 1976 – 89 mins
David Lynch

Indebted to *The Alphabet* (1968) and *The Grandmother* (1970), the director's early shorts that similarly explored themes of repression, fear and psychological paranoia, Lynch's experimental and provocative debut feature remains one of the most distinctive, blackly comic and disturbing of modern pictures. *Eraserhead* was shot at the American Film Institute over a five-year period on a micro-budget (the cast and crew mostly comprised friends and associates). The film's abstract, other-worldly visual style evokes vintage Americana (an abiding obsession with Lynch), European expressionist film, surrealism, the horror genre and the American avant-garde movement of the 40s.

Set in a nightmarish urban landscape ravaged by decay, *Eraserhead* largely steers clear of traditional narrative or structure to operate on a more purely sensory and subconscious level, the faintly familiar and very funny family dinner scene that verges on social satire aside. Henry Spencer (Nance) is a hapless and hopeless shock-haired innocent struggling to comprehend the world he lives in. Mostly confined to his dingy, under-lit apartment, Henry draws comfort from his increasingly bizarre sexual dreams and from the soothing song sung by a hamster-faced girl who he imagines to be living inside his radiator. His reveries are, however, punctured by the news that his girlfriend Mary (Stewart) is pregnant. The 'child' is born premature and, unable to stand its constant crying and wretched appearance, Mary is driven back to the bosom of her outlandish family. Henry is left alone with the pestilent creature, and his dreams soon take on a more disturbing complexion, including, in a gruesome sequence that gives the film its title, his own decapitation.

Riddled with images relating to intercourse and castration that connote a morbid interest in sex, physicality and the cycle of birth and death, *Eraserhead* also clearly offers a personal take on the claustrophobic pressures and anxieties of responsibility. It was made while Lynch was a struggling artist-turned-film-maker coping with the birth of his daughter and recent marriage. The director's representation of women as predatory and demanding, and infants as purely monstrous, must have made arresting viewing for his family (the mechanics involved in realising the reptilian 'baby' remain a source of wonder, as does the creation of the tiny chickens that spring to life, oozing blood as Henry carves them). Lynch himself has described *Eraserhead* as 'a dream of dark

Jack Nance as Henry in the nightmarish and surreal *Eraserhead*

and troubling things', undoubtedly the best way to view it when searching for a meaning.

Shot in black and white (with emphasis on the black), *Eraserhead* is imaginatively and expertly executed. The film contains surreal, often grotesque set-pieces and employs a generally disorientating design, exemplified by Henry's decapitated head plummeting through the film frame, the milky pool into which Henry and his neighbour sink after coupling, and the inventive use of architecture. These aspects are complemented by a hugely effective and disarming aural backdrop, which constructively employs a cacophony of industrial hissings, thuds and clanks. Upon release, the film immediately found favour on the late-night cult repertory circuit. It also enraptured Mel Brooks, who hired Lynch to direct his production of *The Elephant Man* (1980).

Dir: David Lynch; **Prod**: David Lynch; **Scr**: David Lynch; **DOP**: Frederick Elmes; **Editor**: David Lynch; **Score**: Peter Ivers, David Lynch **Main Cast**: Jack Nance, Charlotte Stewart, Allen Joseph, Jeanne Bates.

The Evil Dead
US, 1982 – 86 mins
Sam Raimi

One of the most remarkable and infamous horror films of the modern era, *The Evil Dead* originated as a thirty-minute preview titled *Within the Woods* that was used as bait by Raimi to snare contributions from potential investors. Expanding upon the short's infectious blending of horror, gory live-action animation, graphic violence and humour, Raimi completed the film for the relatively low cost of $400,000, which in part explains its grainy visual aesthetic (the result of a subsequent transfer from 16 to 35mm), gleeful irreverence and experimental bent.

Filming on the project, then titled *Book of the Dead*, took place in 1980 in Tennessee and Michigan locations. The film's premise and structure are attentive to the conventions of the horror genre. A group of twenty-something male and females take a sojourn to a remote woodland cabin where they discover a strange book titled the 'Book of the Dead'. An accompanying tape made by an archaeologist reveals that the book was found among the Khandarian ruins of a Sumerian civilisation. Unfortunately, in playing the tape, which also includes ancient incantations, the group unwittingly summon the hitherto dormant demons of the forest, which in turn possess the party one by one. Only Ash (Campbell, future Raimi regular and the film's executive producer) survives the demonic onslaught to single-handedly engage in the battle of good versus evil.

Raimi's film recalls such notable examples of the genre as *The Exorcist* (1973) (from which *The Evil Dead* takes many of its make-up ideas) and *The Texas Chainsaw Massacre* (1974), and also has a knowing reflexivity and black, tongue-in-cheek humour that has informed the recent strain of post-modern contributions to the horror cycle, such as *Scream* (1996). At times exceedingly violent – albeit in a comic-book fashion – the film revels in its shock tactics and low-budget gore, in which Bart Pierce's impressively executed stop-motion special effects form the centrepiece. However, alongside the film's outrageous mayhem there's also palpable suspense and a genuinely unsettling, claustrophobic and nightmarish air. The film is expertly cut (Joel Coen worked on the editing) and atmospherically lit in ominous clouds of fog. The frequent deployment of first-person camera in the film's initial stages successfully evokes the encroaching presence of the marauding demons. Moreover, the use of crane and Panaglide shots lends *The Evil Dead* a momentum and technical flair that masks its meagre economic means and somewhat muted characterisation.

The film caused a sensation at the 1982 Cannes Film Festival, where horror scribe Stephen King described it as 'the most ferociously original horror film of the year' (quoted in King, 1982). *The Evil Dead* was subsequently acquired by risk-taking British distribution outfit Palace Pictures. Only marginally trimmed after a viewing by the British censors, the film was simultaneously launched theatrically and on video. However, some local councils intervened, objecting largely to a distasteful scene in which a tree apparently rapes a woman; videos of the film were banned and seized. One of the first so-called 'video-nasties', *The Evil Dead* nonetheless became the best renting title of 1983 and an instant cult success.

Dir: Sam Raimi; **Prod**: Robert Tapert; **Scr**: Sam Raimi; **DOP**: Tim Philo; **Editor**: Edna Ruth Paul; **Score**: Joseph Loduca; **Main Cast**: Bruce Campbell, Ellen Sandweiss, Betsy Baker, Hal Delrich.

Faster, Pussycat! Kill! Kill!
US, 1965 – 83 mins
Russ Meyer

An independent director-producer-writer-editor-cameraman and distributor, Russ Meyer is popularly credited with inventing the skin flick with the series of unashamedly adult films he produced between 1959 and 1963. These pictures were considerable commercial successes, and films such as *The Immoral Mr Teas* (1959) were harbingers of Meyer's vehicles for buxom Amazonian women. His films from this period are also marked by a technical excellence lacking in those of his contemporaries, and from the mid-60s onwards the director began to explore more ambitious territories, producing a number of stylishly executed, low-budget outlaw action pictures that marry high nudity content with outrageously trashy narratives, tongue-in-cheek dialogue and domineering female characters. *Faster, Pussycat! Kill! Kill!* galvanised Meyer's burgeoning cult standing and arguably remains the most popular and typical of his pre-studio pictures firmly aimed, as it was, at the undemanding drive-in market.

Set in rugged desert terrain, *Pussycat* features Meyer starlets Satana, Haji (as Satana's female lover) and Williams as a trio of homicidal, Porsche-racing go-go dancers blazing their way across California. Kidnapping a young girl (Bernard) after the black-clad dominatrix Satana breaks her boyfriend's back with a single karate chop, the scantily dressed women head for a secluded farmhouse after a talkative gas attendant informs them that the head of the bizarre household (Stuart Lancaster) has a considerable fortune hidden beneath his floorboards. To get it, they must first contend with the father's lustful advances and the equally physical attentions of his slow-witted but strapping son, Vegetable (Dennis Busch).

Shot effectively in black and white, *Pussycat* is an arresting combination of the distastefully lurid, the camp and the highly comic. All three elements frequently combine in the ripe, over-the-top dialogue:

his eyes transfixed on Satana's ample cleavage, the gas attendant extols the virtues of seeing America, eliciting Satana's feisty response, 'You won't find it down there, Columbus!' Proving that Meyer's interests extended beyond bust size, *Pussycat* has a compositional assuredness that combines an eye for the surreal and visually absurd with expertly choreographed fight sequences and suspenseful cross-cutting. An effective and exuberant action picture, the film displays many of the attributes found in the early Don Siegel pictures.

Roundly criticised for objectifying women and pandering to vulgar wish-fulfilment fantasies, Meyer, who was not adverse to using such responses in his marketing campaigns, defended his work, highlighting that not only are women always the heroines but that they have a sexual appetite and physical strength equal to their male counterparts. Women are rarely victims but are frequently powerful victors, and as such offer a sense of empowerment. John Waters, who displays an obvious debt to Meyer, declared *Pussycat* not only the best movie ever made but also the best ever likely to be made. In 1983 and then 1995, the critical reassessment of Meyer's work was bolstered by a major retrospective at the National Film Theatre, where the film was 'revered by riot girls, feminists and dykes alike for its un-PC portrayal of tough, sexy, ironic women in control' (Giles, 1995, p. 11). The circle was completed when *Pussycat* was successfully revived in the US in the mid-90s, playing at prestigious arthouse venues such as New York's Film Forum. On originally seeing the film in the mid-70s, feminist critic B. Ruby Rich was 'appalled', but she overturned her initial dismissal after a second viewing, labelling the film 'an unexpected celebration of bad-girl empowerment' (Rich, 1995, p. 65).

Dir: Russ Meyer; **Prod**: Russ Meyer, Eve Meyer; **Scr**: Jack Moran; **DOP**: Walter Schenk; **Editor**: Russ Meyer; **Score**: Paul Sawtell; **Main Cast**: Turu Satana, Haji, Lori Williams, Susan Bernard.

Gas Food Lodging
US, 1991 – 101 mins
Allison Anders

Anders is a UCLA film school graduate who got her break as a production assistant on Wenders' *Paris, Texas* (1984) after bombarding the director with letters. She used her own upbringing and subsequent first-hand experiences of single parenthood for her breakthrough feature. A deeply felt, unflinching familial drama about two sisters living in a desolate, backwater desert town with their divorced mother, *Gas Food Lodging* avoids offering a sanctimonious homily about the bonds between mothers and daughters (a staple of mainstream fare covering similar terrain), and instead presents a gritty and authentic representation of blue-collar lives edging ever closer to the poverty line.

Nora (Adams) scrapes a living waiting tables at the local truck stop while single-handedly raising her daughters in a cramped, decrepit trailer. Elder daughter Trudi (Skye) has just turned seventeen and, bored with life in Laramie, has taken to skipping school, drinking until late and making out with high-school Lotharios. As Trudi's reputation for raising hell grows, the tension between her and her mother escalates. Younger daughter Shade (Balk) is also undergoing a sexual awakening, but after suffering rejection at the hands of dreamy Darius (Donovan Leitch), she seeks solace at the local Spanish cinema, where she loses herself in the romantic adventures of Mexican matinee siren Elvia Rivero. There's no such escape for the equally romance-starved Nora, though a flirtation with a local satellite engineer may offer temporary respite from her arduous existence.

The film is rigorously unsentimental in tone. Anders' perceptive writing and sense of character capture the frustrations of the two generations of women, offering a powerful if understated depiction of the resilience required for survival. Eschewing dreams for realism, Anders offers no easy conclusion but does intermittently leaven the tone with a series of brief interludes in which glimpses of happiness are revealed,

Generational female angst in *Gas Food Lodging*

most notably in a scene where Shade and her new Mexican-American boyfriend dance with impromptu abandon. Perhaps most impressive, however, are the violent, no-holds-barred confrontations between Trudi and her mother in which Nora's determination that her eldest daughter escape her own fate is palpable.

Contributing to the film's plausibility are the principal performances. Adams impressively conveys a semi-lifetime of drudgery and disappointment, while Skye (of whom much was expected after the film) lends Trudi a sullen petulance born of frustration and ennui. Lower down the acting credits is former Dinosaur Jr songsmith J. Mascis, who also contributes an evocative, suitably frills-free score. (The relationship between lo-fi musicians and American indie pics remains harmonious – witness Lou Barlow's work on *Kids*, 1995, and the collaborative work on *Heavy*, 1995, by Sonic Youth's Thurston Moore.) In formal terms, *Gas* adopts a predominantly simple, low-key approach, with cinematographer Dean Lent (another UCLA graduate) effectively rendering the arid, weather-beaten landscapes that serve as the film's setting and metaphorical parameter.

Gas is another notable example of the relatively few female-directed American independent movies. What is perhaps a more telling statistic is that Anders is one of the few female directors who has gone on to regularly produce subsequent features, including *Mi vida loca* (1993), *Grace of My Heart* (1996) and *Sugar Town* (1999).

Dir: Allison Anders; **Prod**: Bill Ewart, Dan Hassid, Seth Willenson; **Scr**: Allison Anders; **DOP**: Dean Lent; **Editor**: Tracy S. Granger; **Score**: J. Mascis; **Main Cast**: Brooke Adams, Ione Skye, Fairuza Balk, James Brolin, Robert Knepper.

George Washington
US, 2000 – 89 mins
David Gordon Green

The debut feature of then twenty-five-year-old Green, *George Washington* is a beguiling, elegiac coming-of-age drama and a lyrical meditation on the fragility of human existence. An impressive synthesis of unforced cinematic naturalism, the film also displays an astute appreciation for the ethereal strangeness of human interaction and the minutiae of rural small-town life.

The film follows the lives of a group of black teenagers hanging out in derelict buildings and at the local train depot over a long hot summer in a poor North Carolina town. Examining the fickle ties of friendship and the tentative steps towards adulthood and responsibility, the journey is hastened by a brutal accident that leaves one member of the group tragically dead and the others struggling to come to terms with their culpability. Most affected is a superhero-fixated youth (who through one of the humorous, poignant ironies in which the film is abundant is forced to wear an ungainly helmet for medical reasons). He yearns to become the nation's first black American president (the film is obviously pre-Obama), thus emulating his hero from whom the film takes its somewhat elliptical title.

As with many notable US independent debut pictures, finance for the film arose through a mixture of guile, determination and tenacity on the part of the director, who toiled at a variety of blue-collar jobs in order to raise the bulk of the finance. Green credits this period as providing the inspiration for his perceptive, delicately subtle dialogue (and no doubt the fondness for washed-out, industrial locations), which is alive with the nuances of everyday conversation. Perhaps most impressively, Green never falls foul of patronising his ensemble of youthful characters, played mostly by non-professional actors, some of whom are local town denizens. The uniformly excellent performances suggest a mutual respect, cultivated through the communal spirit Green instilled by having the cast and crew live side-by-side throughout the production. Many of the on-screen friendships accurately mirror those that were developing off screen. A covert work in terms of politics, the mainly black cast were chosen simply because the majority of people where Green wanted to shoot just happened to be black.

Choosing to adopt a markedly differential visual aesthetic to many of his contemporaries, Green eschewed working with digital video technology and the utilisation of grainy, hand-held vérité-style camerawork, instead choosing to shoot on anamorphic lenses. Tim Orr's luminous, sun-dappled photography lends the film an enthralling textural beauty that in conjunction with the long, lingering edits does much to evoke the seminal 70s works of Malick, a director whose brand of visual lyricism is much admired by Green. Meanwhile, the steadfast refusal to pander to the clichés of the genre (*Sleazenation* declared it the benchmark by which coming-of-age dramas will come to be judged) and its attempts to intelligently reflect the troubled, poignant path toward adulthood and moral responsibility place *George Washington* in such

George (Donald Holden), the superhero-fixated youth in *George Washington*, David Gordon Green's tender and lyrical coming-of-age drama

exalted recent company as *River's Edge* (1986) and *Gummo* (1997), albeit with added tenderness and beauty.

Dir: David Gordon Green; **Prod**: David Gordon Green, Sacha Mueller, Lisa Muskat; **Scr**: David Gordon Green; **DOP**: Tim Orr; **Editor**: Steven Gonzales, Zene Baker; **Score**: Michael Linnen, David Wingo; **Main Cast**: Candace Evanoiski, Donald Holden, Damian Jewan Lee, Curtis Cotton III.

Girlfight
US, 1999 – 110 mins
Karyn Kusama

Girlfight marked the bristling, tenacious and intelligent debut of Karyn Kusama, a former assistant to John Sayles. Though it undoubtedly deals a disservice to Kusama (who trained as a fighter during her youth) to overstress the Sayles connection, the film is produced by Sayles' long-time collaborator Maggie Renzi, edited by Sayles' assistant editor Plummy Tucker and is executive-produced by and features the man himself in a minor acting role. This is a film outwardly about the precision and control required of pugilists, but there are shades of Sayles in the film's lean and disciplined aesthetic and in the way it focuses upon a socially disadvantaged protagonist who to succeed must do so against considerable odds.

Diana Guzman (newcomer Rodriguez) is a Brooklyn high-school senior with a track record of getting into corridor fights. Her home life is equally fractious and often punctuated by rows with her widowed, bullying father Sandro (Calderon). While accompanying her bookish younger brother Tiny (Ray Santiago) to the gym for the boxing lessons he loathes but which his father insists he takes, Diana discovers a thirst for the sport. Without her father's knowledge, she coaxes an ex-pro, Hector (Tirelli), to train her using the lesson money intended for Tiny. As her natural talent and dedication shine through, Diana develops a new sense of self-worth, quickly rising through the ranks of local male and female fighters. Meanwhile, a mutual attraction develops between Diana and Adrian (Douglas), the gym's most promising male prospect, but is instantly put under pressure when the pair are drawn to face each other in a high-profile bout.

The boxing world is traditionally a male domain. Kusama puts the largely tired, formulaic conventions of the boxing picture through their paces by investing the material with a feminist perspective (Diana's male counterpart is wryly named after Sylvester Stallone's wife in the *Rocky* series). By doing so, she creates a dramatic, intelligent and affecting tale about not only female but also racial and economic empowerment. Moreover, Kusama largely avoids the pitfall of overwrought sentimentality (the scenes in which Diana confronts her father with the physical abuse that drove her mother to suicide are especially hard-hitting and well handled), thanks to her own accomplished script and a towering turn by Rodriguez in the central role. As Diana, Rodriguez exudes a raw, almost feral brooding energy and, with her permanently furrowed brow, gives the sense that she carries the weight of the world. It is a performance of compelling conviction and, given the arduous training patently required, no little dedication. Kusama's boxing background serves her well, lending the gym sequences and pre-bout banter an appropriately downbeat realism that evokes Huston's *Fat City* (1972). It's a sensibility mirrored in the bruising fight sequences, authentically shot with a minimum of sensationalism or excess using stolid medium shots.

Garlanded at Sundance with Best Director and Grand Jury prizes, *Girlfight* is a notable entry to the crowded ranks of sport-as-metaphor films, and hopefully signals the emergence of a distinctive new film-making talent.

Dir: Karyn Kusama; **Prod**: Sarah Green, Martha Griffin, Maggie Renzi; **Scr**: Karyn Kusama; **DOP**: Patrick Cady; **Editor**: Plummy Tucker; **Score**: Theodore Shapiro; **Main Cast**: Michelle Rodriguez, Jaime Tirelli, Paul Calderon, Santiago Douglas.

Go Fish
US, 1994 – 83 mins
Rose Troche

Go Fish is an overtly lesbian debut described by writer-director Troche and actress/co-writer and former partner Turner as being by and for lesbians. The project began life as *Ely and Max*, fifteen minutes of footage screened at the 1993 Sundance Film Festival. Initially directed in Troche's free time, the film was intended to address the lack of films for lesbian audiences (Donna Deitch's *Desert Hearts*, 1985, excepted) and as an antidote to the stereotypical, titillating predominantly male depiction of lesbianism popularised in mainstream pictures such as *The Hunger* (1983).

The project ran into trouble once the meagre funds raised by Troche evaporated, but following a letter from the director, financial support was pledged by Kalin Vachon Productions Inc (formerly Apparatus), the independent film-maker-friendly outfit founded by lesbian producer Christine Vachon and Chicago-born director Tom Kalin. John Pierson's influential Islet (a valuable resource and source of support for American independent film-makers since the mid-80s) provided completion funding.

Named after a children's card game much beloved in the States, the stylishly shot, grainy black-and-white film is a fresh, Chicago-set romantic serio-comedy that frankly portrays the day-to-day lives of five women friends – Max (Turner), Kia (McMillan), Ely (Brodie), Daria (Anastasia Sharp) and Evy (Melendez) – and the search for romance by the perennially single Max. The film's technically mesmerising associative editing style (Troche does her own edits) evidences the director's affiliation with the Chicago avant-garde tradition. It's little surprise to learn that Troche cites the influence of the experimental video work (a key subculture for the lesbian community) of artists such as Cheryl Dunne and Sadie Benning.

Immediately eclipsing its antecedents, *Go Fish* became a 1994 Sundance sensation and the first film to be actually sold during the festival. Islet had whipped potential buyers into a frenzy, pitching the film as threatening to do for lesbian audiences what Lee's *She's Gotta Have It* (1986) did for black audiences; unsurprisingly Goldwyn hungrily took Pierson's bait. With the sexual identity of the characters a given, the film feels refreshingly free of both stereotypes and didacticism. It became a perhaps unlikely box-office success, in part as a result of a canny marketing campaign intended to neither downplay the lesbian content nor exclude male or heterosexual female viewers. *Go Fish* was nevertheless released in Gay Pride month during the auspicious twenty-fifth anniversary of Stonewall.

Go Fish also established a new visibility for lesbian films and lesbian film-makers in the predominantly male domain of the New Queer Cinema movement, as well as finding universal critical favour. Influential gay critic B. Ruby Rich campaigned for the film, citing it as the daughter of Jan Oxenberg's technically raw but politically sophisticated lesbian comedy, *A Comedy in Six Unnatural Acts* (1975) (Hillier, 2001, p. 94).

Dir: Rose Troche; **Prod**: Rose Troche, Guinevere Turner; **Scr**: Rose Troche, Guinevere Turner; **DOP**: Ann T. Rossetti; **Editor**: Rose Troche; **Score**: Brendan Dolan, Jennifer Sharpe, Scott Aldrich; **Main Cast**: V. S. Brodie, Guinevere Turner, T. Wendy McMillan, Migdalia Melendez.

Gummo
US, 1997 – 89 mins
Harmony Korine

Written for Larry Clark, *Kids* (1995) marked the beginning of an auspicious and controversial career for the cine-literate Korine. The son of a documentary film-maker, Korine partly retained the format's vérité style and use of non-actors for his own directorial debut, mischievously named after the least well-known Marx brother. Made with the rare privilege of final cut, Korine's wildly original *Gummo* polarised critics like few other films in recent American cinema history. Many praised it as the most authentic, inspiring and original work in decades, while others were repelled by its squalid tone and free-form, experimental appearance; Janet Maslin of the *New York Times* dubbed it the worst film of the year (Hillier, 2001, p. 200).

Set among the urban poor of Xenia, an Ohio backwater community, the film eschews linearity and plot (terms Korine despises) to instead offer an expressionistic and fragmented series of snapshots (Korine imagined the film as a collage of still photographs), stories and memories to deal frankly with the ennui of small-town American adolescence. *Gummo*'s protagonists are Solomon (Reynolds) and Tumbler (Sutton), two impoverished and malnourished teenage malcontents from broken homes who evade boredom by shooting stray cats and selling their carcasses. The money they make enables them to buy the glue and aerosol cans that provide respite from their harsh existence.

The subject of adolescent suffering may be a common staple of independent and mainstream American cinema (Solomon and Tumbler also resemble literary figures such as Tom Sawyer and Huckleberry Finn), but Korine's 'teen' movie has a closer kinship to works such as Buñuel's *Los Olvidados* (1950); the director himself cites Alan Clarke as his primary influence. Having spent many months among the community in which he filmed, Korine was keen to avoid a patronising, 'trash-chic' depiction of the people's lives, treating his cast with integrity and affection.

Misspent youth: Solomon (Jacob Reynolds) and Tumbler (Nick Sutton) quell the boredom of small-town life by shooting stray cats and selling their carcasses to buy glue to get high in Harmony Korine's opinion-dividing *Gummo*

There's also a refreshing moral ambivalence and refusal to condemn, achieved in part through an understanding of the social and economic factors that have afflicted an underclass that the director felt had been marginalised or simply ignored by the American media.

At times *Gummo* resembles a home movie (albeit an extremely stylised one) in terms of the spontaneous, private moments it captures, including two skinhead brothers fighting and Solomon's mother (Linda Manz) giving him a bath. Contrastingly, its authentic blue-collar neo-realism is suffused with an intense, lyrical beauty courtesy of Jean-Yves Escoffier's luminous photography, perhaps best evidenced in a transcendent scene in which teenagers frolic in a swimming pool during a summer storm. Dave Doernberg's off-kilter production design heightens the sensory surrealism, most memorably during the opening sequence in which a waif-like boy (Sewell, credited simply as 'Bunny Boy') wanders the grey highways sporting outsized pink rabbit ears.

Gummo fell foul of the censors, who objected to the association of children with drugs and a scene in which the camera reveals the bug bites on the legs of a four-year-old child forced to share his home with a legion of cockroaches. During the hiatus over cuts, the ever-precocious Korine considered junking the project. This now seems unthinkable.

Dir: Harmony Korine; **Prod**: Cary Woods; **Scr**: Harmony Korine; **DOP**: Jean-Yves Escoffier; **Editor**: Chris Tellefsen; **Score**: Randy Poster; **Main Cast**: Jacob Sewell, Nick Sutton, Lara Tosh, Jacob Reynolds.

Half Nelson
US, 2006 – 107 mins
Ryan Fleck

Ryan Fleck's impressive directorial debut neatly sidesteps the pitfalls of the classroom drama and favours an altogether wittier, more credible approach. An honest and understated drama about a disillusioned and self-destructive teacher whose relationship with a precocious student inspires him to reclaim his own wayward life, the film offers a fresh and emotionally charged take on friendship and the possibility of redemption in an unforgiving world.

Dan Dunne (Gosling) is a young, inner-city junior high-school teacher whose ideals wither and die in the face of reality. Day after day in his shabby Brooklyn classroom, he somehow finds the energy to inspire his thirteen- and fourteen-year-olds to examine everything from civil rights to the Civil War with a new enthusiasm. Rejecting the standard curriculum in favour of an edgier approach, Dan teaches his students how change works – on both a historical and personal scale – and how to think for themselves. Though Dan is dynamic and in control in the classroom, he spends his time outside school on the edge of consciousness, his disappointments and disillusionment having led to a serious drug habit. He juggles his hangovers and his homework, keeping his lives separated, until one of his troubled students, Drey (Epps), catches him getting high. From this awkward beginning, Dan and Drey stumble into an unexpected friendship, with both recognising that they have arrived at an important intersection in their lives.

In professional wrestling, a 'half nelson' is an immobilising hold that is very difficult to escape from. Fleck and writer, producer and editor Anna Boden saw the title as a metaphor for being stuck in an uncomfortable position, which is exactly where they place their central

(*Opposite page*) As the Brooklyn teacher in a compromised position, Ryan Gosling excels in *Half Nelson*. Gosling secured an unlikely Academy Award nomination

protagonist. Dunne is a charismatic teacher who has the power to transform the lives of his teenage students. Though his school is in a desolate part of Brooklyn, where everything is drab and depressed, Dunne's classroom is an oasis of enlightenment. When he teaches, he is animated, smart, strong and completely in control. But Dunne's personal life borders on the tragic. The suffocating 'half nelson' he cannot escape is his drug addiction. The siren's call of the crack pipe helps him to forget the terrible truths that haunt him every day: that ideals die, that life presents more dead ends than open doors, and that recovery is always beckoning but never quite attainable. Anchored by a remarkable performance from Gosling, who was nominated for an Academy Award and who has since gone on to make a series of interesting and diverse career choices in films such as *Lars and the Real Girl* (2007), *Half Nelson* avoids simply being another sermon on the perils of addiction. Instead, it uses its flawed but fascinating central character to explore universal political and philosophical themes, such as the impotence of idealism and the failure of the liberal dream.

    The project, invariably compared to David Gordon Green's *George Washington* (2000) though the aesthetic is very different, developed after Fleck and Boden met while attending New York University Film School. Writing the film together in early 2002, they had little money or resources to produce a feature and so decided to refashion their story into a short script and shoot it on digital video with friends and local kids as their cast and crew. Originally titled *Gowanus, Brooklyn* after the industrial Brooklyn neighbourhood Fleck and Boden were living in at the time, the short won the Grand Jury Prize at the 2004 Sundance Film Festival and precipitated the funding to expand to feature length.

Dir: Ryan Fleck; **Prod**: Jamie Patricof, Alex Orlovsky, Lynette Howell, Anna Boden, Rosanne Korenberg; **Scr**: Ryan Fleck, Anna Boden; **DOP**: Andrij Parekh; **Editor**: Anna Boden; **Score**: Broken Social Scene; **Main Cast**: Ryan Gosling, Shareeka Epps, Anthony Mackie, Monique Gabriela Curnen.

Henry: Portrait of a Serial Killer
US, 1986 – 83 mins
John McNaughton

Influenced by a television documentary on convicted mass murderer, Henry Lee Lucas, McNaughton set about creating a film loosely based on his life. Lucas claimed to have killed more than 300 people but has, a caption at the start of the film informs us, recanted many of his confessions.

Released from prison following the murder of his prostitute mother, Henry (Rooker) supplements his job as a bug exterminator with the murders of countless, mostly female strangers. After shacking up in a Chicago apartment with fellow ex-con and sometime drug dealer Otis (Towles), Henry finds a willing accomplice in his murderous pursuits. Seeking sanctuary from her abusive husband, Otis' sister Becky (Arnold) moves in and a tentative bond develops between her and Henry. After an increasingly depraved Otis rapes his sister, he is murdered by Henry, who seems to be on the brink of forming a relationship with Becky. However, the film chillingly concludes with a lone Henry depositing a blood-stained suitcase by the roadside before silently disappearing into the night.

Working from a low-budget aesthetic, McNaughton aims for dispassionate objectivity, adopting a low-key documentary style that the film impressively sustains throughout. Conversation and carnage are rendered with the same detached matter-of-factness that marks out the film's intelligence and the film-maker's resolute refusal to offer the kind of exploitative, cheapo titillation that are the hallmarks of other films of this nature. *Henry* also deploys excellent sound design throughout, perhaps most impressively in the opening panning montage of Henry's victims, which substitutes visceral gore for a discordant soundtrack of screams and cries.

A later DIY video sequence, revealing Henry and Otis invading the home of a young family, is the film's most chillingly realised and excruciating set-piece and McNaughton's formal *coup de grâce*.

The camera is clumsily dropped on its side while Henry slopes off to execute a young interloper; he returns to find Otis attempting to rape the dead mother. Off screen we hear Otis exclaim, 'I want to watch it again', and as the camera pulls back we realise that Henry and Otis are reviewing the tape for their own pleasure. As the tape rewinds on Otis' television screen, McNaughton lingers on the image before thankfully cutting away. A thorn in the side of the censor (and later an inspiration for *Funny Games*, 1997), the moment provokes myriad debates about voyeuristic pleasure and the role of the spectator in connection to on-screen violence.

Henry avoids the presentation of the serial killer as larger-than-life entertainment – a route taken by *The Silence of the Lambs* (1991) – and similarly disavows offering a cathartic, psychological or sociological explanation for Henry's actions. Likewise, there's no sense of moral rectitude concerning the killings, with Henry for the most part presented as the most well-balanced character. A chilling, uncompromising and intelligent vision, the film was dealt a dreaded X certificate in the US and remained unreleased for four years after its original completion.

Dir: John McNaughton; **Prod**: John McNaughton, Lisa Dedmond, Steven A. Jones; **Scr**: Richard Fire, John McNaughton; **DOP**: Charlie Lieberman; **Editor**: Elena Maganini; **Score**: Robert McNaughton; **Main Cast**: Michael Rooker, Tracy Arnold, Tom Towles.

Hoop Dreams
US, 1994 – 171 mins
Steve James

Among the most celebrated of documentary features, *Hoop Dreams* follows four years in the lives of William Gates and Arthur Agee, two black teenage basketball prodigies from the Chicago housing projects who, aged fourteen, are offered semi-scholarship places at the prestigious, largely white St Joseph's College. At almost three hours long (the film-makers vehemently fought to avoid editing to a more conventional length), the film looks at how the fortunes of the two teenagers intersect and diverge as they fight to impress talent scouts, retain the financial and moral support of their respective families and overcome institutionalised racism in a bid to achieve their sporting goals. Once professional status is attained, untold wealth and international recognition tantalisingly await.

Existing within the tradition of the anthropological/ethnographic documentary, *Hoop Dreams* presents a telling, tarnished representation of the American dream and a damning chronicle of the black experience in contemporary America. For young black men such as William and Arthur, excellence in sport seems the only viable means through which to escape their economic and social plight. But being good at sport is not merely enough; academic exams also have to be passed, and the scholarship at St Joseph's brings with it private fees and expenses that ultimately Arthur's family are unable to meet. In perhaps the film's most consciously political moment, Spike Lee gives a talk at William's summer school to reveal how young black men will be exploited by talent scouts and coaches in the name of money and reputation. Another scene in which prospective talents are paraded reinforces Lee's words and evokes the days of slavery and the trading of black men as physical commodities.

Edited from 250 hours of footage, the expansive time frame and narrative trajectory charting the progress of William and Arthur are lent added poignancy and emotional engagement through the intimate interviews with members of the Agee and Gates families. The film offers a positive depiction of black motherhood as it looks at how Arthur's mother Sheila keeps her family together in the face of extreme poverty and her husband Arthur's crack habit. Critics such as bell hooks charged the film with offering a stereotypical view of black families, pointing to the unreliable, largely absent black fathers in the film (hooks, 1995, p. 23). Interestingly, and in contrast to hooks' argument, the film concludes with William, who speaks out against the ethic of competition encouraged by society, becoming a committed, doting parent.

A combination of direct-to-camera interviews and fly-on-the wall footage, *Hoop Dreams* is simply but effectively executed. Filmed largely on Betacam format, which contributes to the film's raw and grainy aesthetic, its main virtue is perhaps its lack of sentimentality and its non-didactic handling of issues of race and class. A critical and commercial success upon release, it enjoyed rave notices following Sundance and New York festival screenings. There was a swelling of support for the film to receive a Best Picture Academy Award nomination, but controversially, the film failed even to secure a nomination in the Best Documentary category. Roger Ebert in the *Chicago Sun-Times* described it as among the greatest viewing experiences of his lifetime (Ebert, 1994).

Dir: Steve James; **Prod**: Fred Marx, Steve James, Peter Gilbert; **Scr**: Fred Marx, Steve James, Peter Gilbert; **DOP**: Peter Gilbert; **Editor**: Fred Marx, Steve James, Bill Haugse; **Score**: Tom Yore; **Main Cast**: William Gates, Arthur Agee, Emma Gates, Ken Curtis.

In Search of a Midnight Kiss
US, 2007 – 90 mins
Alex Holdridge

Combining romance, intelligent dialogue (talk remains cheap) and an ultra-low budget, *In Search of a Midnight Kiss* very much evolved from the spirit and aesthetic encapsulated by the films of Andrew Bujalski. Considered the discovery of its year, in part thanks to the way it won over festivalgoers and critics, the film managed to transcend its humble 'mumblecore' roots to enjoy genuine commercial success and so become the first film of its kind to be actually seen as opposed to merely talked about by the cognoscenti.

Like a spikier *Before Sunrise*, writer-director Alex Holdridge's droll and delightful comedy allows a wholly persuasive relationship to develop before the audience's eyes: flaws, ambiguities, warts and all. Languishing without a New Year's date, and getting his kicks fantasising about his roommate's girlfriend, sweet slacker Wilson (McNairy) is persuaded to place a personal ad. It's answered by beautiful, bossy, egotistical Vivian (Simmonds), who promptly lets Wilson know that he doesn't come up to scratch in her hell-bent search to be with the perfect man come midnight. Yet something binds the two, and the date extends into an impulsive ramble around LA, characterised by bickering, flirtation, competition and just a dash of crime …

The film originated in Austin, Texas, home of Richard Linklater and a hotbed of indie film activity, where Holdridge had made *Wrong Numbers* (2001) and *Sexless* (2003). Encouraged by their relatively favourable reception, Holdrige was motivated enough to move to LA and pursue his dreams of a fully-fledged career in the movies. It was his early days in LA that inspired his plot – namely, what aspiring young Hollywood hopefuls do when the phone refuses to ring. Aware that he would have limited resources, Holdridge wrote the film with several key collaborators in mind, including McNairy, Simmonds and Robert Murphy, who in a money-saving tactic doubles as the film's cinematographer while also shining in an acting role.

A large portion of *In Search of a Midnight Kiss* was shot without permission on the streets of downtown LA, where Holdridge's vision was to utilise its grimy, faded grandeur. While downtown LA has always been considered as the film production hub of the city, this film is unique for shooting the area in a monochrome, vérité style that exposes both its decay and its beauty. The first seventy pages of the script were shot in just nine days, and after the footage was cut together the decision was made to seek financing in order to complete the shooting. The entire production team reconvened one month later for two more weeks of filming and laboured through twenty-hour days to finish on schedule and just as the last of the money ran out.

Gently sprinkled with the melancholy that often trails in the wake of the waning hours of the year and the desperation to find happiness and have a good time, the smart script and wholly effective rendering of the film's locale is married to the sparky performances from McNairy and Simmonds. One awaits Holdridge's next project with some anticipation.

Dir: Alex Holdridge; **Prod**: Seth Caplan, Alex Holdridge; **Scr**: Alex Holdridge; **DOP**: Robert Murphy; **Editor**: Frank Reynolds, Jacob Vaughn; **Principal Cast**: Scoot McNairy, Sara Simmonds, Brian McGuire, Katie Luong.

In the Company of Men
US, 1997 – 93 mins
Neil LaBute

Partly funded by an insurance settlement following a car accident, *In the Company of Men* marked playwright LaBute's transition from stage to screen. LaBute is a practising Mormon and the author of provocative plays such as *Filthy Talk for Troubled Times*, and his unflinching feature debut continued his fascination with the more loathsome, odious aspects of contemporary society and its voracious appetite for cruelty and humiliation.

With a minimalist, pared-down visual style of largely static camera, medium long shots, unfussy, well-lit interior locations and its favouring of acerbic dialogue over action, *Men* immediately drew comparisons with David Mamet's early features, *House of Games* (1987) and *Things Change* (1988). Talk, of course, is cheap to film and the simple formal requirements of these directors' plays ensured that both men were well suited to adapt to the potentially rocky terrain of independent/low-budget film production.

LaBute's film focuses on two white-collar executives, Chad (Eckhart) and Howard (Malloy), chosen by their company to help establish a new out-of-town division. Licking their emotional wounds following the fall-out from recently terminated relationships, the pair conspire to strike a blow for their sex by seducing and abandoning a female target. Office typist Christine (Edwards) fits the bill perfectly. She is beautiful and susceptible to romance, but the fact that she is also deaf makes her the perfect victim and the instrument by which Chad and Howard will exact their revenge. 'Let's do it, let's hurt someone', they cheerfully decide.

Featuring lines such as, 'I don't trust anything that bleeds for a week and doesn't die', the film is a knowingly provocative but astringently intelligent observation of misogyny and male insecurity. By locating the majority of the film in a bland, sterile and patriarchal corporate environment (we rarely see beyond the office walls to the world outside, also of course an economic consideration), LaBute makes an important point about the institutional nature of misogyny. Similarly, a scene in which Chad (one of the most monstrous and irredeemable cinematic creations in quite some time) demands to see the balls of a black underling as proof of his commitment, reveals a simmering undercurrent of racism. The film takes a microscopic look at the contemporary workplace and its gender divisions, and has a distinctly anthropological feel. It is instructive that the only work we see being done is by women, while all the bitching and backbiting is done by men.

The film suffered accusations of misogyny, with its director accused of literally denying women a voice. At the eye of this stormy debate was the film's denouement, in which LaBute perhaps deliberately employs shock tactics to court controversy. Chad, who is revealed as contemptuous of all things as opposed to just a hater of women, is allowed to go unpunished, returning to his life of cosy domesticity. Howard (realised with a weasely intensity by Hal Hartley regular Malloy) is meanwhile revealed as the film's most nauseating, irredeemable character, ultimately reduced to impotently begging an uncomprehending Christine for forgiveness.

Dir: Neil LaBute; **Prod**: Mark Archer, Stephen Pevner; **Scr**: Neil LaBute; **DOP**: Tom Hettinger; **Editor**: Joel Plotch; **Score**: Ken Williams, Karel Roessingn; **Main Cast**: Aaron Eckhart, Matt Malloy, Stacy Edwards, Emily Cline.

Junebug
US, 2005 – 90 mins
Phil Morrison

Originating from debutant director Phil Morrison's interest in the subject of people communicating across great divides and in his and writer Angus MacLachlan's fascination with the moral challenges posed by the relationship between makers and connoisseurs, *Junebug* is a film for which the term 'delightful' could have been invented.

When Madeleine (Davidtz), a British-born dealer in regional, 'outsider' art, travels from Chicago to North Carolina to pursue a local painter for her gallery, she and her brand-new, younger husband George (Nivola) extend the trip to include an introduction to his family: his prickly mother Peg (Weston); his taciturn father Eugene (Scott Wilson); his angry younger brother Johnny (Benjamin McKenzie), who has always suffered in the shadow of his over-achieving brother; and Johnny's very pregnant and innocently garrulous wife Ashley (Adams). Although Ashley immediately takes to the sophisticated Madeleine and embraces her, the other members of George's family are more resistant. With George falling into his old routine of spending time alone, Madeleine relies almost entirely on Ashley to help her navigate the family dinners, Church meetings and Ashley's baby shower, all while desperately trying to close the deal on the artist. Tensions mount when Ashley goes into labour and each family member's priorities, Madeleine's included, are confronted.

The film opens, Werner Herzog-style, with shots of people hollering. Once a practical form of communication in the North Carolina hills, the practice has become aestheticised by its appreciators, who have become its patrons and, often, its practitioners. Thus, Morrison's interest in the connoisseur/maker relationship also extends to an exploration of the difficulties of relationships based on patronage, however well meaning. Beautifully articulating the idiosyncrasies of its setting, the film, shot on Super-16 by Peter Donahue, is rare in its compassion for the people and community it depicts.

This compassion is fully extended to the light Morrison sheds on families, the eccentric behaviour that overcomes them when a stranger enters the nest and the foibles of middle-class respectability. In this regard, *Junebug* is aided no end by a number of exceptional performances. Davidtz is great as the outwardly confident yet inwardly shy intruder, and Weston also shines as the domineering and over-protective matriarch. It is, however, Adams, who secured an Academy Award nomination and set herself on the path to mainstream stardom, who steals the show as the young, kind-hearted innocent smitten with her new 'sister'. Melodiously scored by indie darlings Yo La Tengo and featuring a cameo from Will Oldham as one of Madeleine's primitive art scouts, this is an intelligent, deeply charming and immensely satisfying picture.

Dir: Phil Morrison; **Prod**: Mindy Goldberg, Mike S. Ryan; **Scr**: Angus MacLachlan; **DOP**: Peter Donahue; **Editor**: Joe Klotz; **Score**: Yo La Tengo; **Main Cast**: Embeth Davidtz, Alessandro Nivola, Amy Adams, Celia Weston.

Juno
US, 2007 – 91 mins
Jason Reitman

The second film from Jason Reitman is, like his debut *Thank You for Smoking* (2005), a studio-financed and produced indie. Shepherded through production by a quartet of producers sensitive to writer Diablo Cody's whip-smart script (more of which later), the film was released through Fox Searchlight, Twentieth Century-Fox's boutique division, and followed the success of *Little Miss Sunshine* (2006) in penetrating the mainstream.

Juno MacGuff (Page), a bright teenager with a fine line in sardonic wit, has the misfortune to find herself pregnant after the first and only time she has sex with her equally inexperienced classmate Paulie Bleeker (Cera). With the aid of her supportive best friend (Olivia Thirlby) and the small ads, she finds her unborn child a set of 'perfect' parents: an affluent suburban couple, Mark and Vanessa (Bateman and Garner), longing to adopt. However, things aren't quite as straightforward as they seem, so it's fortunate that Juno has the support of her dad and stepmother (J. K. Simmons and Allison Janney), as she faces some tough decisions, flirting with adulthood and figuring out just where she fits in life.

A former stripper whose partly autobiographical novel *Candy Girl: A Year in the Life of an Unlikely Stripper* won hearts and minds, writer Diablo Cody was pressed into writing a screenplay after producer Mason Novick discovered her salacious, irreverent and wildly funny Internet blog. Recognising in Cody's work a singularly feminine and ultra-contemporary candidness, Novick made contact and the pair discussed an adaptation of Cody's novel. Convincing Cody that a sample script would be necessary in order to assure prospective financiers of her viability as a screenwriter, the writer delivered a first draft of *Juno* and the decision was immediately taken to shoot that instead.

One of Cody's inspirations was the desire to deal in a no-nonsense manner with the issue of teenage pregnancy and adolescent sensibilities, and to avoid the two-dimensional caricatures that traditionally populate other films in the crowded coming-of-age genre. Cody's writing is indeed the main strength of a film that is otherwise fairly pedestrian (but perked up no end by Kimya Dawson's angsty pop songs), and in Juno, beautifully played by Ellen Page, who has since become very much in demand as an actress, she has created a character who is frank, funny, charming and self-confident. In short, a genuinely realistic teenager grappling with the uncertainties of the world. Cody's ear for dialogue is also particularly attuned and perhaps the main strength of *Juno* is that it is a teen movie that doesn't talk down to its target audience. Drawing on the situations and conversations she witnessed growing up in Minneapolis, where she was employed as a phone-sex operator/insurance adjuster while working on the script, Cody was keen to stress at press interviews that her central character was very much an extension of herself.

Dir: Jason Reitman; **Prod**: Lianne Halfon, John Malkovich, Mason Novick, Russell Smith; **Scr**: Diablo Cody; **DOP**: Eric Steelberg; **Editor**: Dana E. Glauberman; **Score**: Kimya Dawson; **Main Cast**: Ellen Page, Michael Cerra, Jennifer Garner, Jason Bateman.

Kids
US, 1995 – 91 mins
Larry Clark

Written by an eighteen-year-old Harmony Korine, *Kids* shares a clear lineage with Clark's controversial collections of photographs (the most notorious of which is perhaps 1971's *Tulsa*) of bored, disaffected, adolescent speed-freaks. Informed by a similarly uncompromising sensibility, *Kids* also adopts a pseudo-documentary realist aesthetic, namely the use of hand-held camera, grainy film stock and a naturalistic, unforced approach to editing. *Kids* is the tale of a group of promiscuous, misogynistic New York teenage boys. Led by Telly (Fitzpatrick), whose particular peccadillo is seducing virgins, the group enjoys the occasional spot of skateboarding but mostly passes the time by taking whatever drugs are available, stealing beer, indulging in mindless violence and sleeping around. However, AIDS casts its menacing shadow when Jenny (Sevigny), one of Telly's conquests, is diagnosed as HIV-positive.

The film polarised critics and audiences alike, with many finding Clark's clarion call to the parents of America a sleazy, sensationalist and exploitative exercise that allowed the director, repeatedly labelled an ageing reprobate by the right-wing press, to indulge on screen a predilection for adolescent flesh. Moreover, the AIDS subplot was viewed as a spurious attempt to lend the material a morality it otherwise lacked. *Kids* was heavily scrutinised by the censors, and created a media furore in America, with parents (oblivious to the fact that Clark is a parent himself) objecting to the unwholesome picture the film paints of American youth and their absent, uncaring parents. Cannily citing objective detachment, Clark claimed to have merely held a mirror up to American society; it didn't like the view one bit. Various 'Do you know where your Kids are?' articles appeared to fan the flames of controversy, all of which were used in the marketing of a film that went on to achieve considerable commercial success. In Britain, an outraged *Daily Mail* led the calls for the film to be banned.

The film's supporters, in part seduced by its somewhat forced realist credentials (*Kids* exhibits an almost inconsequential approach to sound quality), found the film to be a gritty, essential meditation on the horrors of youth in a society marked by casual attitudes to and the easy availability of sex and drugs. *Kids*' characters may be ruled by their lusts but they are still too naive to understand the consequences of their actions. Clark certainly doesn't pull his punches; the sex scenes, in which the female is normally non-compliant, are as frank, messy and determinedly unerotic as the frequent outbursts of gang-related beatings are sickeningly violent. Moreover, the relentlessly grim and sordid tone is a persuasive argument against accusations that the film glamorises the activities on display. The fittingly lo-fi score comes courtesy of Folk Implosion's Lou Barlow.

Kids is provocative, troubling, taboo-tackling and undeniably powerful. Its main legacies are a committed reworking of documentary techniques in the name of fiction and a gloves-off approach in a series of increasingly explicit films dealing with the corruptibility and malaise of America's youth. Clark would himself return to similar territory with *Bully* (2002).

Dir: Larry Clark; **Prod**: Cary Woods; **Scr**: Harmony Korine; **DOP**: Eric Edwards; **Editor**: Christopher Tellefsen; **Score**: Lou Barlow, John Davis; **Main Cast**: Leo Fitzpatrick, Justin Pierce, Chloë Sevigny.

Killer of Sheep
US, 1977 – 84 mins
Charles Burnett

Burnett emerged from the 70s' movement of university-based Los Angeles film-makers who through the establishment of independent black productions sought to challenge and formally and politically oppose Hollywood's discriminatory structure and the blaxploitation films it sanctioned. Focusing on the authentic depiction of the common working-class black experience and the gritty realism of inner-city life, Burnett and his contemporaries had little interest in existing within a commercial framework but instead strove to establish a conscious black audience and initiate social change.

Photographed in frills-free black and white with a largely non-professional cast on the very slenderest of budgets, *Killer of Sheep*'s compelling immediacy and determinedly gritty aesthetic owes much to the Italian neo-realist cinema of the 40s. Its disjunctive approach to character and structure and its raw, uncompromising tone also recall Cassavetes. Set in an impoverished black neighbourhood in South Central LA, Burnett's feature debut 'focuses' (it largely eschews a traditional trajectory) on Stan (Sanders), a black slaughterhouse worker whose monotonous, miserable existence engenders increasingly intense feelings of alienation and disconnectedness. An insomniac increasingly removed from wife (Moore) and troublesome son (Jack Drummond), Stan's life assumes the characteristics of a tiresome dream from which he is powerless to stir.

A project that bears Burnett's signature in every department (he wrote, produced, edited and shot the film), *Killer of Sheep*'s dreamy, often transcendental and to some problematically unfocused tone (for Richard Combs, Cassavetes' 'rambling encounter sessions are models of cohesion' by comparison [Combs, 1977]) frequently gives pause for brief vignettes and seemingly minor interludes and reminiscences. In this regard, Burnett's approach can be viewed as audaciously replicating his

Henry Gayle Sanders as Stan, a disaffected slaughterhouse worker in *Killer of Sheep*

central protagonist's partly somnambulant state as he drifts from one encounter to the next. An essentially decent man 'working myself into my own hell' in a hostile and emotionally barren climate, Stan at one point in conversation with a colleague holds a warm coffee cup to his cheek, wistfully explaining that its heat reminds him of making love to a woman. The moment offers a reminder of the small pleasures that in hardship often serve to sustain the human spirit.

Rich in metaphor (the relationship between sheep and sleeplessness and Stan's performing of a job in which he is mired in hopelessness and hideousness), *Killer of Sheep*'s inventive editing technique further enhances its allegorical power. This is perhaps most tellingly achieved in a juxtaposition of shots of a victimised child with the Judas sheep leading the other animals to slaughter. Detailing with insight, eloquence and without resort to stereotype the plight and loss of self suffered by members of the black community, Burnett also makes explicit reference to its rootedness and cultural heritage in the assemblage of a phenomenal soundtrack featuring the ilk of jazz and blues artists such as Paul Robeson and Little Walter. A film that continues to exert its influence in the field of American independent cinema, it was cited by David Gordon Green as a major influence on his similarly mesmeric *George Washington* (2000). Previously written about rather than seen (the soundtrack clearance rights seemingly causing a mountain of rights red tape and bureaucracy), the film enjoyed a 2008 theatrical re-release and is now widely available, together with a number of Burnett's shorts, on DVD.

Dir: Charles Burnett; **Prod**: Charles Burnett; **Scr**: Charles Burnett; **DOP**: Charles Burnett; **Editor**: Charles Burnett; **Score**: Various; **Main Cast**: Henry Gayle Sanders, Kaycee Moore, Charles Bracy, Angela Burnett.

The Kill-Off
US, 1989 – 97 mins
Maggie Greenwald

The Kill-Off concerns the inhabitants of a grim, wintry East Coast resort who are at the mercy of the malicious and salacious town gossip, Luane Devore (Gross). It was adapted by Greenwald from pulp novelist Jim Thompson's characteristically hard-boiled, misanthropic look at the seedy underbelly of American life. Communicating her venomous missives via telephone, the bed-ridden Devore merrily spreads news of the latest scandals involving her neighbours, making public incestuous relationships, drug dependencies, teenage pregnancies and the like. It's only a matter of time before one of the paranoid victims of her idle tittle-tattle decides to silence her vicious tongue once and for all.

The film was Greenwald's second feature outing following *Home Remedy* (1988), a popular festival screener that acted as a calling card for *The Kill-Off*, which was acclaimed at Sundance. Earning comparisons with the Coens' *Blood Simple* (1983), the film suggested the emergence of a confident, forthright female voice. Pamela Woodbridge's intensely claustrophobic and oppressive production design contributes to the film's suitably hard-bitten tone, while Declan Quinn's atmospheric camerawork evokes an authentically downbeat, Thompsonesque tone of seediness, pernicious moral decay and general despair. Evan Lurie's discordant, jazz-infused score is similarly effective in suggesting a small-town world deviant and twisted to its very core. *The Kill-Off* also makes a compelling virtue of its sound design (efficiently edited by James Kwei), aurally forewarning through dial tones and sound waves (accompanied by panning shots of overhead telephone wires) the moments when Devore is about to make her poisonous calls. Gross is convincingly repugnant and sadistic as Luane and is well supported by a cast of relative unknowns.

Perceived as a lower-budget Kathryn Bigelow due to her tendency to work within genres more popularly mined by male film-makers,

Greenwald was perhaps inevitably feted as a feminist director upon the release of the film. Such views were largely predicated on both the relative dearth of female directors working in the medium, indie or otherwise, and the writer-director's talent for creating strong female characters able to compete on an equal footing with their male counterparts. In terms of assessing the extent of feminist sensibility in Greenwald's work, her follow-up films, the idiosyncratic Western *The Ballad of Little Jo* (1993) and *Songcatcher* (1999), are perhaps more instructive. Gender polemics and the merits of her later work aside, *The Kill-Off* is certainly a highly distinguished, brooding and intelligent contribution to the modern noir genre to compare with Stephen Frears' highly praised *The Grifters* (1990) as one of the finest, most faithful and evocative big-screen Thompson adaptations.

Dir: Maggie Greenwald; **Prod**: Lydia Dean Pilcher; **Scr**: Maggie Greenwald; **DOP**: Declan Quinn; **Editor**: James Kwei; **Score**: Evan Lurie; **Main Cast**: Loretta Gross, Andrew Lee Barrett, Jackson Sims, Steve Monroe.

The Last Seduction
US, 1993 – 110 mins
John Dahl

Dahl had made two impressive if derivative additions to the neo-noir genre, *Kill Me Again* (1989) and *Red Rock West* (1992). His modestly budgeted *The Last Seduction* combined the malevolent, avaricious femme fatale of the 40s with a more explicit and unrestrained eroticism to become one of the most notable modern thrillers since the similarly dark-hearted *Blood Simple* (1983). *Red Rock West* failed to secure a theatrical release in the States (partly because of short-sighted financing), premiering on cable and video; *The Last Seduction* looked set to suffer the same ignominious fate. However, European critics were beguiled by the film's world-weary cynicism and steadfast amorality and, following a rapturous reception at the London Film Festival, *The Last Seduction* was rapidly restored to American theatres, becoming a sleeper hit.

Fleeing from New York after double-crossing her husband Clay (Pullman) on a lucrative cocaine deal, ruthless career criminal Bridget Gregory (Fiorentino) goes to ground in the small town of Beston. Advised by her lawyer to keep a low profile, Bridget takes a job with an insurance company and begins a casual affair with Mike Swale (Berg), an attractive but none too bright white-collar local. Bridget crushes Mike's overtures towards a deeper relationship, but the arrival of a private investigator (Bill Nunn) sanctioned by Clay causes Bridget to realign her affections towards her 'designated fuck'. Having disposed of the investigator in a cleverly staged accident, Bridget then manipulates Mike into a scheme involving the murder of the unfaithful spouses of wealthy clients. Coerced into a contract killing as a means of securing Bridget's devotion, Mike is unwittingly dispatched to New York to kill her husband.

The first of Dahl's films that he did not write, *The Last Seduction* boasts a wickedly dark and blackly comic script courtesy of Steve Barancik that creates one of the most compelling, hard-faced and sexually frank on-screen female characters in recent memory.

Described by her own lawyer as 'a self-serving bitch', Bridget is entirely unafraid of using men as a means of achieving financial gain or physical pleasure. After bluntly telling Mike to 'fuck off' when he tries to hit on her, she is intrigued by his boast that he is 'hung like a horse' and invites him to stay after checking his claim by hand. Bridget also uses the physical failings and weaknesses of men to her advantage, goading Mike when she uncovers the reason for his humiliating return to Beston's humble surroundings: a hitherto hidden marriage to a transvestite. Fiorentino is a revelation, oozing cold-hearted disdain for the weak, dim-witted males she contemptuously crushes beneath her heels.

Although authentically replicating the stylistic motifs of the genre (disorientating compositions, expressionistic lighting etc.), the film somewhat brazenly and entertainingly exists outside any need for moral rectitude. Thoroughly rotten to the core, Bridget, in a scene reminiscent of the closing moments of *Body Heat* (1981), prospers while her duped male counterparts either die or rot in jail.

Dir: John Dahl; **Prod**: Jonathan Shestack; **Scr**: Steve Barancik; **DOP**: Jeffrey Jur; **Editor**: Eric L. Beason; **Score**: Joseph Vitarelli; **Main Cast**: Linda Fiorentino, Peter Berg, Bill Pullman, J. T. Walsh.

The Living End
US, 1992 – 84 mins
Gregg Araki

Having taught a course titled 'Independent-Guerilla-Underground-American New Wave Neo-realist Cinema' at UC Santa Barbara, Araki put his teaching experience to good use when he went on to direct two micro-budget features. Unconventional in form, experimental in structure (sometimes self-consciously so) and born of a willingness to engage with the artificiality of the medium, both *Three Bewildered People in the Night* (1987) and *Long Weekend (O' Despair)* (1989) were over-burdened by an almost suffocating claustrophobia and cloying ennui.

Bolstered by a moderately increased budget and using equipment loaned by the resolutely independent, increasingly marginalised Jon Jost, Araki seemed to really find his voice – and his audience – with *The Living End*. A punkishly political, agitating and notoriously hard-hitting work, it was another seminal moment in the emerging New Queer Cinema movement of the early 90s. Proudly dubbed 'irresponsible' by the director, the spunky and energetic film wears its cine-literacy proudly, playing hard and fast with the conventions of the couple-on-the-run/road movie genre while frequently referencing Godard's *Pierrot le fou* (1965). Godard's influence is profound, both in terms of the diverse counterculture aesthetics and mimicking of mainstream film-making practices the film employs, and in Araki's 'cute' deconstruction of sound-bite culture.

Confrontational, savagely funny (in places the film resembles a screwball comedy) and frequently just savage, *The Living End* tells the story of Luke (Dytri), a gay hustler prone to outbursts of brutal violence, and Jon (Gilmore), a disenchanted Los Angeles movie critic. Both HIV-positive and fiercely attracted to each other, the pair are forced to flee the patently plastic LA environment when Luke carelessly shoots a cop. To the accompaniment of a jagged score from the likes of Braindead Sound Machine, KMFDM and Coil, a fucking and killing rampage through the wastelands of Middle America ensues.

Shot by Araki with a raw tonal intensity, *The Living End* daringly and with heartfelt conviction confronts America's fear of AIDS, existing in stark contrast to Hollywood-sanctioned pictures on the subject, such as Demme's *Philadelphia*, which emerged the following year. The film is also propelled by Araki's rage and indignation, and he ultimately dedicates it to 'the hundreds of thousands who've died and the hundreds of thousands more who will die because of a big white house full of Republican fuckheads'. Roundly antagonistic, Araki even takes a swipe at his US indie peers with a sequence in which Luke murders two gay bashers wearing *Drugstore Cowboy* and *sex, lies and videotape* T-shirts.

Like Todd Haynes and Tom Kalin, Araki also refuses to offer positive, sanitised representations of gay characters. Perhaps as a result, *The Living End* (part of a 'teen apocalypse trilogy' completed by *Totally F***ed Up*, 1993, and *The Doom Generation*, 1995) received a largely muted response from gay critics. Feminists also found fault with *The Living End*'s stereotypical depiction of female characters, particularly the film's two inept lesbian serial killers.

Dir: Gregg Araki; **Prod**: Marcus Hu, Jon Gerrans; **Scr**: Gregg Araki; **DOP**: Gregg Araki; **Editor**: Gregg Araki; **Score**: Cole Coonce; **Main Cast**: Craig Gilmore, Mike Dytri, Darcy Marta, Mary Woronov.

Living in Oblivion
US, 1995 – 90 mins
Tom DiCillo

DiCillo was formerly a cinematographer, most notably for Jarmusch, who made the move to directing with the slight if engaging *Johnny Suede* (1991). Much indebted to Jarmusch's work in tone and structure, the film introduced two defining themes in DiCillo's career: masculinity in crisis and the pressures of maintaining artistic principles in a society where philistinism rules. Largely funded through the financial input of many of the cast and crew, most notably Michael Griffiths and Hilary Gilford who put up the $500,000 required to complete the project, *Living in Oblivion* represents DiCillo's most cogent exploration of these themes.

Written when DiCillo was 'the most disillusioned with every aspect of the film-making process; from raising the money to the technical nightmares of shooting' (DiCillo, 1995, p. ix), it's an entertaining look at an idealistic New York director. Nick Reve, played by the talismanic Buscemi (later to reprise his role in DiCillo's *The Real Blonde*, 1997), is struggling to complete his arty, low-budget movie. Despite the best efforts of leading lady Nicole (a film-stealing performance from Keener, one of the most consistently interesting and audacious actors to emerge from the US indie scene), the anxious director is plagued by a cavalcade of malfunctioning machines, the attentions of his overbearing mother and on-set fighting between cameraman Wolf (Mulroney) and petulant, hammy leading man Chad Palomino (LeGros).

Beginning with a black-and-white dream sequence that was originally a stand-alone short titled *Part One*, *Oblivion* largely proceeds through numerous point-of-view fantasy sequences that instructively reveal the numerous paranoias causing an already fraught shoot to become that bit more difficult. This technique also serves to blur art and life, and fantasy and reality, and creates uncertainty within audience expectations concerning what is 'real' and what is part of the film-within-the-film. A sequence where Keener has to continually re-enact a scene with diminishing returns also marks out both the ardour and the artificiality of the film-making process, stripping it of its mystique and inviting the spectator to consider what actually constitutes performance.

Oblivion has become a classic of its kind, offering a microcosm of the trials and tribulations of independent/low-budget production and its propensity for offering the stuff of both dreams and nightmares. The plot incorporates elements of farce. The fractured and fractious relationships among the cast and crew are, of course, due to the constrictive lack of time and money, but they are exacerbated by a director secretly in love with his leading lady and a philandering, egotistical method-loving actor slumming it in an indie production in order to sharpen his arty credentials (Chad reveals in a fit of pique that he only took the part because he mistakenly believed Nick to be 'tight with Tarantino'). The film is a revealing insight into the currency of 'name' independent directors and a perceptive commentary on how the independent sector is a parasite's paradise offering a short cut to kudos. DiCillo, whose self-penned, Sundance-winning script deftly sidesteps any trace of self-indulgence, also shows that he is not averse to making a number of well-aimed jabs at the egos of would-be auteurs, sending up Nick's more ludicrous pretensions to art in a Felliniesque dream sequence involving a precocious dwarf.

Dir: Tom DiCillo; **Prod**: Michael Griffiths, Marcus Viscidi; **Scr**: Tom DiCillo; **DOP**: Frank Prinzi; **Editor**: Camilla Toniolo; **Score**: Jim Farmer; **Main Cast**: Steve Buscemi, Catherine Keener, James LeGros, Dermot Mulroney.

Lonesome Cowboys
US, 1968 – 110 mins
Andy Warhol

One of the major artists of the twentieth century, Warhol had a strong commitment to cinema, devoting equal time to his Factory Studio and to his conceptual art between 1963 and 1968. Warhol had been weaned on classic Hollywood and gay porn films of the 50s, and was later introduced to Jonas Mekas' Film-makers' Co-op. Thereafter, he added to his list of cinematic influences the work of American avant-garde directors Jack Smith, Kenneth Anger, Stan Brakhage and Marie Menken.

Warhol's early films (1963–4) were Bolex-shot, frills-free silent shorts in which the camera – explicitly acknowledged – remained static. Making concession neither to drama nor narrative, nor indeed the avant-garde, the films were viewed as audacious and provocative. Warhol subsequently worked with scriptwriters Chuck Wein and Ronald Tavel and Factory 'superstars' Edie Sedgwick, Viva and Mario Montez (the approach to performance was idiosyncratic), and his films from 1964 to 1966 began to incorporate both sound and more complex staging, though little in the way of actual plot. Offering a fetishistic depiction of the human body and explicit and destabilised presentations of sex and gender, the films marked Warhol's engagement with fringe cultures of many kinds.

A collaboration with Paul Morrissey, *Lonesome Cowboys* reflects Warhol's attempt to build upon both this and the critical and commercial success of *The Chelsea Girls* (1966), regarded as being as formally important as Godard's work in its use of split-screen technique. Shot on cheap 16mm stock in Arizona, *Lonesome Cowboys* is a synthesis of Western and sexploitation conventions and ultimately resembles an unorthodox pornographic home movie. Featuring a sheriff sporting a black bikini, it's fair to say that the loose incorporation of more traditional realist cinema elements such as characters, plot and costumes is not a tilt at authenticity. The film is frequently hilarious and fleetingly surreal (at one point a cowboy performs ballet exercises), and the props, use of popular songs and the open representation of homosexuality suggest a bold post-modernity. His camera voyeuristically lingering on the muscular torsos of his Western studs (including Hompertz and Joe Dallesandro) as they fuck, frolic, take drugs and generally check each other out, Warhol both popularised cultivated camp (at one point the preening group discuss the correct use of mascara) and provided visual stimuli for the male homosexual gaze.

Moreover, as Peter Gidal comments in *Millennium Film Journal*, in showing the naturalness of sex between men living in close confinement, Warhol posited a far more truthful depiction of the early pioneering days than that revealed in traditional Westerns (Tartaglia, 1979, p. 56). Warhol withdrew from cinema following the attempt on his life by Valerie Solanas, and *Lonesome Cowboys* proved to be his final film as sole director (arm's-length Morrissey collaborations aside). But his radicalism and innovatory pioneering spirit endured throughout the late 60s and 70s.

Warhol withdrew his films from circulation in 1972, claiming they were better talked about than seen, but he was later persuaded to donate all existing materials to the Whitney Museum so that they could be preserved and re-exhibited. When they were collectively shown as part of a major retrospective in 1988, the films provided inspiration for a new generation of formally inquisitive and culturally diverse film-makers willing to vocalise their social, racial and sexual experiences and desires.

Dir: Andy Warhol; **Prod**: Andy Warhol; **Scr**: Andy Warhol; **DOP**: Uncredited; **Editor**: Uncredited; **Score**: Uncredited; **Main Cast**: Viva, Taylor Mead, Tom Hompertz, Louis Waldon.

The Machinist
US, 2004 – 90 mins
Brad Anderson

Two major distinctions characterise Brad Anderson's *The Machinist*. The first is that despite being set in an unnamed West Coast American city, it was actually shot in its entirety just outside of Barcelona. It is both a testimony to the technicians who worked on the film – which was largely Spanish-funded and is cloaked in washed-out industrial greys and blacks – and an indictment of how homogenised the world has become that the difference is not noticeable. The second is an astonishing Christian Bale, who really does take the notion of 'performance' to extremes.

For reasons he is unable to fully fathom, Trevor Reznik (Bale) has not slept for a year. Ravaged by fatigue, Reznik has lost more than sixty pounds and resembles a living skeleton. Wracked by exhaustion, his weary mind increasingly plays tricks on him and he finds only fleeting refuge in the bed of a tender prostitute (Leigh). Then, one fateful day at the machine shop where he works, he's involved in an accident in which a fellow worker (Ironside) loses an arm. Reznik's guilt turns to paranoia when he discovers cryptic notes in his apartment and a ghostly apparition begins to haunt his every move. Is it someone out to exact revenge for the gruesome accident? In a desperate attempt to save his sanity, Reznik, who tentatively connects with a pretty airport waitress (Sanchez-Gijon), must uncover the truth … but the more he learns, the more terrifying his sleepless nightmare becomes.

There are innumerable filmic references, most notably in the Bernard Hermannesque score and the creeping sense of unease and neurosis recognisable from the early films of Roman Polanski, and Scott Kosar, the film's writer, cites Dostoevsky and Kafka as his primary inspirations. Reznik is shown reading literature by both. Though adequately functioning as a somewhat derivative thriller, it is in creating a creeping and almost suffocating sense of paranoia that the film is most successful, evoking its central character's mindset and deteriorating mental and physical state with some conviction. While the film-makers are undoubtedly very strong on tone and atmosphere, ultimately it is Bale who must accept the credit for drawing us into Reznik's nightmarish hinterland.

The actor went to absolute extremes for the role, starving himself for over four months prior to filming. Allegedly, Bale's diet consisted of one cup of coffee and an apple each day and he lost 62 pounds, reducing his body weight to 120 pounds. Bale's appearance frequently causes a sharp intake of breath: in one overhead shot of him laid out on a bed, his utterly emaciated frame, protruding ribcage and pitifully shrunken cheekbones are particularly shocking. The notion of physical performance as spectacle is nothing necessarily new in cinema – think of Robert De Niro's weight gain for *Raging Bull* (1980) – but Christian Bale here undoubtedly explores dangerously new and unchartered terrain.

Dir: Brad Anderson; **Prod**: Julio Fernández; **Scr**: Scott Kosar; **DOP**: Xavi Giménez; **Editor**: Luis de la Madrid; **Score**: Roque Baños; **Main Cast**: Christian Bale, Jennifer Jason Leigh, Aitana Sanchez-Gijon, Michael Ironside.

Man Push Cart
US, 2005 – 87 mins
Ramin Bahrani

This impressive first feature from Iranian-American Ramin Bahrani offers a naturalistic, low-key but dramatically compelling account of the immigrant experience. Beautifully observed and making distinctive use of its New York locations and combination of trained and non-trained actors, the film also reveals a community and a way of life rarely depicted on screen, rarer still in American productions.

Written, produced, directed and edited by Bahrani, who deploys understatement in all departments, the film tells the story of Ahmad (Razvi), a former Pakistani rock singer who ekes out a living selling coffee and doughnuts to morning commuters from his pushcart in Midtown Manhattan. Ahmad supplements his income by selling bootleg porn DVDs, carefully saving his money in the hope of one day purchasing a place to live for himself and his estranged young son. It is a harsh, often humiliating life, but Ahmad carries on with a stoic dignity and sensitivity, seemingly determined to find his way. Then the dull routine is brightened by two developments: the arrival of a young Spanish woman (Dolera) working down the street in a newspaper kiosk; and an offer of assistance from a wealthy fellow Pakistani (Sandoval), who remembers Ahmad's unlikely former life.

While Ahmad strives to pursue these two new opportunities for a better life, Bahrani returns repeatedly to the routine of setting up the cart in the early morning darkness: the preparations he makes for opening, the other immigrants who prepare the city in the dead of night, the exchanges with his customers as they buy their coffee, tea and bagels. This imparts a deliberate rhythm to *Man Push Cart*, as the film explores the complex and hidden depths of a central protagonist we later learn is desperately hanging on to his small dreams in the midst of grief and despair. Concerned with the intricacies of character and mood, and gradually uncloaking subtle power-shifts that speak volumes about desire, loneliness and regret, Bahrani delivers an impressive and effective look at the opportunities available to newcomers in strange cities.

Inspired by the true story of Ahmad Razvi, a former pushcart operator who as well as acting in the film helped source extras and authentic locations, *Man Push Cart* is also informed by Bahrani's love of Persian poetry, *The Myth of Sisyphus* by Albert Camus and the issue-led American movies of the 70s. Having lived on and off in Manhattan and Brooklyn for nearly a decade, Bahrani has witnessed many changes in the city, especially since 9/11, and was desperate to craft a film that not only looked at America with fresh eyes but that also showed that not everyone who looks like Ahmad is a terrorist. Made during a volatile climate that precipitated numerous verbal attacks from New Yorkers during filming, this is a compelling and compassionate work that in its own unassuming and modest way stands as a remarkable testimony to human endurance.

Dir: Ramin Bahrani; **Prod**: Ramin Bahrani; **Scr**: Ramin Bahrani; **DOP**: Michael Simmonds; **Editor**: Ramin Bahrani; **Score**: Peyman Yazdanian; **Main Cast**: Ahmad Razvi, Letica Dolera, Charles Daniel Sandoval, Ali Reza.

Me and You and Everyone We Know
US, 2005 – 90 mins
Miranda July

The feature-length debut of Miranda July, *Me and You and Everyone We Know*, wowed critics and audiences from the moment it premiered at the 2005 Sundance Film Festival. Originally workshopped at the Sundance Screenwriting and Film-making labs in 2003 and 2004, the film ably reflects July's background as an artist who works across a variety of disciplines. Her short pieces have been screened at venues including The Museum of Modern Art and The Guggenheim, while a sound installation

In conversation with the world: Miranda July's *Me and You and Everyone We Know*

piece, *The Drifters*, was presented in the 2002 Whitney Biennial. July is also a widely acclaimed short story writer and her radio performances can be heard regularly on NPR's *The Next Big Thing*. In the production notes prepared for the film, July claims that she regards it all as a single medium and that the performances, short stories, radio plays and moving images are interchangeable and evidence of a desire to simply be in conversation with the world.

Richard Swersey (Hawkes), a newly single shoe salesman and father of two boys, is prepared for amazing things to happen. But when the captivating and utterly spontaneous Christine (July) enters his life, he panics. Christine is an artist and 'Eldercab' (a taxi service for the elderly) driver who alternates between heartbreak and faith. Life is not so oblique for Richard's seven-year-old son Robby (Ratcliff), who is having a risqué Internet romance with a stranger, and his fourteen-year-old brother Peter (Thompson), who becomes the guinea pig for the neighbourhood girls as they practise for their future of romance and marriage. All of them are seeking togetherness in the small moments that connect them to someone else on earth.

Though the above synopsis makes the film sound rather dry, while also fully reflecting July's desire to deal with fractured relationships and the brief and unexpected sparks of intimacy that sometimes occur between strangers, the reality is that it couldn't be more engaging, witty and worthy of affection. An intensely personal work, inspired by a childhood sense of longing and the belief that somebody, at any moment, can enter a person's life and transform everything, the film also offers an intelligent and brilliantly inventive take on the rituals of togetherness. July is also relatively unique in her ability to work effectively with child actors (Ratcliff, in particular, is a minor revelation) and to deal with the intersection between innocence and experience with candour, insight and sensitivity. In one celebrated sequence, Robby, via email, engages in a spot of talking dirty. The scene is both hilarious and an accurate and honest portrayal of how children begin to explore sexuality through thought and language.

Strikingly designed and beautifully photographed in bold, primary colours by noted Mexican cinematographer Chuy Chávez (*Chuck and Buck*, 2000), this is a film that deals with self-isolation and yet manages to radiate optimism, hope and warmth. July is yet to make a follow-up but there is no doubting that *Me and You and Everyone We Know* is a true American original.

Dir: Miranda July; **Prod**: Gina Kwon; **Scr**: Miranda July; **DOP**: Chuy Chávez; **Editor**: Andrew Dickler, Charles Ireland; **Score**: Michael Andrews; **Main Cast**: John Hawkes, Miranda July, Brandon Ratcliff, Miles Thompson.

Mean Streets
US, 1973 – 110 mins
Martin Scorsese

Post-*Easy Rider* (1969), Scorsese and his New Hollywood contemporaries found themselves in a climate receptive to liberty and daring. Scorsese was advised by mentor John Cassavetes to extricate himself from producer Roger Corman's exploitation movie *Boxcar Bertha* (1972), Cassavetes offering a typically curt, 'You're better than the people who make this kind of movie' (Thompson and Christie, 1989, p. 38). Shot on a low budget with many of the *Boxcar* crew, *Mean Streets* bristles with the director's ferocious energy and commitment. On-screen urgency was compounded by a compact shooting schedule involving up to twenty-four set-ups a day and the frequently aggressive chemistry of its actors. Ultimately produced and distributed by Warner Bros. (but owing much to Corman and his associate Paul Rapp), the film represents the cinema of Scorsese in its purest form.

It is set in the violent Little Italy streets of the director's childhood. Returning to the thematic terrain of Catholicism and Italian-American male camaraderie, covered in Scorsese's earlier *Who's That Knocking at My Door* (1968), *Mean Streets* examines the conflicts affecting a closely knit but volatile group of aspirant Italian-Americans. Prominent among them is the relatively respectable Charlie (Keitel), whose ascendancy to the running of an ailing restaurant is haunted by his religious sense of the evil around him and his feeling of duty towards his reckless, destructive young friend, Johnny Boy (De Niro, in a towering performance of flawed masculinity). Charlie's illicit affair with Teresa (Robinson), Johnny Boy's cousin, ultimately proves the flashpoint that leads to a bloody denouement involving a sharpshooter (Scorsese in a characteristic cameo) hired by the brooding moneylender (Richard Romanus) that Johnny Boy has unwisely antagonised.

Given the restrictive conditions under which the film was made, the expressive and experimental approach to editing, sound and camerawork is all the more amazing. Though regarded as a quintessential New York movie, the interiors were largely shot in Los Angeles with only rehearsals and eight days of actual shooting taking place in NYC. Frequently filming in extremely long takes with a mobile camera (as in the prolonged fight scene in a pool hall), Scorsese also uses slow-motion sound and cinematography allied with bold tracking shots – to celebrated and imitated effect. This is most evident in the sequence where Johnny Boy enters a bar to the sounds of 'Jumpin' Jack Flash'. Just one of many such moments (accredited by the director to the tracking camera style

Johnny Boy (Robert De Niro) and Charlie (Harvey Keitel) violently clash in *Mean Streets*

pioneered by Sam Fuller), it moreover illustrates the film's long-lasting influence in the incorporation of popular music as an integral part of its structure.

Scorsese made a powerful connection with his audience, a quality that Michael Powell (a direct influence on the film) cites as being 'the rarest gift given to a movie director. Most directors, however wise, however experienced, however resourceful, however bold, don't have it and never will have it. Marty has always had it' (ibid., p. xiv). Scorsese's expressiveness also prevailed upon a freshly emerging generation of film-makers, both independent and otherwise, later dubbed the 'sons of Scorsese' (Hillier, 2001, p. 92) by critic Amy Taubin. The film is undoubtedly one of American cinema's defining moments. On seeing an initial rough cut of *Mean Streets*, Cassavetes exclaimed, 'Don't cut it whatever you do' (ibid., p. 48).

Dir: Martin Scorsese; **Prod**: Jonathan Taplin; **Scr**: Martin Scorsese, Mardik Martin; **DOP**: Kent Wakeford; **Editor**: Sidney Levin; **Score**: Various; **Main Cast**: Harvey Keitel, Robert De Niro, David Proval, Amy Robinson.

Medium Cool
US, 1969 – 110 mins
Haskell Wexler

A heady fusion of cinéma vérité and political radicalism, Oscar-winning cinematographer Haskell Wexler's debut as a director erodes the barriers between fiction and documentary. Capturing the political unrest of the late 60s with clarity and passion, the film's title is a reference to media theorist Marshall McLuhan's description of the required relationship between viewers and the broadcast image.

In a role originally intended for John Cassavetes, Robert Forster gives a career-defining performance as John Cassellis, a TV cameraman whose motto is 'I love to shoot film'. Practising his craft with cold dispassion, Cassellis considers himself a mere recorder of circumstances and in the film's opening sequence shoots a gruesome car accident with complete detachment. If his soundman (Bonerz) is unable to penetrate his frosty demeanour, what hope has Cassellis' girlfriend (Marianna Hill)? However, as he documents a number of political incidents, including a verbal attack on media racism by members of the Black Panthers, Cassellis slowly becomes more aware of the world around him and the implications of his job. Fired for refusing to hand his Black Panther material over to the FBI, Cassellis develops a deepening relationship with Eileen (the magnificent Bloom), a Vietnam War widow living in the Chicago slums. Accompanying her to the 1968 Democratic National Convention where she searches for her missing son (Blankenship), Cassellis witnesses first hand the violence of the state as demonstrators on the Chicago streets come under intense physical attack.

Wexler adapted the script from a novel by Jack Couffer, and it was his intention to make the heart of his film the footage he and his small crew would capture at the Convention. The resulting brutal police action, condoned by Mayor Richard Daley, resulted in rioting and carnage and made the material more powerful and prescient than Wexler could ever have imagined. This footage, which has an eye-of-the-hurricane urgency and features authentic shots of protestors being clubbed by police, is then combined with staged scenes in which Wexler encouraged his actors to improvise. Partly self-funded, *Medium Cool*'s experimental approach and synthesis of fact and fiction recalls the mid–late 60s films of Jean-Luc Godard (with the final shot a direct homage to *Le Mépris*,

Robert Forster is the man with the movie camera in director Haskell Wexler's radical and politicised *Medium Cool*

1963), but they horrified Paramount, the film's distributor, who significantly delayed the release, undoubtedly blunting the film's potent polemical power. Its reputation, however, subsequently flourished and as well as remaining perhaps the most coherent and committed political feature ever released by a Hollywood studio, it has become accepted as an essential document in terms of its technique, its conviction and in its illustration of a moment of civic and political unrest in American history.

Contemporary audiences were recently able to revisit the film through Paul Cronin's insightful *Look out Haskell, It's Real!* (2001), a documentary that features interviews with almost all the cast and crew of the original production, and never-before-seen out-takes from the UCLA Film and Television Archive. The title of Cronin's film is taken from a voice on the soundtrack during the filming of the riots and is a reference to the tear-gas canisters that were exploding all around.

Dir: Haskell Wexler; **Prod**: Haskell Wexler, Jerrold Wexler; **Scr**: Haskell Wexler; **DOP**: Haskell Wexler; **Editor**: Verna Fields, Marcia Griffin; **Score**: Mike Bloomfield, Wild Man Fisher; **Main Cast**: Robert Forster, Verna Bloom, Peter Bonerz, Harold Blankenship.

Metropolitan
US, 1989 – 98 mins
Whit Stillman

Ushering in a new decade, Stillman's *Metropolitan*, his writing-directing debut, proved to be one of the key independent films of the era and a catalyst for the renaissance in intelligent, understated and knowingly literate low-budget comedy dramas. Emerging alongside Soderbergh's *sex, lies and videotape* (1989) and Hartley's *The Unbelievable Truth* (1989), the picture also established Ira Deutchman (who began his career with Faces films and the release of Cassavetes' *A Woman under the Influence*, 1974) as a ubiquitous figure in American independent distribution and led to the forming of Fine Line features. The 'classics' division of New Line Cinema and a Mecca for established and emerging talents such as Gus Van Sant and Jim Jarmusch, Fine Line contributed to the forming of similar 'classics' divisions at studio-owned companies.

Filmed for just $80,000, it's a smart, articulate, satirical look at the anachronistic children of the 'UHB: the urban haute bourgeoisie', as one character defines them, that's partly informed by Stillman's preppy upbringing as the son of a Republican Democrat on New York's Upper East Side. Into a tightly knit group of privileged Park Avenue bluebloods navigating the endless dinner dress soirées of the debutante season comes Tom Townsend (Clements), an impoverished Princeton student from the Lower West Side whose Socialist principles and hired evening attire conflict sharply with the sensibilities and backgrounds of the self-christened 'Sally Fowler Rat Pack'. However, when Audrey (Farina) develops a crush on him, Tom is persuaded to act as an escort and enjoy food, drink and companionship for the remainder of the season.

The film is beautifully performed by its unknown ensemble cast (many of whom became Stillman regulars), while practicalities dictated that *Metropolitan* make a virtue of pithy, perceptive dialogue dripping in social nuances. Recalling Edith Wharton and F. Scott Fitzgerald (by way of Woody Allen), Stillman reveals characters desperately trying to hide their

Against his socialist principles, impoverished Princeton student Tom Townsend (Edward Clements) mixes with a member of the UHB ('urban haute bourgeoisie') in *Metropolitan*

insecurities under social and intellectual facades, along the way offering valuable insights on the desperate need for acceptance and standing. Commendably, Stillman takes an egalitarian approach to superiority, gently revealing Tom as a 'public transportation snob who looks down on people who takes taxis' and a pseudo-intellectual whose opinions on literature are informed by other people's critiques.

Metropolitan makes a virtue of its festive Manhattan backdrops and economically evokes through the 20s' jazz score and the stylised intertitles the sense that its characters belong to a previous time and are merely adhering to customs and traditions outmoded before they were born. Stillman keeps his compositions relatively simple and just so, filming the largely static scenes in uninterrupted medium close-ups. In a telling irony of low-budget production, while the characters are often shot leaving the plush Plaza hotel, prohibitive filming costs put paid to filming inside it.

Described by Rita Kempley in her *Washington Post* review as a 'smart comedy of conversation … like *My Dinner with André* but with eight place settings', *Metropolitan*'s generally warm critical reception was matched by a respectable box-office performance (just under $3 million on a limited release) that once again alerted the industry to the potential profits to be made from low-budget productions. As well as accruing its director an Academy Award nomination for Best Original Screenplay, *Metropolitan* also netted Stillman a prestigious production deal with Castle Rock. The deal quickly soured after 1998's *The Last Days of Disco* and Stillman all but disappeared. However, a revival of *Metropolitan* renewed interest in his work and at the time of writing, a new project, *Little Green Men*, is in production.

Dir: Whit Stillman; **Prod**: Whit Stillman; **Scr**: Whit Stillman; **DOP**: John Thomas; **Editor**: Chris Tellefsen; **Score**: Mark Suozzo; **Main Cast**: Carolyn Farina, Edward Clements, Christopher Eigerman, Taylor Nichols.

Mutual Appreciation
US, 2005 – 108 mins
Andrew Bujalski

Andrew Bujalski's follow-up to *Funny Ha Ha* (2005) is again characterised by its ultra low-budget production, offhand and seemingly improvised script, use of non-professional actors and wryly amusing musings on the personal relationships between a group of gently drifting twenty-somethings. A key film in the new talkie generation of movies dubbed the 'mumblecore' movement, the film, which was self-distributed in the US and released only after the ripples caused by Bujalski's engaging debut (sold initially on VHS tapes from his website) saw its multitasking creator invariably compared with such indie stalwarts as Jim Jarmusch and Hal Hartley. A lower-fi Woody Allen served as another point of comparison, while Bujalski himself cited Eric Rohmer as a key influence.

Alan (Rice) shows up in New York to pursue his burgeoning rock 'n' roll career. He starts by searching for a drummer and half-heartedly goes about the mechanics of self-promotion. He finds a champion in Sara (Lee), a radio DJ who finds him a drummer. In his down time, Alan drinks and strategises with his old friend and eternal student, Lawrence (Bujalski), and Lawrence's journalist girlfriend, Ellie (Clift). Alan endeavours to keep his shoulder to the wheel, while Ellie finds herself quietly compelled by him. The attraction is mutual, but both parties are reluctant to take the next step.

Slightly broader in scope than its predecessor and a little surer of itself, *Mutual Appreciation* is a wonderfully astute and pleasingly intimate character study in which the pithy one-liners and insightful observations never feel forced or rushed. Boston-born and Harvard-educated, Bujalski had no film-making experience when he shot *Funny Ha Ha* and describes the film as being made with friends in a vacuum. The film came to public attention only after numerous festival screenings, and *Mutual Appreciation* continues the sense that this is a film-maker who is uninhibited by the prescribed notion of doing things.

Though the film often appears to be making itself up as it goes along, it is actually quite carefully structured, wholly scripted and gently rigorous in its analysis of unfocused lives and the creeping ennui that takes hold after the thrill of college is over and the fear of responsibility begins to take hold; and while Bujalski allows the film to travel off in numerous directions, it always returns to the triumvirate of Alan, Lawrence and Ellie. Despite its micro-budget origins, the film also looks a treat, benefiting from excellent use of New York locations, Bujalski's understanding of the struggling artist milieu (apartments are sparsely furnished with just mattresses instead of beds) and Matthias Grunsky's luminous black-and-white 16mm photography.

Dir: Andrew Bujalski; **Prod**: Morgan Faust, Dia Sokol, Ethan Vogt; **Scr**: Andrew Bujalski; **DOP**: Matthias Grunsky; **Editor**: Andrew Bujalski; **Score**: Bishop Allen; **Main Cast**: Justin Rice, Rachel Clift, Andrew Bujalski, Seung-Min Lee.

Napoleon Dynamite
US, 2004 – 86 mins
Jared Hess

The toast of Sundance, where it provoked a furious bidding war, the off-kilter *Napoleon Dynamite* signalled the introduction of an original new voice in Jared Hess. Capturing the comedy, tragedy and disorientation of trying to make it through life and high school, the film, co-written by Hess with his wife Jerusha, creates a character who begins as the ultimate outcast before becoming something of an unlikely and reluctant hero.

Hailing from Preston, Idaho, Napoleon Dynamite (Heder), with his tight red 'fro, moon boots and skills that can't be topped or taught, is a new kind of enigma. Napoleon lives with his Grandma (Sandy Martin) and his thirty-year-old, unemployed brother Kip (Ruell), who spends his days looking for love in Internet chat rooms. When Grandma hits the road, Napoleon and Kip's meddling Uncle Rico (Jon Gries), a door-to-door salesman who's mentally stuck in 1982 – the year his football team 'almost won state' – comes to stay with them and ruin their lives. But then Deb (Majorino), the artisan behind the 'boondoggle key chain', and Pedro (Ramirez), with his sweet bike and talent with women, come to the rescue and Napoleon finds goals outside of being a star milk-tasting judge. Together the trio launches a campaign to elect Pedro for class president and make the student body's wildest dreams come true. But if Pedro is to beat the stuck-up Summer Wheatley (Haylie Duff), Napoleon will have to unleash his secret weapon …

Napoleon Dynamite originated from *Peluca*, a short film Hess had made based on his own distinctive experiences growing up an outsider in the rural American backwater town of the film's setting. While studying at Brigham Young University, Hess, who always hoped to shoot a feature, made his short in just two days for a mere $500, using mostly locals rather than professional actors. He hired a few of his talented classmates to fill in the remaining cast and crew roles, enlisting Jeremy Coon as his producer and Jon Heder (then an animation student and a master of deadpan ennui in the central role) as his star. The short became a minor sensation, and inspired by a packed Slamdance screening, Hess felt ready to turn it into the full-length feature comedy he'd always envisioned. With the support of Coon and a private investor, Hess set out to write a script that would lovingly reinvent the tired structures of the typical teen comedy. A writing collaboration so tight that Hess claims it is impossible to attribute any one character either to himself or Jerusha, the process sparked memories of friends and acquaintances who happily lived on life's weirder side, in a nearly alien small-town world of time machines, martial arts mastery, unselfconscious dance numbers, exasperated sighs and encyclopaedic knowledge of cows.

Though the film inspired cult worship and an affectionate place in recent popular culture (the 'Vote Pedro' T-shirt became de rigueur), it was

Not your typical teen comedy: the eponymous Napoleon Dynamite (Jon Heder, centre) with brother Kip (Aaron Ruell, left) and bothersome guest Uncle Rico (Jon Gries, right)

not without its detractors. Defending the film against accusations that it merely mocked its parade of waifs and strays, Hess was quick to point out that many of the incidents emerged from reality (including the cow shooting) and that the characters were directly inspired by Hess' five younger brothers and by his friends from school. It must have been some childhood.

Dir: Jared Hess; **Prod**: Jeremy Coon, Chris 'Doc' Wyatt, Sean C. Covel; **Scr**: Jared Hess, Jerusha Hess; **DOP**: Munn Powell; **Editor**: Jeremy Coon; **Score**: John Swihart; **Main Cast**: Jon Heder, Aaron Ruell, Efren Ramirez, Tina Majorino.

Nashville
US, 1975 – 161 mins
Robert Altman

Following the production of industrial training films in his native Kansas City, a successful career in television (credited as the source of his improvisational methodology) and numerous low-key features, Altman finally rose to prominence during the creatively liberating period ushered in by the revelatory critical and commercial success of *Easy Rider* (1969). Beginning with *M*A*S*H* (1970), Altman enjoyed studio benefaction, producing throughout the 70s an unparalleled body of work that combined stylistic and technical daring with an unflinching reflection of the pervading air of disenchantment clouding American society.

A dazzling country music opus set against the political backdrop of an independent presidential candidate's election campaign, *Nashville* follows the intertwining lives, loves and longings of twenty-four disparate protagonists (including performers, agents, groupies, journalists and locals) during an ill-fated, weekend-long music festival in Nashville, Tennessee. Sprawling, ambitious and epic in tone, it is commonly viewed as representing the pinnacle of Altman's achievements in regard to import and execution, and certainly acts as a summation of the director's interest in myriad free-form narratives. Frequently co-existing in parallel, these divergent strands are tentatively woven through an impressive marshalling of ensemble scenes and the intelligent and liberating manipulation of sound and image. The film is further noted for Altman's pioneering incorporation of overlapping dialogue and the use of multiple hidden microphones as opposed to booms.

The apogee of Altman's decentred, multi-character dramas, *Nashville* also offers through its mock-documentary aesthetic a compelling aside on the increasingly blurred boundaries between fiction and reality. Moreover, filmed at the Mecca of country music and made under the shadow of the Vietnam War, it typifies Altman's habit of imbuing his subjects – often made under the guise of genre conventions – with a revisionist approach to American history. This refusal to perpetuate mythologies would later see him cast out of the system (*Buffalo Bill and the Indians*, 1976, destroyed his Hollywood standing), but on this occasion it brought him five Academy Award nominations, including Best Director and Best Picture. Impeccably acted by a densely populated and notable repertory cast (Lily Tomlin, Geraldine Chaplin and Shelley Duvall appear; Elliot Gould and Julie Christie offer cameos), the film strikes

Nashville: a dazzling, multi-narrative country music opus set against the political backdrop of an independent presidential candidate's election campaign

another perfect note with its evocative use of country music. Many of the actors wrote and performed their own material, with Altman mainstay Keith Carradine winning a Best Song Oscar for 'I'm Easy'.

Popularly viewed as one of the most iconoclastic, maverick and influential talents to emerge in post-war American cinema (Paul Thomas Anderson is particularly indebted to him), Altman, until his death in 2006, remained a true independent whose tremendous longevity spanning over five decades could be attributed to his ability to adapt to the economic vagaries of his film-making environment. When the studios deserted him, refusing to adhere to his stipulation of complete creative control after a number of commercial failures, Altman turned to alternative funding. Ironically, it was *The Player* (1992), a blackly comic précis of industry morals (or rather lack of them) that saw the director welcomed back to Hollywood.

Dir: Robert Altman; **Prod**: Robert Altman; **Scr**: Joan Tewkesbury; **DOP**: Paul Lohmann; **Editor**: Sidney Levin, Dennis Hall; **Score**: Various; **Main Cast**: Ned Beatty, Ronee Blakley, Henry Gibson, Keith Carradine.

Night of the Living Dead
US, 1968 – 96 mins
George A. Romero

Widely considered to be 'arguably the most influential contribution to
the modern horror genre' (Andrew, 1998, p. 23), *Night of the Living
Dead* is a landmark of late-60s' cinema. Permeated by a nihilistic sense of
abject hopelessness and frantic despair, Romero's film presents a radical
and subversive re-reading of horror genre conventions to reflect, like
contemporaries such as *The Wild Bunch* (1968) and *Easy Rider* (1969),
the pervading mood of pessimism engulfing American society.

The film was independently produced on a meagre budget by a small
Pittsburgh company specialising in industrial films and political TV spots.
Romero (who personally invested in the project) and his small army of
multitasking friends and co-workers were forced to be extremely
resourceful. Co-writer John Russo and producers Russell Streiner and Karl
Hardman were coerced into featuring in the film, alongside a cast of
amateur actors and Pittsburgh locals. Filming slowed to a halt on
numerous occasions while Romero secured additional financing by
showing potential investors completed stock and offering them shares in
the picture.

Night is a powerful social allegory dealing with the collapse of society
that reflects a growing resentment towards authority, the media and
American involvement in Vietnam. It immediately destabilises horror
customs when a marauding ghoul kills the male hero in the opening
sequence. The man's surviving sister Barbara (O'Dea) flees, finding refuge
in an apparently abandoned farmhouse. Shocked into silence, she finds
herself among a group of fellow survivors under attack from what a
television report reveals to be marauding, cannibalistic flesh-eaters
created following a freak molecular mutation. Reluctantly led by the
largely inefficient Ben (black actor Jones, though there is no allusion to
his colour), the band, which includes members of the same family (later
to devour each other), rapidly disintegrates into backbiting and bickering,

creating a volatile atmosphere bracketed by the threat of danger from without and within.

Night's relentless, unsparing terror (rendered by eerily effective monochrome cinematography) and gruesome new moral order is carried through to its profoundly despairing conclusion. Having survived the onslaught, Ben, the only character who offers any possible identification for the disorientated spectator, is mistaken for a zombie and shot by a gung-ho policeman.

Rejected by Columbia, allegedly because it wasn't in colour, the film played at out-of-town drive-ins and as part of triple features, accruing a word-of-mouth reputation among horror aficionados. Latterly a fixture on the midnight movie circuit, it attracted the attentions of a number of critics and academics of the time who became convinced of its social relevance and unerring power. *Night*'s was the immediate inspiration for an emerging legion of horror directors keen to merge intellect and gore to allegorical effect. Sam Raimi, Tobe Hooper, David Cronenberg and Wes Craven were perhaps the first to take up *Night*'s gauntlet. The film spawned a number of sequels directed by Romero and make-up artist Tom Savini, and nourished the 70s' cycle of Italian exploitation films such as Lucio Fulci's *Zombie Flesh Eaters* (1979) and those of Dario Argento.

Dir: George A. Romero; **Prod**: Russell Streiner, Karl Hardman; **Scr**: John A. Russo; **DOP**: George A. Romero; **Editor**: George A. Romero; **Score**: Uncredited; **Main Cast**: Judith O'Dea, Duane Jones, Karl Hardman, Keith Wayne.

Old Joy
US, 2006 – 73 mins
Kelly Reichardt

A gentle study of masculinity in modern America, Kelly Reichardt's Sundance-winning *Old Joy* also offers a poignant, if minimalist, portrayal of friendship, loss and alienation in the Bush era.

Mark (London), settled down and expecting his first child, takes a call from his old friend Kurt (Oldham), still very much the unencumbered drifter, whom he has not seen for some time. The pair team up for a camping trip to the Cascade Mountains, east of Portland, Oregon. For Mark, the weekend outing offers a respite from the pressure of his imminent fatherhood; for Kurt, it is part of a long series of carefree adventures. As the hours progress and the landscape evolves, the twin seekers move through a range of subtle emotions, enacting a pilgrimage of mutual confusion, sudden insight and recurring intimations of spiritual battle. When they arrive at their final destination, a hot spring in an old growth forest, they must either confront the divergent paths they have taken, or somehow transcend their growing tensions in an act of forgiveness and mourning.

Executive-produced by Todd Haynes, *Old Joy* began as a collaboration between three artists: photographer Justine Kurland, writer Jonathan Raymond and film-maker Kelly Reichardt. The short story was originally conceived as a creative partnership between Raymond and Kurland for Artspace Books, a forum for partnerships between visual artists. Having read Raymond's novel *The Half-Life*, and sympathising with its lyrical depiction of the American landscape, and its treatment of the legacy of 60s utopian communities, both themes in her own work, Kurland invited him to join forces. Reichardt, another artist interested in depictions of the American landscape and narratives of the road, read the story in the summer of 2004, and saw in it the template for a meditative, naturalist cinematic project. Also, she recognised a starring role for her dog and constant companion, Lucy, who returns to the

Will Oldham (left) and Daniel London (right) take a walk on the wild side for director Kelly Reichardt in *Old Joy*

screen in the director's next feature, *Wendy and Lucy* (2008). Reichardt and Raymond proceeded to adapt the story, adding a character and a few scenes, but largely retaining the piece's subtle emotional pivots, forest setting and much of the original dialogue.

Deciding to cast musician Will Oldham as Kurt after hearing Raymond do a read-through of the short story in New York (Oldham tried to persuade a number of his friends who closely resembled Kurt to play the part but they proved too Kurt-like to pin down), Reichardt also enlisted the services of cinematographer Peter Sillen at a very early stage. Shooting from a fifty-page script that allowed scope for improvisation,

Reichardt arranged for Oldham and London to meet for the first time the day before shooting began. Principal photography was completed in just ten days with a minimal crew and using only available daylight and favoured atmosphere over action. This intimate approach shines through in the film itself, eloquently echoing the frailties of the central relationship.

Dir: Kelly Reichardt; **Prod**: Neil Kopp, Lars Knudsen, Jay Van Hoy, Anish Savjani; **Scr**: Jonathan Raymond, Kelly Reichardt; **DOP**: Peter Sillen; **Editor**: Kelly Reichardt; **Score**: Yo La Tengo; **Main Cast**: Will Oldham, Daniel London, Tanya Smith.

On the Bowery
US, 1956 – 65 mins
Lionel Rogosin

A landmark of modern realism and of independent film-making, *On the Bowery* is an inventive and influential chronicle of urban street life. Emulating both Italian neo-realism and the documentaries of Robert Flaherty, Lionel Rogosin's film would itself go on to exert a major influence on the Direct Cinema or cinéma-vérité movement of the 60s. Rogosin was also friendly with a young John Cassavetes, who remained a fervent *Bowery* admirer. And yet perhaps the clearest precedents are not other films or film-makers but the toxic photographic essays snapped by Weegee and Joseph Mitchell depicting the New York lowlifes and eccentrics that populated the small neighbourhood in the southern portion of New York City known as the Bowery. It also feels like all the early songs of Tom Waits rolled into one.

One of the quintessential New York movies but a million miles from *Manhattan* (1979), *On the Bowery* offers a pungent glimpse into a world of bars, booze, brawling and fleapit flophouses. An experiment in improvised drama and found scenes that organically grew out of an intense collaboration between the film-makers and non-professional actors, the film was nominated for an Academy Award in 1958 for Best Documentary, though it is not a documentary in the strictest sense of the word. Perhaps the closest contemporary parallel would be *Ghosts* (2006) and *Battle for Haditha* (2007), two recent films by acclaimed documentarist Nick Broomfield in which he applied documentary techniques to a fictional structure.

The film follows Ray (Salyer), an itinerant railman with a battered suitcase who walks into a Bowery bar, orders a beer and then finds himself all too quickly swallowed up in a forgotten pocket of the world that barely sustains itself through a meagre diet of desperation and hopelessness. As he stumbles drink-sodden through a largely nocturnal milieu of sparsely furnished gin joints and ramshackle apartments, Ray's journey takes in a distinctly unromantic encounter with a hatchet-faced female barfly and, more significantly, bust-ups and arguments with various neighbourhood denizens. Most prominent among them is one Gorman Hendricks (whose dialogues with Salyer were prepared by Rogosin from previously observed conversations), a pot-bellied old-timer and real-life Bowery resident with more than a few tricks up his sleeve.

Boxing, baseball and boozing: a trawl through the boulevard of broken dreams in the quintessential *On the Bowery*

Extensively researched and shot using extremely discreet filming techniques, this kerbside trawl through the boulevard of broken dreams has an absolute and quite remarkable tang of authenticity. As impressive as Rogosin's evocation of place and character is, a resolute adherence to objectivity and a refusal – despite the film's patent social conscience and obvious sympathy for the plight of the community it portrays – to manipulate compassion or sentiment on behalf of the viewer is perhaps the most striking achievement.

Though the film acquired a prestigious reputation in certain circles, it was never widely screened and to this day remains rarely revived. Hendricks died shortly after filming was completed, and Salyer, who began the project with an actor's contract, never worked again, the apocryphal story going that he disappeared into the Bowery woodwork, turning down subsequent acting assignments in order that he could be left alone to drink. Rogosin used comparable clandestine filming efforts in *Come Back Africa* (1960) but similarly largely retreated from view. No matter, *On the Bowery* is one hell of a legacy.

Dir: Lionel Rogosin; **Prod**: Lionel Rogosin; **Scr**: Richard Bagley, Lionel Rogosin, Mark Sufrin; **DOP**: Lionel Rogosin; **Editor**: Carl Lerner; **Score**: Charles Mills; **Main Cast**: Gorman Hendricks, Frank Matthews, Ray Salyer.

Parting Glances
US, 1985 – 90 mins
Bill Sherwood

According to John Pierson, prior to *Parting Glances*, overtly gay films could largely be reduced to three distinct types: bitchy banter (*The Boys in the Band*, 1970); broad physical farce (*La Cage aux folles*, 1978); and explicit, hardcore 'freak shows' (*Taxi zum Klo*, 1981) (Pierson, 1996, p. 35). Studio attempts to deal with gay sexuality led to predatory caricatures such as *Cruising* (1980) and the insipid *Making Love* (1982). Sayles' impressive lesbian drama *Lianna* (1982) was perhaps alone in presenting an unpatronising and perceptive account of a gay relationship, though it was the product of a straight director.

Independently financed by director Sherwood, a former Juilliard-trained classical musician, *Parting Glances* offers a non-political, but nonetheless from-the-horse's-mouth presentation of gay sexuality. It depicts realistic, fully rounded characters struggling to deal with the universal trials and tribulations that are the by-product of any relationship. Michael (Ganoung) and Robert (Bolger) are two young, well-adjusted, prosperous, New York professionals who consent to put their relationship on hold when Robert decides to spend a year in Africa. Michael remains in New York to comfort Nick (Buscemi), a former lover and mutual close friend dying of AIDS.

Though undeniably stylistically conservative with overly bright production values and, Buscemi aside, performances that echo a daytime soap, *Parting Glances* exhibits a droll humour. There is, too, an endearing affection for and tenderness towards its characters and a refusal to locate its gay characters merely in relation to the heterosexual world around them. A portentous insight into the threat of AIDS and its impact upon the gay community, the film has the distinction of being the first theatrically produced feature to deal with the disease, precipitating a flurry of like-minded pictures such as the TV-produced *An Early Frost* (1985) and the largely anodyne *Longtime Companion* (1990).

The film was treated with kid gloves in the US by its somewhat tentative distributor Cinecom, which played down the explicit gay/AIDS angle and instead firmly positioned the film as another low-budget US indie. *Parting Glances* also brought to the fore the thinly veiled homophobia in the industry. Many companies passed on the film because of its refusal to simply marginalise the sexuality of its characters, and on one infamous occasion a screening theatre projectionist threatened to pull the plug after viewing an early scene featuring two men kissing.

The legacy of the film cannot be undervalued. As well as giving Buscemi his first starring role and acting as the springboard for his enduring association with the US independent scene, *Parting Glances* certainly opened the doors for a new influx of openly gay, in-your-face directors who fought to have their increasingly experimental and uncompromising films positively positioned as such. The ensuing emergence of the New Queer Cinema movement was in no small part due to the activities of Christine Vachon, an assistant editor on *Parting Glances* who went on to form feisty producer alliances with directors such as Gregg Araki, Todd Haynes and Tom Kalin.

Sadly, Sherwood never got to complete another feature, succumbing to AIDS in 1990.

Dir: Bill Sherwood; **Prod**: Oram Mandel, Arthur Silverman; **Scr**: Bill Sherwood; **DOP**: Jacek Laskus; **Editor**: Bill Sherwood; **Score**: Uncredited; **Main Cast**: Richard Ganoung, John Bolger, Steve Buscemi, Adam Nathan.

π *(Pi)*
US, 1997 – 84 mins
Darren Aronofsky

Drawing upon inspirations as diverse as Shinya Tsukamoto's body horror classic *Tetsuo: The Iron Man* (1991), the novels of William Gibson and the theories and philosophies of Baudrillard and Hegel, Aronofsky's π (the Greek symbol that in terms of mathematics is commonly used to represent a doorway to the infinite) marked a literate, challenging and highly original debut.

Maximillian Cohen (Gullette, who, with Aronofsky and producer Eric Watson came up with the premise for the film) is a reclusive mathematician and electronics whizz kid who believes that mathematics is the language of nature and that everything can be expressed in mathematical terms. From his chaotic Chinatown apartment, Cohen and his self-assembled computer Euclid apparently discover a number that signifies the underlying numerical pattern behind the global stock market. Befriended by Lenny (Shenkman), a Hasidic Jew who believes that the Kabbalah and the Torah are numerical codes sent from God, Max's findings also arouse the intense attentions of pushy businesswoman Marcy Dawson (Hart). Plagued by migraines and subsisting on a diet of painkillers and exhaustion, Max, despite the warnings of his former teacher Sol (Margolis) to give up his work, teeters on the brink of physical and mental meltdown.

The film is an intense, uncomfortable and often unsettling viewing experience, in which Aronofsky conveys Max's off-kilter psychosis and apparent descent into a paranoid, psychological hinterland with a sustained and inventive employment of visual and aural techniques that recalls Lynch's similarly striking *Eraserhead* (1976). Effectively and cheaply shot on high-contrast black-and-white 16mm stock, the film's surreal drug-induced hallucinatory sequences also display a Buñuelian eye for the disturbingly absurd. Brian Emrich's impressive, cacophonous sound design further compounds the sense of millennial doom, corporate skulduggery and impending madness, and is augmented by a largely electronic, avant-garde soundtrack featuring the likes of Autechre and Banco De Gaia. Describing the project as a digital take on the story of Faust, Gullette completes the aesthetic, giving a haunted, nervy performance that conveys anxiety and instability with an intensity unmatched on screen since Peter Greene in Lodge Kerrigan's *Clean, Shaven* (1993).

Scholars have questioned the film-makers' understanding of some of the basic tenets of maths and physics that are so essential to its plot and structure and π is certainly guilty of regurgitating certain cinematic stereotypes that constantly equate genius with, in the first instance, eccentricity and, in the second, madness. But, such criticisms aside and at times in spite of the film's wish to stress its undeniably impressive IQ, π succeeds as both a compelling examination of the destructive nature of obsession and as a surprisingly assured, albeit metaphysical, thriller. Sealing the film's reputation as that year's must-see independent movie and provoking a bidding war for distribution rights was a hugely successful Sundance screening that also netted the talented Aronofsky the Best Director award. *Requiem for a Dream* (2000) offered confirmation of both Aronofsky's pessimistic worldview and his abilities. A major return to form after the overambitious *The Fountain* (2006), *The Wrestler* (2008) marked a significant comeback both for its director and its grizzled star Mickey Rourke. Though hardly upbeat, the film also suggests that Aronofsky may have compromised his downbeat worldview just a little. The film never suffers for it.

Dir: Darren Aronofsky; **Prod**: Eric Watson; **Scr**: Darren Aronofsky; **DOP**: Matthew Libatique; **Editor**: Oren Sarch; **Score**: Clint Mansell; **Main Cast**: Sean Gullette, Mark Margolis, Ben Shenkman, Pamela Hart.

Pink Flamingos
US, 1972 – 95 mins
John Waters

Born in Baltimore, which, portrayed as a gloriously OTT hotbed of degeneracy, has continued as the setting for his films, Waters cites his middle-class, Catholic upbringing and frequent forays into local sex cinemas as formative influences. Waters initially experimented with 8mm shorts in which no subject or act was too profane to represent, and drew together a motley repertory company, including Mink Stole, local legend Edith Massey and larger-than-life transvestite Divine. (Waters continued to work with many of his cohorts long after his assimilation into the Hollywood mainstream as the king of kitsch.)

Pink Flamingos was to act as Waters' breakthrough picture and remains his signature piece, expanding upon the negligible production values, gloriously poor taste and excessive vulgarity of his previous features, *Mondo Trasho* (1969) and *Multiple Maniacs* (1970). The film takes as its premise the attempts of Raymond and Connie Marble (Lochary and Stole), two pornographers, heroin dealers and all-round sexual deviants, to wrest from local rival Divine, aka Babs Johnson, the coveted title of the filthiest person in the world. As the competition hots up, the Marbles throw down the gauntlet by sending Divine a year-old turd before burning down the trailer home she shares with the egg-guzzling Mama Edie (Edith Massey) and her chicken-fixated son Crackers (Danny Mills). Swearing revenge, Divine captures the Marbles and tars and feathers them before slaying them in front of reporters, declaring, 'I am God … killing and blood make me cum.' The film famously concludes with Divine reaffirming her right to the title by devouring freshly laid dog excrement, an act that one hopes required but a single take.

(*Opposite page*) 'I am God … killing and blood make me cum.' Divine, aka Babs Johnson, as the self-proclaimed 'filthiest person in the world' in *Pink Flamingos*

Waters has on occasion insisted that for him the act of someone throwing up during one of his movies would be the equivalent of a standing ovation; *Pink Flamingos* delivered a hearty and sustained round of applause. Not for sensitive souls, though! In addition to the memorable final shot, there are also numerous other notable and vaguely disgusting moments, including copulation with a chicken (Waters quipped that it was subsequently cooked and eaten), a plethora of scatological references, a close-up shot of a youth flexing his anus and references to rape, torture and incest. Those not seduced by Waters' gleeful revelling in abominable behaviour and general irreverence have pointed to fascistic overtones in the film and deemed its unique brand of humour corrupting and irresponsible.

Pink Flamingos is defined by a primitive visual style, performances that are intentionally camp and uneven, and an at-best rudimentary grasp of film skills. The frills-free camerawork, editing and production values befit the film's guerrilla-style aesthetic and $12,000 budget. Upon release, the film assumed instant cult status, becoming an immediate underground success on the late-night repertory circuit. Gleefully promoted as the most disgusting picture ever made, the film turned New Line from a fledgling outfit into one of the most innovative, daring and successful American independent distributors.

Dir: John Waters; **Prod**: John Waters; **Scr**: John Waters; **DOP**: John Waters; **Editor**: John Waters; **Score**: Uncredited; **Main Cast**: Divine, David Lochary, Mink Stole, Mary Vivian Pearce.

Poison
US, 1990 – 85 mins
Todd Haynes

Having shown considerable promise with the subversive and formally daring *Superstar: The Karen Carpenter Story* (1987), a witty and perceptive meditation on how popular culture affects society on multiple levels, former art, semiology and psychology student Haynes was courted by Disney and United Artists. Resisting their overtures, Haynes opted to establish an independent partnership with *über* producer Christine Vachon. The result was *Poison*, Haynes' $200,000 debut feature. Conceived as a tribute to the work of Jean Genet and expressing an explicit gay sensibility, the provocative and intelligent film won Sundance's 1991 Grand Jury Prize and placed Haynes at the vanguard of the emerging New Queer Cinema movement.

In part prompted by the American Right's dismissal of the AIDS crisis and a rejection of a 'positive' image of gay cinema in favour of a more complex and ambitious analysis of what society regards as transgressive or deviant, *Poison* calculatedly but enigmatically adopts a disparate range of styles and genres. Tripartite in structure, each separate narrative segment interweaves with little apparent overlap, allowing the spectator a refreshing autonomy regarding the issues and meanings with which Haynes engages (namely sexuality, oppression, alienation, non-conformity and persecution) and the at times vicarious manner in which each segment relates to another.

Poison begins with *Hero*, a mockumentary that adopts the form of a suburban TV news location report into the disappearance of Richie Beacon, a seven-year-old boy, who apparently ascends into the sky after murdering his father. The statements of Richie's peers reveal the retaliatory nature of the crime, committed in response to the beatings his father administered to his mother on discovering that his wife was sleeping with their Hispanic gardener (shades of Haynes' more recent *Far from Heaven*, 2002, abound). Concerned with violence and small-town hysteria, *Hero* remains the most elusive segment. The black-and-white *Horror* is a historically acute pastiche of 50s' B-movie sci-fis in which a scientist researching the mysteries of the sex drive accidentally imbibes his own serum. Suffering hideous physical mutations that make him repellent to society, Dr Graves becomes the subject of a police witch-hunt after he kills a woman in a bar whom he has infected with his condition. The most accessible section, *Horror* serves as a parable about AIDS and about mainstream cinema's and popular culture's tendency to stigmatise illness as an object of horror and equate sex – particularly of the non-heterosexual variety – with disease and decay.

The only sequence that relates directly to Genet's work (it's based on the autobiographical *Thief's Journal*), *Homo* is part claustrophobic, grim prison drama and part lyrical homage to a more innocent era of sexuality that traces the ever-shifting sexual relationship between two inmates

Dr Graves (Larry Maxwell) with his sex-drive serum in the *Horror* segment of *Poison*. An evocation of the 50s horror movie, *Horror* meditates on the stigmatisation of illness and the equation of sex with disease within the mainstream media

who knew each other as youths in reformatory school. Concluding with a brutal rape, *Homo* examines contrasting notions of 'masculine' and 'feminine' behaviour in the rigidly codified prison environment.

Compelling and challenging viewing, *Poison* was condemned as pornography by the American Family Association led by Reverend Donald Wildmon, who also conducted a campaign against the National Endowment for the Arts, which had contributed completion funding. Ironically, his objections merely increased *Poison*'s media profile and added to its impressive commercial performance in the States, where the film (initially released on a single print but later increased to seven) took just under $790,000. Haynes has remained a film-maker of great vision and consistency, with the aforementioned *Far from Heaven* and imaginative Dylan 'biopic' *I'm Not There* (2007) being particular recent career highlights.

Dir: Todd Haynes; **Prod**: Christine Vachon; **Scr**: Todd Haynes; **DOP**: Maryse Alberti; **Editor**: James Lyons, Todd Haynes; **Score**: James Bennett; **Main Cast**: Edith Meeks, Scott Renderer, James Lyons, John R. Lombardi.

Portrait of Jason
US, 1967 – 100 mins
Shirley Clarke

Portrait of Jason is the engrossing final part of a 60s' trilogy of films in which former experimental film-maker Clarke challenged practices of the American cinéma vérité movement. In works such as 1961's *The Connection* (Clarke's first collaboration with her black lover Carl Lee) and 1963's *The Cool World*, Clarke purposefully blurred the line between documentary and fiction, and offered compelling portraits of under-represented and marginalised African-American figures. This approach called into question the position of natural authority and objective reality asserted by vérité documentarists such as D. A. Pennebaker and Richard Leacock.

Entirely self-funded and filmed in Clarke's room at the Chelsea Hotel, *Portrait* stands as Clarke's most sustained critique of vérité techniques, and shares Warhol's distrust of artifice and his preference for frills-free filming techniques. The 100-minute film evolved from a continuous twelve-hour, single-take interview with Jason Holliday (real name Aaron Paine), a black, thirty-three-year-old homosexual prostitute and would-be raconteur. Filmed on a single camera in real time as a response to Pennebaker and co.'s offering of climactic, edited highlights, Jason's initially highly entertaining and colourful monologue recounting his childhood, service as a houseboy and 'white boy fever' is punctuated only by brief, out-of-focus, extreme close-ups followed by fades to black. These moments signal Clarke's changing of the camera magazine.

Jason smokes and sips scotch, his reminiscences initially encouraged and guided by the off-screen voices of Clarke and Lee (Clarke makes explicit her role as director by issuing technical instructions and directions regarding Jason's positioning). They prompt, 'Hey Jason, do one of your nightclub routines'. However, as Jason's histrionics for the benefit of the camera increase, Clarke and Lee become aggressive and antagonistic, questioning the authenticity and veracity of his comments with mocking slurs such as 'be honest, motherfucker'. At this point, Jason is reduced to tears. Displaying a continued preoccupation with ghetto subcultures (the film profoundly influenced Marlon T. Riggs in its willingness to engage with issues of black maleness and sexuality), *Portrait* serves as a provocative investigation and riff on the manipulative nature of performance and the supposedly impartial mediation of 'truth' in documentary film-making.

Jason Holliday (real name Aaron Paine) reaches breaking point in *Portrait of Jason*

Despite the validity and intelligence of Clarke's intentions there are, however, undoubtedly moments in which *Portrait* feels uncomfortably exploitative. Holliday is no doubt seduced by the opportunity to regale an audience with his outrageous, 'autobiographical' tales, and the suspicion remains that his trust is somewhat betrayed by Clarke, who ultimately uses Holliday's personal confessions merely to prove an admittedly cogent point about the nature of filmed reality. Given Jason's showmanship, there's no denying that there is a degree of mutual media manipulation, but Jason's closing comment that he found the experience 'beautiful' would seem to suggest a lack of complicity and an endorsement of the fact that Clarke, as director and editor, ultimately wields the greater power.

Dir: Shirley Clarke; **Prod**: Shirley Clarke; **Scr**: N/A; **DOP**: Jeri Sapanen; **Editor**: Shirley Clarke; **Score**: N/A; **Main Cast**: Jason Holliday (Aaron Paine).

Reservoir Dogs
US, 1991 – 99 mins
Quentin Tarantino

Acquired by Miramax following a frenzied Sundance screening at which even US indie sage John Pierson admits to having been 'blown away' (Pierson, 1996, p. 213), the impact of *Reservoir Dogs* on the industry was as radical as *sex, lies and videotape* (1989). Similarly, the film placed its celluloid junkie director – a former clerk at LA's Video Archives store – at the forefront of a new wave of aspirant young film-makers.

Imbued with a vast array of stylistic and structural references to the works of others, it's a tale of honour among a bunch of nameless, low-life crooks assembled by an old-time hood. The spirit of *Mean Streets* (1973) looms large, as does *The Killing* (1956), *City on Fire* (1987) and *The Wild Bunch* (1969). The exaggerated, amoral violence and nihilistic denouement also recalls Takeshi Kitano. This tendency to pay homage to or freely borrow from the work of others inspired conflicting critical reaction. Some saw Tarantino as a cine-literate and inspired genre stylist or *metteur en scène* in the style of Godard; others, such as Geoff Andrew, have discerned a disregard for originality and tendency to 'sample' the work of others that for older viewers 'may smack of plagiarism' (Andrew, 1998, p. 317).

Skilfully crafted originality does, however, characterise Tarantino's daring and elaborate approach to narrative and structure. *Reservoir Dogs* unfolds as a series of elaborate tales within tales allowing for minutely detailed and seemingly inconsequential but ultimately intrinsic plot and character digressions. Audaciously, the heist is never revealed; Tarantino's real interest lies in events leading up to its thwarted execution and bloody aftermath. Thus, from the opening diner sequence, the film abruptly cuts to the sounds of a fatally wounded Mr Orange (Roth) being driven by Mr White (Keitel, who alongside Monte Hellman co-produces) to the abandoned warehouse where the criminals reconvene. As Orange slowly bleeds to death, Tarantino inserts episodes from the past to reveal the machinations of the recruitment process and intersecting lives of the criminals. Of equal note and influence (perhaps the most recognisable motif of his career) is Tarantino's gift for snappy, conversational dialogue, which riffs on popular culture. *Reservoir Dogs* begins with the sharp-suited criminals expansively discussing the connotations of the lyrics to Madonna's 'Like a Virgin'.

Bolstered by a recognisable cast, including Buscemi and Keitel, and a modest budget funded by a home video company, the film generated controversy for its visceral violence. To the ironic radio airing of 'Stuck in the Middle with You', Michael Madsen's psychopathic Mr Blonde goes to work on a policeman's ear with a razor. The film's most infamous moment, and unpleasant though the scene is, Tarantino pans the camera to avert the actual act. Indeed, though Tarantino could be said to use violence as a means of providing spectacle, it is more often purely a generic convention and a further component in his gleeful approach to the art of storytelling.

Though only a modest commercial success in part due to its restrictive rating, *Reservoir Dogs*' appearance on home video ensured that it became a cultural phenomenon. A loyal legion of dedicated Tarantino admirers sprang up and, seduced by the stylised violence and hip post-modern dialogue, crowned him the future of American cinema. Similarly awed and inspired by the film's potentially lucrative appeal, the industry frantically looked for duplicates, precipitating an unwelcome and prolonged period that produced a slew of brash, knock-off imitations and second-rate copyists. Grindhouse homage *Death Proof* (2007) would seem to suggest that Tarantino is now little more than a skilled copyist himself.

Dir: Quentin Tarantino; **Prod**: Lawrence Bender; **Scr**: Quentin Tarantino; **DOP**: Andrzej Sekula; **Editor**: Sally Menke; **Score**: Karyn Rachtman; **Main Cast**: Harvey Keitel, Tim Roth, Michael Madsen, Steve Buscemi.

Return of the Secaucus Seven
US, 1979 – 110 mins
John Sayles

Having penned a number of short stories and two ambitious novels while working as an actor in summer stock, Sayles carved out a name for himself as an intelligent, literate writer of superior, humanist exploitation pictures produced by Corman's New World Pictures. Diligently accruing the proceeds earned on *Piranha* (1978), *The Lady in Red* (1979) and future contracted titles *Alligator* (1980) and *The Howling* (1980), Sayles, in the manner of Cassavetes before him, ploughed them into his own self-financed, written and directed $60,000 debut feature, *The Return of the Secaucus Seven*.

Shot on free locations with actors drawn from the writer-director's Eastern Slope Playhouse – and providing their own wardrobe and make-up – the 16mm film, partly inspired by Alain Tanner's *Jonah, Who Will Be 25 in the Year 2000* (1975), is an affectionately observed ensemble drama that deals with the annual New Hampshire reunion of several college friends. Formerly bound by the shared moral and political activism of 60s' campus life (Sayles subtly reveals the origin of their radical titular collective: a night spent in jail en route to a Washington demonstration), the group have all chosen different paths since graduation, but despite the passage of time and the changing nature of their relationships remain linked by a shared experience and common humanity.

Displaying a rare willingness to focus on the concerns of the thirty-something generation, whose values were all but dismissed by Reagan-era America, the film's acuity arises from Sayles' intelligent, ironic dialogue that combines insight and perceptivity with a surprising lack of sentimentality and didacticism. The stock-in-trade of the resourceful low-budget writer-director, the evocative dialogue and sense of character in part mask Sayles' technical limitations (since overcome) and economic constraints. With camera movement kept to a relative minimum, Sayles cites *Nashville* (1975) as the inspiration for the frequent cutting between characters as fresh allegiances and interrelationships evolve.

Made pre-Sundance, the film was screened at various American festivals before being transferred to 35mm and commercially released in a grass-roots fashion on the East and West Coast. A critical and commercial success (making a profit of $120,000), it bought Sayles the Los Angeles Film Critics Best Screenplay award and a 'genius' grant from the MacArthur Foundation. With its liberal sensibilities, psychologically rounded characters and an interest in communities under threat from society, *Secaucus Seven* set the template from which Sayles has continued to work. This is not only true thematically and aesthetically, but also because Sayles independently finances the projects himself through his intermittent journeyman script work on Hollywood pictures (*Apollo 13*, 1995, and *The Spiderwick Chronicles*, 2008, are recent credits). The film was also important in establishing a continuing repertory group of collaborators, including his partner and producer Maggie Renzi, composer Mason Daring and actors David Strathairn and Gordon Clapp.

Over and above the role the film played in shaping Sayles' career, which is one of surprising longevity, productivity and integrity, *Secaucus Seven* is a milestone picture in the history of American independent cinema. Becoming one of the first films to actively promote the virtues of its minuscule budget in relation to its domestic gross in its marketing campaign, it provided a timely reminder of a cinema that was aesthetically, politically and economically at odds with mainstream Hollywood film-making practices.

Dir: John Sayles; **Prod**: Jeffrey Nelson, William Aydelott; **Scr**: John Sayles; **DOP**: Austin De Besche; **Editor**: John Sayles; **Score**: Guy Van Duser, Bill Staines, Timothy Jackson, Mason Daring; **Main Cast**: Bruce Macdonald, Adam Lefevre, Gordon Clapp, Maggie Renzi.

(*Opposite page*) Made for just $125,000 and successfully released in a grass-roots fashion on the East and West Coast, John Sayles' *Return of the Secaucus Seven* represents a milestone moment in American independent cinema

Roger & Me
US, 1989 – 90 mins
Michael Moore

In the same year that Soderbergh's *sex, lies and videotape* (1989) was changing perceptions of low-budget features, former investigative journalist turned film-maker Moore was about to have a similar effect on the documentary. Shot on 16mm (but blown up to 35mm) for an approximate budget of $160,000, *Roger & Me* not only ignited a heated debate concerning documentary aesthetics but also transformed the ways documentaries were distributed, marketed and consumed.

Filmed under the title of *A Humorous Look at How General Motors Destroyed Flint, Michigan*, the film is an often hilarious and scathing examination of industrial ruthlessness that traces the decline of Moore's hometown of Flint, Michigan, after General Motors' systematic and poorly implemented closure of its production plants. Sanctioned by General Motors' chairman Roger Smith, this action resulted in social and economic deprivation, most directly through the loss of thousands of local jobs. *Roger & Me* was filmed over a three-year period. Archive footage and interviews with local celebrities, dignitaries and former General Motors' employees are inventively interspersed with Moore's dogged attempts to track down and confront Smith with the consequences of his actions.

Viewed as a precursor of the 'subject pursued' style of documentary refined by figures such as Nick Broomfield (similarly chastised for being too prominent a figure in his work), *Roger & Me* is ostensibly simplistic. It is even at times primitive in style (basically Moore tracked by a very small camera crew). The alchemy and subsequent controversy arose from Wendy Stanzler and Jennifer Beman's stylish editing that, in providing the film with a distinctive narrative thrust, plays fast and free with chronology in favour of humour, metaphor and exaggeration. The film premiered to ecstatic notices at the Telluride Film Festival and subsequently enjoyed significant critical and public support.

However, Moore's approach also led to accusations that he'd sacrificed the principles of journalistic accuracy and betrayed the documentary format. Moore, as John Pierson describes in *Spike, Mike, Slackers and Dykes*' excellent chapter on the film, was understandably defensive, making no apologies for breaking the cardinal rule of documentary by being entertaining and accessible (Pierson, 1996, pp. 137–76). Moore described the work as belonging to a new subgenre: the 'docucomedy'.

Roger & Me's irreverent attitude to chronology and its emphasis on entertainment may have sabotaged what appeared to be a sure-fire Academy Award nomination in the Best Documentary category, but this did the film no harm in terms of securing a lucrative distribution deal. Warner Bros. eventually won the race for distribution rights, after agreeing to the asking price of $3 million, and Moore's principled list of contract clauses (including 25,000 free tickets for unemployed auto workers and one empty seat to be left available at every single show in every single theatre for Roger Smith). Aggressively marketed with little mention of the fact that it was a non-fiction work, the film avoided the limited release route (at one point the film was on 307 screens) and was instead promoted to mainstream, multiplex audiences, who, in the climate of intense dissatisfaction with Reaganite politics, ensured that with a first-run theatrical gross of $7 million it became one of the most successful non-concert documentaries in history.

Dir: Michael Moore; **Prod**: Michael Moore; **Scr**: Michael Moore; **DOP**: Christopher Beaver, John Prusak, Kevin Rafferty, Bruce Schermer; **Editor**: Wendy Stanzler, Jennifer Beman; **Score**: Uncredited; **Main Cast**: Michael Moore, Roger Smith.

Salt of the Earth
US, 1953 – 94 mins
Herbert J. Biberman

Salt of the Earth is a subversive, courageous and profoundly radical work. Its independence lies not only in the adverse circumstances surrounding its production and the autonomous spirit in which it was made but also in its rigorous ideological and political opposition to McCarthyism.

Director Biberman, producer Paul Jarrico, screenwriter Michael Wilson, composer Sol Kaplan and actor Will Geer were among the 'Hollywood Ten' blacklisted because of their refusal to co-operate with the House Un-American Activities Committee. Biberman declined to answer Congressional questions on First Amendment grounds, a stance that resulted in a stay in federal prison. *Salt of the Earth* therefore represents nothing less than acute defiance. Independently financed by the Mine, Mill and Smelter Workers of America (one of eleven unions expelled by the Congress of Industrial Organisations in 1949 because of Communist sympathies), the production suffered not only continual harassment from the FBI but the repatriation of veteran leading Mexican actress Rosaura Revueltas before filming could be completed. Opposition to the picture continued post-production and it was largely the intervention of Electrical Workers Union film-maker Haskell Wexler that enabled the finished film to be processed. Wexler would go on to become one of America's most renowned cinematographers, working on John Sayles' *Matewan* (1983), a picture owing a huge debt to *Salt of the Earth* in both subject matter and sensibility.

Set in the New Mexican community of Zinc Town and based on actual historical events, *Salt of the Earth* deals with the uprising of Mexican mineworkers in protest against the unbearable conditions in which they are forced to live. In stark contrast is the reasonable quality of life enjoyed by their Anglo co-employees. Featuring among its cast many non-professional actors and real mineworkers, and efficiently shot in black and white to capture the grime of its environment, the film focuses on a downtrodden Mexican worker, Ramon Quintero (Chacon), and his long-suffering pregnant wife (Revueltas). Targeting racism, workers' rights and the rapidly developing divide emerging in the wake of America's post-war economic boom, the film's modern, forward-thinking sensibility is also reflected in its proto-feminist undertones. The women are initially forced to defer to a traditional macho male ethos, but as the strike and the violent actions of company-employed officials intensify (Geer, incidentally, plays a venal local sheriff), they begin to take a more active role in events, standing side by side with their husbands both on the picket line and in jail.

The decision of the Projectionists' Union to refuse to screen it ensured that *Salt of the Earth* was effectively banned in America. Consigned to independently owned drive-ins and a smattering of sympathetic theatres, the film received only nominal distribution and exhibition in its homeland (wider circulation was secured in Latin America) and so passed largely unseen. However, the film was greeted with acclaim in Communist circles (it was apparently approved of at the highest levels in Moscow) and in more liberal publications, and retrospectively its reputation and impact have continued to grow.

Dir: Herbert J. Biberman; **Prod**: Paul Jarrico; **Scr**: Michael Wilson; **DOP**: Stanley Meredith, Leonard Stark; **Editor**: Ed Spiegel, Joan Laird; **Score**: Sol Kaplan; **Main Cast**: Rosaura Revueltas, Juan Chacon, Will Geer, Mervin Williams.

The Savages
US, 2007 – 113 mins
Tamara Jenkins

Emerging alongside *Thank You for Smoking* (2005), Adrienne Shelly's *Waitress* (2007), *Little Miss Sunshine* (2006) and *Juno* (2007), *The Savages* is another of the recent Fox Searchlight pictures that manages to successfully merge an independent sensibility with the luxuries – stars and a marketing spend that offers a shot at mainstream glory – that a decent budget affords. Of these so-called 'Indiewood' hybrids, this irreverent look at family and mortality is one of the most accomplished. It's also one of the darkest, offering a peek through the lens of one of modern life's most challenging experiences: when adult siblings find themselves plucked from their everyday, self-centred lives to care for an estranged elderly parent.

The last thing the two Savage siblings ever wanted to do was look back at their difficult family history. Having wriggled their way out from beneath their father's domineering thumb, they are now firmly cocooned in their own complicated lives. Wendy (Linney) is a struggling East Village playwright, aka a temp who spends her days applying for grants, stealing office supplies and dating her married neighbour. Jon (Seymour Hoffman) is a neurotic college professor writing books on obscure subjects in Buffalo. Then comes the news that the father they have long feared and avoided, Lenny Savage (Bosco), is slowly being consumed by dementia and they are the only ones who can help. Now, as they put their already arrested lives on hold, Wendy and Jon are forced to live together under one roof for the first time since childhood, rediscovering the eccentricities that drove each other crazy. Faced with complete upheaval and battling over how to handle their father's final days, they are confronted with what adulthood, family and, most surprisingly, each other are really about.

Having established her ability to explore dark territory with a devastating wit in *The Slums of Beverly Hills* (1998), the story of a poor

Jewish family trying to make it on the fringes of Beverly Hills in the freewheeling 70s, writer-director Tamara Jenkins goes several steps further in a film that is surprisingly unsparing in its look at the ravages of time and parental abuse. Inspired by both the descent into dementia of her own father and by the fact that she had recently moved to a new house in a neighbourhood close to the kind of cold and characterless nursing facility so authentically depicted in *The Savages*, this is a work that perfectly captures the fear and anxiety that occurs when younger adults are forced to assume the uncomfortable responsibility of deciding where their parents are going to spend the drawn-out period of suffering and humiliation before they die. This is also a biting comment on the American health-care system, where the quality of care you receive is in direct relation to the amount of money you have. The moment when Wendy and Jon deposit Lenny at the prison-style building staffed by uncaring aides is horrifying and will no doubt precipitate an unwelcome shudder of recognition for many viewers.

The extent of Lenny's abuse is also intelligently handled, revealed only later when one of Wendy's plays finally makes it into production. In this moment, it becomes clear that rarely has a character been so aptly named. Beautifully performed, the film evokes the clinically comfortless world of Chris Ware, who was selected to execute the American poster artwork.

Dir: Tamara Jenkins; **Prod**: Ted Hope, Anne Carey, Erica Westheimer; **Scr**: Tamara Jenkins; **DOP**: Mott Hupfel; **Editor**: Brian A. Kates; **Score**: Stephen Trask; **Main Cast**: Laura Linney, Philip Seymour Hoffman, Philip Bosco, Peter Friedman.

Secretary
US, 2002 – 104 mins
Steven Shainberg

Director Shainberg's second feature following the provocatively titled but relatively little seen *Hit Me* (1998), *Secretary* is a love story that also deals with the ambiguities of office politics. Exploring with a bold, unflinching humour and strange yet seductive eroticism the notion that love doesn't always occur in the ways we might expect, it became one of the most talked about and endlessly debated films of its year. And yet for all its potential shock value and the upfront manner in which it was marketed – the film's sadomasochistic content was made explicit – it's a surprisingly tender tale about a complex relationship between complex people.

After a bout of illness and a period in psychiatric care, Lee Holloway (Gyllenhaal) moves back in with her dysfunctional family, ready to start anew. Despite her fragile mental state, she applies for a secretarial position at the law office of E. Edward Grey (Spader). Though she's never had a job in her life, Lee is hired by the mysterious lawyer who appears strangely unconcerned by her lack of experience. At first the work seems quite routine and boring – typing, filing and coffee-making – but Lee tries hard to please him. Slowly Lee and Mr Grey embark on a more personal relationship behind closed doors, crossing lines of conduct into a deep realm of human sexuality, a unique love affair, in which the roles of dominance and submission suit both of them perfectly. When this complex office love becomes apparent to Lee's family and her sometime boyfriend (Davies), the misunderstood lovers have a fight on their hands to protect their happiness and their unconventional connection.

Featuring a strategically placed flashback that occurs just before the central relationship teeters on the brink of genuine romance, the sequence reveals Holloway's troubled family life and escape through self-mutilation. At this point, the strength of *Secretary*'s meticulously conceived production design becomes clear, emphasising that when Holloway followed the 'Secretary Wanted' sign into the offices of Edward

Grey, characterised by its exotic plants and vivid colours, she found a welcome alternative to the terminal greys and muted greens of her dour home. Evocative of the characters and worlds familiar to David Lynch and Atom Egoyan, Shainberg's film is less a kinky two-hander and more a potent examination of intimacy, complicity and vulnerability.

Conveying the substantial dysfunctional emotional baggage of their respective characters and ensuring that the film extends beyond a mere exercise in libertarianism, Spader and Gyllenhaal are exceptional. From *sex, lies and videotape* (1989) through to Cronenberg's *Crash* (1996), Spader has frequently acted as a shorthand for sexual perversity, but he is a far more subtle actor than that, as he demonstrates here by revealing Grey's lacerating self-doubt and susceptibility. Written by a woman and adapted from a short story by Mary Gaitskill, the film's astute understanding of psychosexual issues from a female perspective presented Gyllenhaal with a career-making opportunity that she seized with both hands. Instrumental in propelling the film to a Special Jury Prize for Originality at Sundance and collecting several acting awards herself, Gyllenhaal subsequently took time out from more lucrative roles in projects including Oliver Stone's *World Trade Center* (2006) to revisit another troubled soul in Laurie Collyer's *Sherrybaby* (2006).

Dir: Steven Shainberg; **Prod**: Steven Shainberg, Andrew Fierberg, Amy Hobby; **Scr**: Erin Cressida Wilson; **DOP**: Steven Fierberg; **Editor**: Pam Wise; **Score**: Angelo Badalamenti; **Main Cast**: James Spader, Maggie Gyllenhaal, Jeremy Davies, Patrick Bauchau, Stephen McHattie.

sex, lies and videotape
US, 1989 – 100 mins
Steven Soderbergh

sex, lies and videotape ranks among the most auspicious feature debuts
in contemporary cinema. Few debuts since Hopper's *Easy Rider* (1969)
have had so lasting an effect on the American production landscape in
generating a clamour for low-budget projects. It was also by many
yardsticks the most important and influential American independent
picture in recent memory, though the majority of the film's $1.2 million
budget was provided by the video division of Columbia.

Soderbergh was a cineaste from an early age, with a taste for the
formal and structural characteristics of European cinema. He drew upon
the fall-out from a recent failed relationship and the premise of his earlier
short, *Winston* (1987), for his risqué-titled but subtle, thought-provoking
and insightful ensemble drama. Head on, it tackles sexuality and its
offshoots: inhibition, insatiability and impotence. Moreover, the film calls
into question the way sexuality is portrayed and sold in the media while
also acting as a profound meditation on voyeuristic viewing experiences.

Graham Dalton (Spader), an impotent drifter who makes videotapes
of women recounting their sexual experiences, returns to Baton Rouge to
visit John Mullaney (Gallagher), a successful lawyer whose marriage to
the sexless Ann (MacDowell) is lent added spice by his affair with her
voracious sister, Cynthia (Giacomo). Filmed quickly and relatively cheaply
in Louisiana with relative unknowns and a crew largely made up of
Soderbergh's cohorts from his student days, the film combines an
ostensibly simplistic formal aesthetic (relatively static medium long shots),
a talk-is-cheap philosophy (the writer-director's assured and pithy
dialogue is used to intelligent effect) and an experimental aspect, shown
by the incorporation of the low-density video footage on which Graham
conducts his interviews. It is through this medium that Soderbergh,
belying the film's humble origins and his own relative lack of experience
as a film-maker, is able to explore the concept of dual time frames, the

way in which we seek to catalogue experiences through video documentation and the spectator's desire for visual gratification.

Debuting at the Sundance Film Festival, the film was immediately hailed as the most original American feature in recent memory. Soderbergh was tagged by the press as the successor to figures such as Cassavetes and Sayles as the doyen of indie directors. And it exploded onto the international scene following its 1989 Cannes Palme d'Or success. An unsuspecting Soderbergh, the youngest-ever winner of the award, was catapulted even further into the limelight; 'It's all down hill from here', he was heard to remark bemusedly. As well as helping to establish the US independent distributor powerhouse Miramax, the film also put Sundance on the map, turning it into a major event and an attractive and lucrative shop window for new talent, producers and distributors. John Pierson describes the film as having 'radically and demonstrably changed the business' (Pierson, 1996, p. 2).

The critical fanfare and industry repercussions the film generated were more than matched by its commercial success. In making back its

Life through a lens: Andie MacDowell as Ann in *sex, lies and videotape*

cost many times over (to date it has grossed over $100 million worldwide), *sex* became a key work in the rejuvenation and development of US independent cinema and, according to Pierson, the fluke financial benchmark of potential for an independent film. Precipitating Soderbergh's remarkable film-making career and exhibiting similar thematic concerns so eloquently mined by Canadian film-maker Atom Egoyan, particularly in early work such as *Family Viewing* (1987), it is an enduring triumph of intelligent, low-budget film-making.

Dir: Steven Soderbergh; **Prod**: Robert Newmyer, John Hardy; **Scr**: Steven Soderbergh; **DOP**: Walt Lloyd; **Editor**: Steven Soderbergh; **Score**: Cliff Martinez; **Main Cast**: James Spader, Andie MacDowell, Peter Gallagher, Laura San Giacomo.

Shadows
US, 1959 – 87 mins
John Cassavetes

Viewed as the *Citizen Kane* (1941) of American independent cinema, *Shadows* opened the door for a new kind of uncompromising and self-sufficient film-making: 'There were no more excuses. If he could do it, so could we,' commented Scorsese (Thompson and Christie, 1989, p. 15). Intermittently made between 1957 and 1959, the film evolved from an improvisation dealing with miscegenation in one of Cassavetes' acting workshops.

Intrigued by the notion of 'off-Broadway movies' (Carney, 2001a, p. 56), Cassavetes gave an interview to the *New York Times* announcing his plans to turn the piece into a $7,500 amateur production. 'We had no intention of offering it for commercial distribution. It was an experiment all the way' (ibid., p. 57). After persuading cameraman Erich Kollmar to join up, Cassavetes appeared on Jean Shepherd's 'Night People' radio show, imploring listeners to send donations for a film about the ordinary people seldom seen in Hollywood movies. The irrepressible Cassavetes also talked Deluxe Film Labs into donating stock and processing facilities and borrowed 16mm equipment from fellow film-maker Shirley Clarke. Intended to capture the spontaneity of the actors and lend empowering mobility to the film-maker (much of the film was shot without permission on New York's sidewalks), the lightweight Arriflex camera provided by Kollmar would lend *Shadows* its influential hand-held, free-focus visual aesthetic. It was named after an actor's etching, and shot in black and white with a skeleton six-person crew.

Shadows offers a frank observation of the tensions and lives of three siblings in an African-American family in which two of the siblings, Ben and Lelia, are light-skinned and able to 'pass' for white. Cassavetes demanded that the actors retain their real names to reflect the actual conflicts within the group, but saw the film as being concerned with human problems as opposed simply to racial ones. The film features an elliptical narrative, ten-minute takes and jagged editing. Cassavetes attributed *Shadows*' conception and style to the Italian neo-realists while also professing admiration for Welles' pioneering spirit. Landmark picture though it is, Cassavetes expert Ray Carney describes the common tendency to view the film as the first American independent as displaying an 'ignorance of the history of the American independent film' (ibid.,

The *Citizen Kane* of American independent cinema? John Cassavetes' influential *Shadows*

p. 61) and a disregard for the early 50s' work of Morris Engel, Lionel Rogosin and Shirley Clarke.

Having shot and printed 60,000 feet of material, Cassavetes' inexperience and technical limitations were exposed in the editing process. The sound was so poorly recorded that much of it was unusable. Nobody had kept a record of what was said, so Cassavetes was forced to employ lip-readers so that dialogue could be dubbed. Featuring a bebop score by Charles Mingus and Shafi Hadi, *Shadows* was finally screened in November 1958 at New York's Paris Theatre, almost two years and $25,000 after filming originally began. The screening was not a success, acting, according to Cassavetes, as a 'shattering admission of our own ineptness' (ibid., p. 81). Having destroyed much of the unused footage, Cassavetes was forced to collaborate with screenwriter Robert Alan Aurthur on over an hour of new scenes that were intercut with the original print during the summer of 1959. The final budget rose to $40,000, much of it financed by Cassavetes' studio acting roles. With less than twenty-five minutes of the original version remaining, the version of *Shadows* now known today was blown up to 35mm and screened in a Cinema of Improvisation programme. Shortly before his death, Cassavetes confessed to Carney that little of the finished film was in fact improvised.

Shadows influenced many aspects of independent film-making, redefining film distribution in particular. It was a critical and commercial sensation in Britain and Europe, but the American release was blighted by constant references to its low-budget origins and technical deficiencies by reviewers still largely in thrall to Hollywood production values. Chastened by the experience (and his ill-fated studio sojourns), Cassavetes formed Faces Films to enable him to self-distribute his work and retain ownership of it.

Dir: John Cassavetes; **Prod**: Maurice McEndree; **Scr**: John Cassavetes; **DOP**: Erich Kollmar; **Editor**: Len Appelson, Maurice McEndree; **Score**: Charles Mingus, Shafi Hadi; **Main Cast**: Lelia Goldoni, Ben Carruthers, Hugh Hurd, Anthony Ray.

Sherman's March
US, 1985 – 160 mins
Ross McElwee

A former Richard Leacock student, McElwee evolved from what William Rothman in *Documentary Film Classics* terms the second generation of American cinéma-vérité directors, a group whose work was distinguished by the acknowledgment on camera of their presence and personal participation in the stories they told. For Rothman, the 'grand epic' (1997, p. xii) that is *Sherman's March* also introduces an ironic perspective that makes explicit the extent to which the documentarist has knowingly become the subject in his own story. Michael Moore, Nick Broomfield and Nanni Moretti are key practitioners of this approach; the proliferation of made-for-television video diaries its ugly conclusion.

Described by John Pierson as 'an enormously charming and moving personal essay' (1996, p. 107), *Sherman's March* originated when McElwee received a grant to make a documentary tracing American Civil War General William Tecumseh Sherman's devastating march through the American South and the as yet unhealed wounds of the civilian population. The pervading anxieties of the global politics of the 1980s and the impending threat of nuclear war made suitable parallels for Sherman's destructive trail. Abandoned by his girlfriend on the eve of filming, McElwee returned dejectedly to his family home in Charlotte, North Carolina, with the intention of aborting the project. Encouraged, however, by his sister's promptings that he use his camera as a conversation piece to meet women, McElwee adopted the subtitle *A Meditation on the Possibility of Romantic Love in the South during an Era of Nuclear Weapons Proliferation* and appropriated Sherman's conquering march for his own journey in search of an understanding of Southern womanhood and flickeringly vengeful quest for romantic fulfilment.

Though historical ironies are revealed about the feared general (his obsessive marching was fuelled by a sense of failure following a series of disastrous business ventures), after the Leacock-narrated introduction, Sherman only fleetingly appears as a metaphor for McElwee's own expedition and romantic misadventures. On his travels, McElwee turns his camera on several invariably resilient women, including Mary, a former girlfriend; Pat, an aspiring actress who dreams of meeting Burt Reynolds (a model of the larger-than-life masculinity McElwee feels he lacks); Claudia, a survivalist; Jackie, a nuclear campaigner and Charleen, who advises him, 'This isn't art Ross. This is life.' Each responds differently to the attentions of the camera, with McElwee well aware of its intrusive nature. Towards the conclusion, McElwee – who we later learn finds love with a teacher in Boston – steps out from behind the camera to be filmed by a third party. The moment, which occurs while addressing a statue at the site of Sherman's final victory, is illustrative of what Ellen Draper writing in *Film Quarterly* describes as a 'complex discussion of its own nature as a movie'.

Narrated in McElwee's frequently hilarious and self-mocking voiceover (the *Washington Post*'s Paul Attanasio likened him to Woody Allen), the film's intelligence and interest in structure and representation – a major influence on Nick Broomfield and specifically *Driving Me Crazy* (1988) – are tempered by its comic tone. At the beginning of the film, McElwee appears dressed as the pillaging Sherman but is reduced to addressing his camera in a barely audible whisper so as not to wake his sleeping parents. Widely admired for McElwee's maverick and entertaining approach, there were dissenting voices, notably the *Monthly Film Bulletin*'s Louise Sweet, who criticised the director for treating the Southern preoccupation with war as a backdrop to an 'irritating' personal quest.

Dir: Ross McElwee; **Prod**: Ross McElwee; **Scr**: Ross McElwee; **DOP**: Ross McElwee; **Editor**: Ross McElwee; **Score**: Uncredited; **Main Cast**: Ross McElwee.

She's Gotta Have It
US, 1986 – 85 mins
Spike Lee

With just a student short, *Joe's Bed-Stuy Barbershop: We Cut Heads* (1983), the first film to be selected for the New Directors/New Films series at the Museum of Modern Art, and an aborted 1984 feature, *The Messenger*, to his name, Lee fundamentally altered the landscape for African-American film-makers with his idiosyncratic, independent debut feature, *She's Gotta Have It*. Featuring a cast and crew composed of many of Lee's collaborators from his student days and an evocative, effervescent jazz score from father Bill, the film represented a triumph over economic adversity, exacerbated when the American Film Institute withdrew the funding it had earmarked for Lee's earlier project. Made largely through deferments, the total budget was just under $115,000, a mere $15,000 of which was Lee's writing, producing, directing and acting fee.

An attempt to authentically convey the experiences of the African-American community as Scorsese, a profound influence, had done for Italian-Americans, and to foreground issues such as race, class and gender in an entertaining way, the film's heroine is Nola Darling (Johns). An independent, sexually liberated black woman simultaneously involved with three disparate, though equally needy, male lovers, Nola finally resolves to choose between the caring and sincere Jamie (Hicks), the preening, self-obsessed model Greer (Terrell) and the vivacious though immature courier Mars (Lee).

Eschewing a classical, linear storyline in favour of a more impressionistic, fragmentary approach, Lee's film wears its stylistic debt to the French New Wave with aplomb. Arrestingly shot in high-contrast black and white by Ernest Dickerson (save for a colour interlude the director intended as a homage to Vincente Minnelli and *The Wizard of Oz*, 1939), Lee deploys jump-cuts, documentary-style direct-to-camera address, digressive vignettes, innovative use of sound effects and montage sequences to profound, irreverent and humorous effect. Perhaps most memorable is a riotously funny sequence involving twelve black men recounting for the camera their favoured and often lascivious pick-up lines: 'Girl, I got plenty of what you need, ten throbbing inches of USDA, government inspected, prime-cut, grade-A tube steak.'

Selected as part of Director's Fortnight at Cannes, where it carried off the Prix la Jeunesse, the film was initially greeted with scepticism and incomprehension by the largely white critical cognoscenti. Also, and

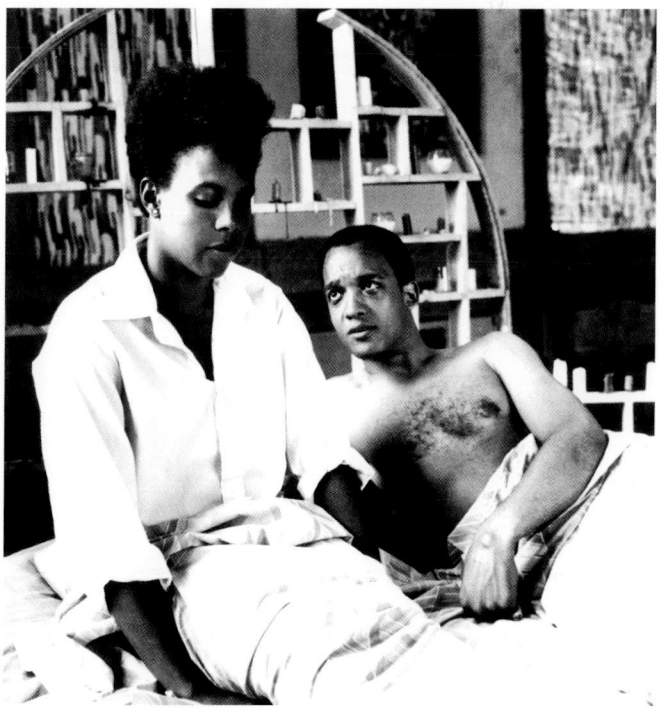

Pillow talk: Nola Darling (Tracy Camila Johns) and Jamie (Tommy Redmond Hicks) in Spike Lee's *She's Gotta Have It*

despite focusing on a strong-willed black female character and revealing men to be absurd and slightly pathetic, it drew criticism from female commentators, most notably Amy Taubin, for what were perceived to be misogynistic overtones. Especially contentious was the scene in which Nola is virtually raped by Jamie, an act of punishment for her promiscuity.

However, after a cannily marketed New York opening, the film rapidly became a cultural and commercial phenomenon, finding favour with both arthouse aficionados and more pertinently African-American audiences unaccustomed to seeing their lives and sensibilities faithfully depicted. Since the demise of blaxploitation, there were few black directors working in the American film industry. Lee, whose *Do the Right Thing* three years later fully established the notion of a commercially viable black cinema and perhaps the most cohesive and successful fusion of his independent sensibilities with studio funding and resources, almost single-handedly opened the door for a new generation of African-American film-makers, with figures such as John Singleton, Leslie Harris and Matty Rich immediately following in his trailblazing wake. For this and for its own particular merits, *She's Gotta Have It* remains one of the most momentous contemporary American independent pictures, and to this day, independent sage John Pierson (who acted as a rep on the film) still cites Lee as his hero.

Dir: Spike Lee; **Prod**: Shelton J. Lee; **Scr**: Spike Lee; **DOP**: Ernest Dickerson; **Editor**: Spike Lee; **Score**: Bill Lee; **Main Cast**: Tracy Camila Johns, Tommy Redmond Hicks, John Canada Terrell, Spike Lee.

Shock Corridor
US, 1963 – 101 mins
Samuel Fuller

Fuller's punchy, straight-to-the-gut narratives and sheer visual ferocity passed unappreciated by the American critics of his day. The director was a former crime journalist and war veteran who worked tirelessly in relative obscurity on quickly shot, low-budget pictures invariably released as B-movies. Focusing on unsympathetic, deeply flawed protagonists comprised of soldiers, cops and bigots, Fuller's work was inaccurately charged with expressing fascistic leanings. He worked outside the studio system as writer, producer and director, and his independence enabled him to deliver subversive and unflinchingly honest critiques of American society in which 'film is a battleground of alienated human energies' (Thomson, 2002, p. 318).

Shock Corridor, deemed trashy, vicious and irresponsible by the American press, is characteristic Fuller fare. Beginning with a quote from Euripides ('Whom God wishes to destroy, he first turns mad'), it examines the attempt by ambitious crime reporter Johnny Barrett (Breck) to win the Pulitzer Prize by solving the murder of a patient at a mental institution. He decides to pose as an inmate at the institution. In order to be committed, Barrett persuades his stripper girlfriend Cathy (Towers) to pretend that she is his sister and has been subjected to his incestuous advances. While undergoing sexual therapy, Barrett interviews the three witnesses to the murder: Stuart (Best), a disgraced American soldier who has returned from the Korean War believing himself to be a Confederate general; Boden (Evans), an atom bomb developer who has regressed to the state of a six-year-old; and Trent (Hari Rhodes), a black student who was among the first to enter an all-white Southern university, but who now believes himself to be a white supremacist. His grip on reality wavering, Barrett himself begins a slow descent into madness.

Originally intended as an exposé of the harrowing conditions in American mental facilities, the film delivers a riveting précis of the fundamental issues troubling a 60s' America awash with paranoia and ideologically enforced anti-communist sentiments. Detractors bemoaned a lack of subtlety in Fuller's sociological observations, but there's no doubting the passion and force with which *Shock Corridor* articulates both the racial divide in American society (continued in Fuller's *White Dog*, 1982) and unease concerning nuclear weapons. Formally, the film heralds an advance on the vibrant use of camera that had already become a signature of Fuller's work (and which was to so influence Scorsese), with the constant tracking shots accentuating the escalating hysteria. Fuller's stylistic achievements are all the more impressive given the parameters within which he worked. Save for two colour sequences, the film is effectively shot in stark black and white by Stanley Cortez (*The Magnificent Ambersons*, 1942) and boasts noir-inspired chiaroscuro lighting pregnant with menace and foreboding.

Fuller became revered as an auteur throughout Europe (in 1977, Wenders cast him in *The American Friend*) and particularly in France. His domestic standing rose following the publication in 1968 of Andrew Sarris' *The American Cinema*, in which the critic described the director as an authentic American primitive and an estimable artistic force. More recently, Fuller has been accorded statesmanlike status by the American independent sector, a position cemented by a full retrospective of his work at the 1988 Sundance Film Festival.

Dir: Samuel Fuller; **Prod**: Samuel Fuller; **Scr**: Samuel Fuller; **DOP**: Stanley Cortez; **Editor**: Jerome Thoms; **Score**: Paul Dunlap; **Main Cast**: Peter Breck, Constance Towers, Gene Evans, James Best.

Shotgun Stories
US, 2007 – 90 mins
Jeff Nichols

Set against the picturesque cotton fields and dusty back roads of
Southeast Arkansas, three brothers discover the lengths to which each
will go to protect their family in director Jeff Nichols' brooding drama.

Son Hayes (Shannon) never speaks of the scars on his back.
The shotgun pellets embedded under his skin form a sporadic pattern of
blue-black dots. The men he works with take bets on how he got them.
His brothers, Boy (Ligon) and Kid Hayes (Jacobs), don't discuss it. But his
past, just like these scars, is never far behind him. This stands true for the
memory of his father, a violent drunk who never bothered to give his
children proper names and left them to be raised by their mother, a
similarly hateful woman. Having left the memory of his children as
completely as he abandoned their home, the father managed to move
on and put his life back together, sobering up, becoming a devout
Christian and remarrying to sire four new sons. They all received proper
names. The past inevitably comes calling when, as grown men, Son, Boy
and Kid attend their father's funeral and initiate a simmering but
ultimately all-consuming feud with their distant kin.

An Arkansas native who wrote *Shotgun Stories* believing that tales
should come from a specific place, Nichols certainly relishes his regional
aesthetic. The director grew up with two older brothers and spent a
considerable amount of time around the places and people that he
documents, which contributes greatly not only to the acute sense of dress,
dialogue and behaviour but also to the quietly compelling authenticity.
A debut feature in which characters keep their sentences brief and their
emotions guarded, the film resembles a Greek tragedy, avoiding the
fireworks and high-calibre violence the material could have elicited in favour
of a residual accumulation of brutality, recrimination and confrontation.

This is also evident in the very deliberate and considered manner in
which the film is shot. Both the people and places portrayed all move at

a very deliberate pace, and this is reflected in the wide shots and very minimal use of camera movement. The vast, open rural landscapes of England, Arkansas, are superbly rendered in an anamorphic-aspect ratio by cinematographer Adam Stone, who shot second unit photography for David Gordon Green's first three films. Green also acts as the film's producer and there are pleasing echoes of both *George Washington* (2000) and *All the Real Girls* (2003) here.

An actor who has threatened but never quite attained mainstream success (he was superb in a key but minor role in Lumet's *Before the Devil Knows You're Dead*, 2007), Michael Shannon is an edgy and exciting screen presence, excelling here in a rare central role. Insular and withdrawn, he conveys the sense that the suffering and bitterness of Son Hayes is spiritual as well as physical and likely to destroy any happiness that he might have enjoyed with his own young son. The likely repetition of the sins of the father is one of the key themes in this honest portrayal of hard-working people responding to the pain and heartbreak they find, and at times create, in their own lives. Perhaps most tellingly, however, *Shotgun Stories* also skilfully dramatises the notion that there is no victory in revenge and that violence should never be considered cathartic.

Dir: Jeff Nichols; **Prod**: David Gordon Green; **Scr**: Jeff Nichols; **DOP**: Adam Stone; **Editor**: Steven Gonzales; **Score**: Ben Nichols/Lucero; **Main Cast**: Michael Shannon, Douglas Ligon, Barlow Jacobs, Glenda Pannell.

Slacker
US, 1991 – 97 mins
Richard Linklater

Seldom seen, Linklater's debut feature, *It's Impossible to Learn to Plow by Reading Books* (1988), helped establish the youth-specific motifs that would recur throughout the largely self-taught director's career: fractured attempts at communication; disenchantment; an agonising over choices; and travel. His breakthrough picture, *Slacker*, consolidated these themes and precipitated a coherent run of films, including *Dazed and Confused* (1993) and *Before Sunrise* (1995), that briefly placed the director at the forefront of the American independent scene.

Slacker's unconventional, freewheeling and essentially plotless narrative offers a *True Stories* (1986)/documentary-style snapshot of a town's various obsessive and eccentric slacker inhabitants. It is set over a twenty-four-hour period in Linklater's home town of Austin, Texas. Surprisingly, the film is in fact entirely scripted. Included in the often bewilderingly expansive mix of characters (the poster for the film simply listed the cast as 'a lot of people') are hipsters, barroom philosophers, conspiracy theorists, anarchists and general oddballs, one of whom is selling what she claims to be Madonna's cervical smear. The film begins with a frantic traveller (Linklater himself) theorising on parallel realities, and then unfolds as a series of ostensibly random and largely comic vignettes. The intersection between episodes is provided by the fleeting moment of contact between one subject and the next. In one instance, this occurs mid-scene when the restless, attentive camera simply picks out a passing figure of greater interest than the one currently shadowed.

Almost entirely self-financed (completion money was provided by a $35,000 German television sale), the film was produced by Linklater's own Detour Productions (named after the 1945 Edward G. Ulmer classic). The simply but effectively 16mm-shot film suffered initial rejection by almost every major and, indeed, minor festival. Undeterred, Linklater was confident that the film could succeed in his home town, having nurtured a burgeoning film community through the formation of the Austin Film Society (a self-confessed cineaste, Linklater cited the arthouse sensibilities of Antonioni, Ophuls, Buñuel and Fassbinder as influences). Acting as his own distributor, he opened it at an on-campus cinema, where it was a phenomenal success, enjoying consecutive sell-out weeks. Orion Classics acquired the film for national release one year after its Austin platform, sensing the film's *Zeitgeist* factor in its ability to directly connect with the rapidly emerging Generation X types being heavily hyped by the media. As a result, *Slacker* not only enjoyed a commercial and critical resurgence but also coined a new lifestyle approach, in the process ensuring the title's term an indelible place in the modern lexicon.

Slacker exerted a profound influence on a new generation of emerging directors (Linklater was himself barely into his twenties), including Kevin Smith who, dragged from his traditional multiplex haven to a downtown art cinema, suffered something of an epiphany. It made a highly visible and esoteric mark on the post-*sex, lies and videotape* (1989) independent landscape. As detailed by John Pierson, another of the film's legacies was the blow it struck at a grass-roots level in its daring launch strategy (Pierson, 1996, p. 185).

Dir: Richard Linklater; **Prod**: Richard Linklater; **Scr**: Richard Linklater; **DOP**: Lee Daniel; **Editor**: Scott Rhodes; **Score**: Uncredited; **Main Cast**: Richard Linklater, Rudy Basquez, Jean Caffeine, Jan Hockey.

Smithereens
US, 1982 – 93 mins
Susan Seidelman

The debut feature from New York Film School graduate Seidelman, *Smithereens* was an independent triumph in the face of adversity. Largely self-funded through the forming of limited partnerships, the film was shot for $80,000 in three stints over a year-long period in less than salubrious Lower East Side locations. Mas'ud Zavarzadeh in *Film Quarterly* described the film as a 'postmodern classic' (Zavarzadeh, 1984, p. 54).

Smithereens follows Wren (Berman), a punkish, working-class girl from the wrong side of the Hudson River, who descends upon Lower Manhattan in search of an express ticket to rock 'n' roll fame. By day, she ekes out a menial living; by night, she trawls the clubs and bars of the New York punk scene, stubbornly promoting her flimsy talents. Wren is partly embroiled in a potentially fulfilling relationship with Paul (Rinn), an artist from Montana, but her ruthlessly ambitious streak, and her eviction from her apartment for non-payment of rent, leads to a chance encounter with Eric (Hell), the self-obsessed lead singer of much-fancied band the Smithereens. Could a ride on Eric's coat-tails turn Wren's dreams to reality?

With only limited previous acting experience, Berman is astonishing in an unattractive central role. Wren is fed by an almost tyrannical ego and narcissism: she is seen early on in the film pasting pictures of herself inscribed with the enigmatic question, 'Who is this girl?' Paul describes her as being morally deficient, in that people only matter to her in so far as they can be of use to her prospective career. Wren's abject lack of talent is emphasised by the fact that she works in a copy shop, 'a job characterised by re-production instead of production' (ibid.). Having set out ostensibly to portray the New York punk rock scene and its subculture, Seidelman accurately exposes a movement in its dying embers, when it was barely sustained by waning media attention and irreparably tarnished by a perversion of values and artistic and ethical decay.

Seidelman has said in a *New York Times* interview that she 'wanted to people the film with characters who were products of the mass culture of the 1970s and 80s kids who grew up on rock and roll' (Armstrong, 1984, p. 4). She resonantly cast charismatic Richard Hell as a last-minute replacement for another unnamed actor. The author of the 1976 album *Blank Generation* and an acclaimed punk performer, Hell was one of the most visible figures of the era. Playfully aware of the hierarchies of cool involved in any creative movement, Seidelman also cast New York underground associates such as Amos Poe and Cookie Mueller in cameo roles.

Seidelman herself edited the film, which has a soundtrack that includes tracks by seminal New York acts The Feelies and ESG. Chirine El Khadem's realistic cinematography and its functional aesthetic authentically capture the squalor underpinning the facade of bohemian living. The film was acquired for domestic distribution by New Line, following an impressive showing at Telluride and its surprising selection for the main competition at Cannes. Marketed as a film with a lot of attitude, *Smithereens* played to packed houses on New York's alternative cinema circuit. Describing her goal to the *New York Times* as achieving a balance between Hollywood and non-Hollywood film-making, Seidelman perfected the formula for the following year's *Desperately Seeking Susan*.

Dir: Susan Seidelman; **Prod**: Susan Seidelman; **Scr**: Ron Nyswaner, Peter Askin; **DOP**: Chirine El Khadem; **Editor**: Susan Seidelman; **Score**: Glenn Mercer, Bill Million; **Main Cast**: Susan Berman, Brad Rinn, Richard Hell, Nada Despotovich.

Strange Culture
US, 2007 – 75 mins
Lynn Hershman-Leeson

In this moving, innovative and unconventional documentary, director Lynn Hershman-Leeson tells the terrifying true story of how one man's personal tragedy turns into persecution by a paranoid and overzealous government and a US Justice Department unwilling to admit that it has made a mistake.

Everything changed for conceptual artist and outspoken critic of the US Food and Drug Administration Steve Kurtz on the morning of 11 May 2004, when he awoke to discover that his forty-five-year-old wife, Hope, had died in her sleep after suffering a heart attack. A domestic tragedy turned into a Kafkaesque nightmare after the paramedics summoned by Kurtz, alarmed by the Petri dishes, scientific paraphernalia and books in the house, reported him to the FBI as a suspected bioterrorist. The founders of the Critical Art Ensemble, Kurtz and his wife had been working on an installation about the emergence of biotechnology for the Massachusetts Museum of Contemporary Art. The live cultures they were using were as harmless as yogurt, but a Hazmat team from Quantico descended on their home, arrested Kurtz, carried away his equipment, computers and papers, and seized his wife's body from the coroner.

Told through a unique blend of interviews, documentary footage and reconstructed scenes, *Strange Culture* offers a sophisticated look at how the traumatic events of 9/11 altered American society and undermined its long-held values. Avoiding standard documentary techniques, Hershman-Leeson also circumvents any legal restrictions on a defendant discussing an ongoing case by having real-life characters played by real-life actors. Kurtz was cleared of the charges of bioterrorism but still faces federal indictments that could result in a long prison term and is therefore played by Hal Hartley regular Thomas Jay Ryan. His voice does, however, feature in a number of telephone conversations.

Displaying both her political convictions and her proclivity for offbeat roles and challenging projects, Tilda Swinton, who also worked with the director on the equally conceptual *Conceiving Ada* (1997) and *Teknolust* (2002), is arguably the film's anchor and moral compass as Hope.

The film frequently blurs the lines between reality and fiction, with actors openly discussing their characterisations with the people they are playing. At one point, Swinton also asks aloud what the film might achieve once it is projected to a public audience. Interested in asking as many questions as it does provide answers, Hershman-Leeson also goes beyond the frankly Kafkaesque persecution of Kurtz to look at the art installations the couple produced and how these contributed to the continuing discourse and debate about genetic food modification.

Though largely relegated to the festival circuit, and rarely seen in the UK at all (it is now available on DVD through its US website), this is an invigorating and quietly unsettling film that is bursting with ideas and intelligence.

Dir: Lynn Hershman-Leeson; **Prod**: Steven C. Beer, Lisa Swenson; **Scr**: Lynn Hershman-Leeson; **DOP**: Hiro Narita; **Editor**: Lynn Hershman-Leeson; **Score**: The Residents; **Main Cast**: Tilda Swinton, Thomas Jay Ryan, Peter Coyote, Steve Kurtz.

Stranger Than Paradise
US/W. Germany, 1984 – 89 mins
Jim Jarmusch

One of American independent cinema's defining moments, *Stranger Than Paradise* was directly responsible for pushing many new films and directors into production and for auguring what John Pierson perceives as a halcyon period (1984–94) in intelligent, esoteric but accessible low-budget movies. Moreover, the film (Jarmusch's second after 1982's disappointing *Permanent Vacation*) coined a laconic, minimalist visual style and general sensibility in part informed by the works of Bresson, Ozu and Rivette but also borrowing from avant-garde and punk rock aesthetics. Kevin Smith recognised the 'look' to which he aspired, thanking Jarmusch in the *Clerks* (1993) credits for 'leading the way'.

Originating as a 30-minute short shot over a weekend on leftover stock gifted by Wenders following the completion of *The State of Things* (1982), the film screened on portable projectors at clubs throughout New York in order to attract further finance. Later shown at the Hof Festival in Germany, the short captured the attention of director Paul Bartel and chocolate impresario Otto Grokenberger, with the latter stepping forward to provide the completion funding that extricated Jarmusch from his soured relationship with Gray City Films, Wenders' distribution company.

Exploring the effects of an unwanted visit from a Hungarian cousin (Balint) on detached, taciturn New Yorker Willie (Lurie) and his gambling buddy Eddy (Edson), the film offers a perceptive look at exile, existential solitude and the possibilities of communication beyond cultural differences. Jarmusch also studies the effects of geography on human emotions, tracking the trio as they travel from

(*Next page*) Welcome to Florida. From left to right, Eddie (Richard Edson), Eva (Eszter Balint) and Willie (John Lurie) playing it cool in *Stranger Than Paradise*

New York, to snowy Cleveland and then on to an out-of-season Florida. These elements, alongside the collision between American culture and foreign elements, have persisted throughout the director's work and are at the forefront of subsequent pictures, including *Down by Law* (1986, and apparently Jarmusch's favourite among his own movies), *Night on Earth* (1991), *Dead Man* (1995) and *Ghost Dog: The Way of the Samurai* (1999).

Shot for $110,000, $10,000 of which went towards securing the use of Screamin' Jay Hawkins' 'I Put a Spell on You', *Paradise* was immediately set apart by Tom DiCillo's elegant black-and-white photography and its part poignant, part comic minimalism that serves to magnify the import of every gesture and wry comment. The film is divided into three chapters, 'The New World', 'One year later' and 'Paradise', and Jarmusch employs a very discrete approach to style and grammar, with no dissolves, cuts or wipes in the long, uninterrupted stationary scenes that characterise the film. Drawing on understated, deadpan performances, the film made a telling contribution to the casting process, with Jarmusch avoiding Screen Actors Guild members in favour of character types and figures with whom he was familiar from the downtown punk scene.

Jarmusch became the first American to win the Camera d'Or for best first feature at Cannes and was the recipient of sustained critical approval. Zeroing in on the *Zeitgeist*, *Paradise* was picked up for distribution by the Samuel Goldwyn Company and played for over a year in cinemas, racking up a profitable domestic gross of $2.5 million. It was subsequently a cultural and commercial event throughout Europe and Japan (a sustained source of funding for future Jarmusch productions), where Jarmusch was immediately canonised as a guru of cool.

A seismic influence on the way American independent films were made, distributed and marketed (the poster audaciously proclaimed 'a new American film by Jim Jarmusch'), the determinedly economical style perfectly captured the relationship between aesthetics and economy, with executives seizing upon the realisation that small budgets bring increased profit potential.

Dir: Jim Jarmusch; **Prod**: Sara Driver; **Scr**: Jim Jarmusch; **DOP**: Tom DiCillo; **Editor**: Jim Jarmusch, Melody London; **Score**: John Lurie; **Main Cast**: John Lurie, Richard Edson, Eszter Balint, Cecillia Stark.

Suture
US, 1993 – 96 mins
Scott McGehee, David Siegel

Though they have met just once at the funeral of their murdered father, wealthy, unprincipled sophisticate Vincent Towers (Michael Harris) invites his identical half-brother Clay (Haysbert), a lowly construction worker, to spend some time with him in Phoenix, Arizona. The visit is ostensibly a bonding exercise, but Clay is dismayed to learn upon arrival that an unannounced business trip necessitates Vincent's immediate attention. After dropping his preoccupied brother at the airport, Clay is involved in a terrible car explosion that leaves his face burned beyond recognition and his memory erased. With the aid of Freudian psychoanalyst Dr Shinoda (Shimono) and leading plastic surgeon Renée Descartes (Mel Harris), Clay is slowly pieced back together. The only problem is, he's reconstructed as Vincent, the prime suspect in his father's death.

Executive-produced by Soderbergh, *Suture* is a sophisticated, post-modernist and intertextual first feature that borrows freely from the B-movie thriller, the American avant-garde, and the thematic and stylistic staples of film noir. There is highly stylised chiaroscuro lighting, a complex flashback structure and a focus upon a moral landscape predicated by corruption and greed. The directors acknowledge *Spellbound* (1945) as a key structural influence. *Suture* nonetheless brings its own intoxicating and inventively cerebral embellishments to the Hitchcockian mix.

Suture is an intelligent analysis of identity, class, the duality of mind and body (the film alludes to Lacanian psychoanalysis, which, in part, also lends the film its title), and the physical and mental means by which we define ourselves. It features at its core two compelling, non-naturalistic performances by Harris and Haysbert. Harris is slight and white, Haysbert is muscular and black – facts that go unmentioned within the film. For the spectator, the men's racial differences highlight the illusory nature of identification. 'Our physical resemblance is striking' remarks Vincent at one point, in a moment that is indicative of the film's deadpan dialogue

Clay (Dennis Haysbert) and Vincent (Michael Harris) in *Suture*, a film in which nothing is simply black and white

and entertainingly existentialist sensibilities. The naming of a character after the philosopher Descartes and the engaging use of Johnny Cash's 'Ring of Fire' as a charred Clay is rushed to emergency offer further evidence of the film-makers' mischievous but effective daring.

Shot in austere black and white by Greg Gardiner (who won the Cinematography Award at 1994's Sundance) and boasting Kelly McGehee's stunning production design (the use of modish 60s' office interiors evokes Godard's *Alphaville*, 1965), *Suture* is also visually arresting in its spatial dexterity and compositional assurance. The final face-off between Vincent and Clay, shot from high above in an ornate bathroom, is especially memorable. Also memorable are the film's disjunctive editing and the overlapping use of sound to intrude from one scene to another, techniques that reference the pioneering work of the late-60s' theorist Jean-Pierre Oudart, who drew parallels between the psychic processes that establish subjectivity and the structuring language of cinema.

Suture can be enjoyed on multiple levels. A gripping thriller where nothing is black and white (both literally and metaphorically), it's an ambitious example of the possibilities of the medium and a notable entry to the pantheon of inspired American independent movies.

Dir: Scott McGehee, David Siegel; **Prod**: Scott McGehee, David Siegel; **Scr**: Scott McGehee, David Siegel; **DOP**: Greg Gardiner; **Editor**: Lauren Zuckerman; **Score**: Cary Berger; **Main Cast**: Dennis Haysbert, Mel Harris, Sab Shimono, Michael Harris.

Sweet Sweetback's Baadasssss Song
US, 1971 – 97 mins
Melvin Van Peebles

A watershed film in the history of black American cinema, *Sweet Sweetback's Baadasssss Song* was an act of great defiance that had major ideological repercussions in its polemical treatment of white oppression and its challenge to the discriminatory regime of Hollywood and American society in general. Independent by any definition – production, politics, aesthetics and economics – its signficance and influence cannot be overstated.

Van Peebles was not surprisingly unable to obtain studio funding for the project. A former novelist blessed with entrepreneurial flair, Van Peebles acted as his own producer to raise a shoestring budget largely composed of contributions from wealthy black businessmen and entertainment figures, including Bill Cosby. As well as undertaking writing and directing duties, Van Peebles would also go on to star, edit and, alongside Earth, Wind and Fire, compose the R & B score.

The film is dedicated to 'all the Brothers and Sisters who had enough of the Man' and billed simply as 'starring The Black Community'. The simple plot concerns an apolitical black stud, Sweetback (Van Peebles), who becomes a reluctant hero after impulsively beating two white cops guilty of brutalising Mu Mu (Hubert Scales), a young black revolutionary. Sweetback is forced to go on the run, his escape to Mexico being punctuated with various altercations with the law and encounters with numerous women, who are suitably chastened by his sexual prowess.

The film is set amid the Los Angeles ghettos frequently glossed over on screen. While *Sweetback*'s narrative may at times border on the repetitive and its central character, whose actions lack any real political motivation, reinforces stereotypes of black male potency, the film is still an uncompromising and provocative vision that begins with the epigraph, 'these lines are not an homage to brutality that the artist has invented, but a hymn from the mouth of reality'. Perhaps the film's single most transgressive gesture is that Sweetback's anti-authoritarian stance is met not with death (as would traditionally be the case) but with liberty and a final warning shot emblazoned on the screen: 'Watch Out! A baadasssss nigger is coming back to collect some dues.' The film's activism is mirrored by Van Peebles' striking formal approach. Making a mockery of his budget and his limited film-making experience, he vigorously employs multiple experimental new-wave techniques such as split screen, freeze-frames, overlapping images and the exposure of the film negative.

Sweetback's impact was immediate and enduring, despite it being rated X by the Motion Picture Association of America. Van Peebles personally ordered the addition to the posters of the statement, 'rated X by an all-white jury', and largely condemned the film to limited circulation by an industry fearful of its content and repercussions. Deemed mandatory viewing by the Black Panthers, the film is credited with fathering the blaxploitation movement of the early 70s and offered a positive advance in terms of the cinematic visibility of African-Americans. Moreover, it opened the door for subsequent black film-makers, including Haile Gerima, Billy Woodberry, Charles Burnett and, latterly, Spike Lee. It also opened up the potential for such figures to ply their trade both within and independent from the Hollywood system.

Dir: Melvin Van Peebles; **Prod**: Melvin Van Peebles; **Scr**: Melvin Van Peebles; **DOP**: Robert Maxwell; **Editor**: Melvin Van Peebles; **Score**: Melvin Van Peebles; **Main Cast**: Melvin Van Peebles, Rhetta Hughes, John Amos, Simon Chuckster.

Swoon
US, 1991 – 94 mins
Tom Kalin

A former producer for AIDSFILMS, a prevention education organisation, and the director of the provocative and experimental short *They Are Lost to Vision Altogether* (1989), a look at the media's treatment of AIDS information within America, Kalin made a compelling feature debut with the self-written and edited *Swoon*. Produced by Christine Vachon (with initial funding from Apparatus, the company established by Vachon and Todd Haynes) after Kalin had himself raised $100,000 by personally writing to granting organisations, the film became one of the key pictures of the New Queer Cinema movement and, alongside works such as Haynes' *Poison* (1991) and Greg Araki's *The Living End* (1992), was active in establishing a clearly recognisable gay cinematic aesthetic and sensibility.

Swoon offers a bold and modernist account of the 1924 Leopold and Loeb murder case in which eighteen-year-old Nathan Freudenthal Leopold Jr and Richard Loeb, two aesthetes from wealthy Chicago Jewish families, kidnapped and murdered fourteen-year-old Bobby Franks purely for the intellectual stimulation of the crime. Bound by Nietzschean concepts of superiority and by a sadomasochistic sexual relationship (Leopold was a homosexual, Loeb a sociopath who allowed himself to be used sexually in return for Leopold's involvement in his criminal activities), the pair were sufficiently arrogant as to be clumsy in their execution and thus were quickly brought to justice.

The case had been filmed on two previous occasions, first by Hitchcock as the famously one-take *Rope* (1948), which did explore the pair's fascism and grounding in Nietzschean philosophy, and then by Richard Fleischer as *Compulsion* (1959), a more conventional thriller based on Meyer Levin's novel. Kalin's revisiting of the material was inspired by his desire to 'state publicly, once and for all, in an unabashed and direct fashion the facts of the case' (Kalin interview, in Hillier, 2001, p. 88), namely Leopold and Loeb's homosexual relationship. Perhaps unsurprisingly this facet was consciously avoided by the earlier productions, which were made in a more sexually and morally proscriptive climate. Determinedly eschewing positive representation – which later led to criticism from some sections of the gay media concerning the depiction of homosexuality – *Swoon* begins with an examination of the sadomasochistic nature of the sexual relationship and the transgressive games the pair played to show just how important a factor it was in regard to their subsequent actions. For Kalin, the crime did not directly evolve because of the sexuality of the perpetrators, but it was undeniably linked to it. He recently returned to similar terrain with *Savage Grace* (2007), an outstanding account of the incredible story of Barbara Daly, an aspiring socialite who marries above her class to Brooks Baekeland and then develops an unnaturally close relationship with their son.

Exhaustively researched and factually accurate to the extent that almost all the confession speeches and courtroom material of *Swoon*'s latter half were literally transcribed, the film expands upon defence attorney Clarence Darrow's argument that the pair's homosexuality was a sign of pathological deviance and his belief that they could not be held fully accountable for their crimes. As such, a fascinating depiction of racism, repression and rabid homophobia emerges. Relaying what Kalin has described as a 'revisionist aesthetic' influenced by the photographs of Bruce Weber, *Swoon*'s impressive and non-naturalistic collage of fictional footage and courtroom re-enactments, all beautifully captured in monochrome by Sundance Cinematography Award-winner Ellen Kuras, also boasts a decadent, well-tailored retro style that communicates the atmosphere and extravagance of the period, and Leopold and Loeb's just-so glamour.

Dir: Tom Kalin; **Prod**: Tom Kalin, Christine Vachon; **Scr**: Tom Kalin, Hilton Als; **DOP**: Ellen Kuras; **Editor**: Tom Kalin; **Score**: James Bennett; **Main Cast**: Daniel Schlachet, Craig Chester, Ron Vawter, Michael Kirby.

Synecdoche, New York
US, 2008 – 124 mins
Charlie Kaufman

As difficult to pronounce as it is to comprehend, the directorial debut of one of America's finest and most imaginative screenwriters ultimately collapses under the weight of its own ideas and ambition. But, what an astonishing and audacious effort this is. Part dream and part puzzle (and one that proves ultimately unsolvable), *Synecdoche, New York* offers a look at the burden of dreams and the emotional and physical chasm that exists between the hurt and confused inhabitants of twenty-first-century society.

Philip Seymour Hoffman is heartbreaking as Caden, a neurotic theatre director whose problems include a failing marriage to Adele (Keener) and a career that seems to be speeding nowhere. When Adele leaves him to pursue her own art career in Berlin, Caden throws himself into his new Broadway show, turning his every living moment into painfully exposed material. Attempting to fill his domestic void with dramatic recreations, Caden casts an actor (Tom Noonan) as his doppelgänger, a beautiful actress (Williams) as his wife and a quirky lookalike (Watson) as his love interest, who in real life is an even quirkier box-office attendant named Hazel (Morton). As the players attempt to reproduce the goings-on in Caden's life at a 1:1 ratio, complications multiply. The real and the simulacrum start talking to one another, and Caden becomes both puppeteer and puppet on his own stage.

The name of graphic artist Chris Ware has been invoked elsewhere in these pages, but his brand of bare-bones emotionalism and depiction of miserable, ruined lives, as brilliantly realised in his *Jimmy Corrigan* series, is once again an entirely apt point of comparison here. Kaufman, whose previous, award-winning scripts include *Being John Malkovich* (1999), *Adaptation* (2002), *Confessions of a Dangerous Mind* (2002) and *Eternal Sunshine of the Spotless Mind* (2004), is, of course, known for writing material that manages to be both lucid and, in terms of narrative, a total mind-fuck. The sense of sad, disconnectedness and the failure of his protagonists to cope with loss or separation has been another dominant feature of his work. However, not even those earlier writing assignments, two of which were so skilfully wrestled onto the screen by Spike Jonze, a producer here, could have given an inkling of *Synecdoche*, a work that is quite towering in its scope and melancholy. As a philosophical reflection on the futility of life and creative endeavour, it is perhaps unmatched by anything in contemporary American cinema.

Kaufman has obviously learned much from working so closely in collaboration with his previous directors and peppers his film with the visual flourishes characteristic of both Jonze and *Eternal Sunshine* director and kindred spirit Michel Gondry. Some of the sequences are inspired: the fact that Hazel's house is permanently on fire, and the huge and

Will a spot of spring cleaning help Caden Cotard (Philip Seymour Hoffman) make sense of his life? Charlie Kaufman's ambitious and quietly epic *Synecdoche, New York*

ever-increasing and oppressive set that seems to be in danger of engulfing the whole of New York. He's good with actors too, and quite apart from the magnificent Hoffman, corrals an impressive ensemble of supporting players, including Hope Davis, Jennifer Jason Leigh and Dianne Wiest. A poignant, tragic reflection on the degree to which life imitates life (and vice versa), this is a film that will only increase in stature with the passing years.

Dir: Charlie Kaufman; **Prod**: Anthony Bregman, Charlie Kaufman, Spike Jonze, Sidney Kimmel; **Scr**: Charlie Kaufman; **DOP**: Frederick Elmes; **Editor**: Robert Frazen; **Score**: Jon Brion; **Main Cast**: Philip Seymour Hoffman, Samantha Morton, Michelle Williams, Catherine Keener, Emily Watson.

Targets
US, 1968 – 90 mins
Peter Bogdanovich

Bridging the gap between classic and contemporary horror, the unconventional *Targets* transcends its genre origins to offer a complex commentary on US mythology and the pervading culture of violence and paranoia. The first film from Peter Bogdanovich, it is less celebrated than *The Last Picture Show* (1971), which revisits similar themes concerning a changing America, but arguably remains his most enduring contribution to cinema.

O'Kelly plays Bobby Thompson, a seemingly mild-mannered husband and son. But Bobby has a penchant for collecting firearms and thinking murderous thoughts, which translate into action when he becomes a deadly sniper, picking off drivers from an oil tank high above the LA freeway. Meanwhile, Byron Orlok (Karloff), an ageing horror film star, plans his retirement, convinced that the atrocities wrought by daily human global existence have numbed the public to the movie monsters he plays. As fate and movies will have it, the worlds of Thompson and Orlok collide at the Reseda Drive-In, where Orlok is reluctantly making his final public appearance.

Scripted by Bogdanovich and his then wife Polly Platt, *Targets* was inspired by the 1966 killing spree of Texas Tower sniper Charles Whitman. Counterpoising Karloff's screen monster against the young sociopath, the film intelligently explores the relationship between the imagination and unexplained and unexpected violence, and emerged at a time when the national psyche was reeling from political events at home and abroad. Utterly chilling and shot with cold detachment by celebrated cinematographer László Kovács, the film also precipitated a debate that has continued to fixate the media: the possible desensitising impact of a continued exposure to violent images.

As well as writing, producing and editing, Bogdanovich also appears on screen as Sammy Michaels, a fledgling film director caught in the clutches of an opportunistic producer. It was Roger Corman, Bogdanovich's mentor, who had encouraged his young charge to try his hand at directing, donating footage from 1963's *The Terror* (sequences featuring a young Jack Nicholson of which appear at the drive-in) and its leading man, whose contract stipulated that he still owed the low-budget *über* mogul two days' worth of work for the picture. Karloff reputedly became so caught up in the twenty-nine-year-old Bogdanovich's enthusiasm that he agreed to work additional days at a minimum rate. Often erroneously cited as Karloff's final work – four films in which he featured were in fact hastily edited after his death – it is undoubtedly the last significant contribution from one of the titans of horror.

Less than enthusiastically received by Paramount, who were wary of a film dealing with such a sensitive subject in the wake of the recent Martin Luther King and Kennedy assassinations, *Targets* received a muted release. It finally came to wider attention and critical regard after a reissue programme that saw it play to fervent and appreciative crowds at college campuses and film societies.

Dir: Peter Bogdanovich; **Prod**: Peter Bogdanovich; **Scr**: Peter Bogdanovich; **DOP**: László Kovács; **Editor**: Peter Bogdanovich; **Score**: Charles Greene, Brian Stone; **Main Cast**: Boris Karloff, Tim O'Kelly, Nancy Hsueh, James Brown.

Tarnation
US, 2003 – 88 mins
Jonathan Caouette

A raw, extremely personal and sensual display of self-destruction and rebirth that announces the arrival of an exceptional new cinematic visionary, *Tarnation* marks the feature debut of Jonathan Caouette. The film interweaves a psychedelic whirlwind of snapshots, Super-8 home movies, answering-machine messages, video diaries, snippets of 80s pop culture and dramatic re-enactments to create an epic portrait of Caouette's American family, one torn apart by dysfunction and reunited through the power of love. Structured so as to evoke the film-maker's own depersonalisation disorder, the film has been variously compared to David Lynch, *Capturing the Friedmans* (2003) and avant-garde artists such as Stan Brakhage and Jack Smith. A personal love letter to the film-maker's mother Renee, who spent much of her youth undergoing electroshock therapy for a form of schizophrenia, *Tarnation* redefines the possibilities of documentary, and of film-making in general.

A project that began when Caouette was just eleven years old, *Tarnation* was screened at the 2004 Sundance Film Festival to considerable acclaim and went on to enrapture audiences worldwide with is visual audacity and undiluted emotion. One of the main talking points was its initial $218.32 budget, a figure made possible by the use of Apple's iMovie editing software. Included free with most Macintosh computers, since its introduction in 1999, iMovie has evolved into a comprehensive editing suite for aspiring movie-makers, allowing the capability to edit image, mix sound, add effects and filters, generate titles and even create screening DVDs. It was on a screening DVD that Caouette first circulated a version of *Tarnation* to American festival organisers. On seeing copies of these DVDs, established figures such as John Cameron Mitchell and Gus Van Sant came on board the project as executive producers, endorsing the film's striking aesthetic and its gay sensibility.

Jonathan Caouette's digital DIY confessional, *Tarnation*

By film industry standards, iMovie is a very basic program that was initially considered best-suited for non-professionals learning to edit home movie footage. However, because of its affordability, accessibility and simple interface, many digital film-makers turned to iMovie to edit their projects. Veterans such as Walter Murch have followed suit and so in one fell swoop, *Tarnation* ushered in a new respect and excitement for do-it-yourself film-making, forcing the entertainment industry to pay more attention to potent but unproven film-making talent.

Incorporating over 160 hours of digitised material, *Tarnation* – the compilation of two concepts, tarnished and eternal damnation, and also the name of one of its creator's favourite bands – was described by Van Sant as the first cinematic masterpiece of outsider art. Having stated that he has enough material stored away for a sequel, Caouette is very aware of the likely democratising effect his efforts will have:

I feel that *Tarnation* will make cinema more accessible for film-makers and for audiences. I don't think that everybody will necessarily be able to make good films, just like not everybody is able to make films using more traditional methods either, but this is certainly going to offer a new, more achievable way of making films for considerably less money. And thank God for it. (Boorman and Donohue, 2006, p. 364)

Dir: Jonathan Caouette; **Prod**: Jonathan Caouette, Stephen Winter; **Scr**: Jonathan Caouette; **DOP**: Jonathan Caouette; **Editor**: Jonathan Caouette, Brian A. Kates; **Score**: John Califra, Max Avery Lichtenstein; **Main Cast**: Jonathan Caouette, Renee Leblanc, David Leblanc, David Sanin Paz.

The Thin Blue Line
US, 1988 – 101 mins
Errol Morris

The Thin Blue Line evolved from *Dr Death*, another much-mooted and fastidiously researched Morris project that took as its subject Dr James Grigson, a Dallas psychiatrist who often appeared as a witness for the prosecution in death penalty cases. It was while interviewing death row inmates for that project that Morris first encountered and interviewed Randall Adams, a young drifter imprisoned in 1977 for the fatal shooting of Dallas police officer Robert Wood, a case in which the authorities had been under pressure to deliver an assailant. The chief witness against Adams was David Harris, also on death row for an unrelated murder. Adams had continually professed his innocence, and slowly Morris began to believe him, realising that tracking the situation on film was an opportunity to clear Adams' name and spare him from execution.

The film takes its title from the judge recalling the prosecutor's summary concerning 'the thin blue line' that maintains the social fabric, and is described by the director as 'the first murder mystery that actually solves a murder'. It is an impressive and provocative piece of photojournalism that serves as a sobering meditation on the failings of the American justice system, and also offers an at times blackly comic, decidedly Lynchian peep into the troubled American psyche. Fascinated more by incongruities than the facts themselves, Morris painstakingly interviews all the principal figures in the case, slowly piecing together an alternative and more probable picture of the fateful events from multiple perspectives. Though conventionally framed, Morris' interview technique is captivating and unique. Honing in on idiosyncratic word choices and patterns of speech, he draws the most intimate, revealing and previously suppressed details from his subjects, including, ultimately, Harris' audio confession to the crime.

Morris eschews the low-key aesthetic conventionally associated with the documentary (an approach that offended purists, hence the film was

a no-show in the Academy Award nominations), characteristically adopting a more visually arresting and inventive approach to structure, design and execution. The distinction between documentary and fiction is blurred (acquired by Miramax, the film was aggressively marketed as a 'non-fiction feature'), as immaculately conceived reconstructions (including a dramatic slow-motion re-enactment of Woods' bullet-ridden body slumping to the floor), actual footage and close-ups of objects and hitherto overlooked details blend to cogent and seductive effect. When excerpts from *Swinging Cheerleaders* (1974), the late-show B-movie that was used as an alibi, are incorporated, shots of a ticking clock are intercut to reveal glaring discrepancies in chronology (Morris unearths the fact that there was no late show on the night of the murder). Sensitively scored by Philip Glass, *The Thin Blue Line* also boasts felicitous sound design, including strikingly repeated amplified gun shots, that contributes to the overall rhythmic thrust. Little wonder that J. Hoberman described the film as 'impressive, haunting and brilliantly stylised' (Hoberman, 1988, p. 60).

The film was entered as evidence when Adams was granted a retrial, which became a media furore that contributed to the film's notable home video popularity. The instant impact of the film was magnified when it aired on American Playhouse – one of the project's financiers – to coincide with Adams' release from prison.

Dir: Errol Morris; **Prod**: Mark Lipson; **Scr**: N/A; **DOP**: Stefan Czapsky, Robert Chappell; **Editor**: Paul Barnes, Elizabeth King; **Score**: Philip Glass; **Main Cast**: Randall Adams, David Harris, Edith James, Dennis White.

(*Opposite page*) Documentary evidence: Errol Morris' *The Thin Blue Line* was pivotal in the retrial of convicted cop killer Randall Adams and indirectly led to the quashing of his conviction

Tongues Untied
US, 1989 – 55 mins
Marlon T. Riggs

Along with Isaac Julien's *Looking for Langston* (1988), *Tongues Untied* was one of the first black independent productions to openly address the thorny issue of black homosexuality. Intelligently and passionately exploring the intersections of racism and homophobia, the film gives a committed and defiant voice to the previously silenced black gay male community.

Tongues Untied is hugely politically charged, being set in the shadow of AIDS. The film is largely autobiographical, beginning with a childhood spent among the rednecks of Georgia where the director remembers being referred to as a 'motherfuckin' coon'. It depicts numerous racist and homophobic encounters as Riggs subsequently comes out into a largely white gay environment, shedding 'shades of nigger boy for pigments of faggot and queer'. The initial wonder of San Francisco's Castro area soon dissipates when Riggs realises his invisibility remains because 'I was a nigger boy still'. Giving evidence of a shared black gay male experience and mutual recognition, while further tapping into the African-American tradition of witness and testimony, Riggs eloquently structures the film around the poetry of a chorus of black gay voices, including Essex Hemphill, Reginald Jackson and Steve Langley. The music of the a cappella outfit the Lavender Light Quartet also features prominently, as does, on the film's soundtrack, artists such as Sylvester, Roberta Flack and Nina Simone.

The film impressively draws upon Riggs' experience of working within disparate media, resembling an at times complex and skilfully edited kaleidoscopic collage. Among the inserts intercut with the poetry and personal reminiscences are an Eddie Murphy routine in which homosexuals are roundly condemned, a street mime performed by a troupe of young black kids and a profoundly lyrical, slow-motion sequence of a black man smoking a cigarette wearing a look of pained contemplation. Accompanying the latter sequence is Billie Holiday's 'Loverman', here transformed into a paean for black gay longing.

Despite attracting criticism from black gay women and feminist critics for its seemingly segregative closing coda of 'black men loving black men is the revolutionary act' (Amy Taubin labelled it 'heedlessly misogynistic': Taubin, 2001, p. 91), *Tongues Untied* nonetheless articulated a new collective sexual and racial identity and placed Riggs at the vanguard of the renaissance of black culture in the 80s and early 90s. Made on a tight budget with a grant from the National Endowment for the Arts, the film, also produced, edited and shot by Riggs, achieved a recognition far beyond black or gay audiences when its airing on US television was used by far-right sympathisers to attack George Bush for what they regarded as his misuse of tax-payers' money to fund a rainbow coalition. Riggs fired back, defending the right of all to representation, while highlighting the anti-gay bigotry with which the political establishment now laced its racial slurs.

Dir: Marlon T. Riggs; **Prod**: Marlon T. Riggs; **Scr**: Reginald Jackson, Steve Langley, Alan Miller, Donald Woods, Joseph Bream, Craig Harris, Marlon T. Riggs, Essex Hemphill; **DOP**: Marlon T. Riggs; **Editor**: Marlon T. Riggs; **Score**: Alex Langford, Steve Langley, Marlon T. Riggs; **Main Cast**: Kerrigan Black, Blackberri, Bernard Brannier, Gerald Davies.

Trees Lounge
US, 1996 – 95 mins
Steve Buscemi

Buscemi's nervous, haunted presence graced seemingly every self-respecting 90s' US independent picture, making his 'king of the indies' title (Kemp, 2001) seem entirely appropriate. His understanding of and association with the indie milieu was extended by having played low-budget directors in Alexandre Rockwell's *In the Soup* (1992) – which also gave him the opportunity to helm the short film contained therein – and DiCillo's *Living in Oblivion* (1995). Buscemi's familiarity with the territory therefore ensured that it came as little surprise when he made his impressive writing-directing debut with the partly autobiographical *Trees Lounge*.

Shot in Valley Stream, the blue-collar suburban belt of Long Island where Buscemi grew up, it's a well-observed and ultimately quietly poignant character study of Tommy Basilio (Buscemi), an unemployed mechanic whose life has fallen apart since his girlfriend Teresa (Bracco) left him for his former boss, Rob (LaPaglia). Tommy wastes his days hanging around the garage and his nights drinking himself into oblivion at the Trees Lounge bar, conveniently situated right below his apartment. Finally finding work driving an ice-cream truck, his downward spiral nonetheless continues when he beds his seventeen-year-old niece, Debbie (Sevigny).

Described by Buscemi as a projection of 'what would have happened if I'd stayed in Valley Stream' (ibid., p. 16), *Trees Lounge* is a perceptive and authentic account of barroom blue-collar life and the perils of constant libation. Vividly realised by Buscemi's credible, world-weary dialogue and its coterie of well-drawn leather-skinned bar lizards drunkenly pontificating on life, the Trees Lounge bar is a wonderfully murky, beer-sodden creation of the kind Charles Bukowski may have frequented. Tommy's attempts to rally his co-drinkers into a hospital visit to see Bill, the Lounge's longest-serving patron, immediately collapse

Barflies Tommy Basilio (Steve Buscemi) and Bill (Bronson Dudley) in the director-star's autobiographical *Trees Lounge*

under the collective weight of apathy; a moment that perhaps encapsulates the central concern of the film.

The film is beautifully performed by its ensemble cast, not least Buscemi's former stand-up comedy partner Mark Boone Junior, and the director himself, who brings a wounded sympathy to two-time loser Tommy. *Trees Lounge* is appropriately shot in a relaxed, understated and unhurried deadpan style that suggests that Buscemi's time with Jarmusch and the Coen brothers was formally instructive. The defining influence and sensibility is, however, that of Cassavetes, whose spirit is evoked through the film's unforced naturalism and its favouring of colourful, digressive and often painfully funny character-driven vignettes in place of a rigid structural cohesion. Moreover, a well-judged cameo from Cassavetes' stalwart Seymour Cassel apart, *Trees Lounge* also maintains a lineage with Cassavetes in its willingness to engage with the underbelly of American life. Like many indie directors of his generation, Buscemi is forthright in his admiration for Cassavetes and of his alternation of an independent film-making career with lucrative acting parts in Hollywood movies. This is a tactic increasingly employed by Buscemi himself, with his subsequent feature, *Animal Factory* (2001), being partly built upon fees accrued for work in fare such as *Con Air* (1997) and *Armageddon* (1998).

Told by a Valley Stream barfly during shooting that *Trees Lounge* was a terrible idea because it was not remotely commercial, Buscemi took the comment as a compliment, replying 'that's the point' (ibid., p. 16). Nominated for two Independent Spirit Awards (Best First Feature and Best First Screenplay), the film was actually no slouch at the US box office either. Initially opening on just two screens, the film took $39,830 on its opening weekend, and later expanded to fifty-one screens and a final box-office gross of $749,741.

Dir: Steve Buscemi; **Prod**: Brad Wyman, Chris Hanley; **Scr**: Steve Buscemi; **DOP**: Lisa Rinzler; **Editor**: Kate Williams, Jane Pia Abramovitz; **Score**: Evan Lurie; **Main Cast**: Steve Buscemi, Chloë Sevigny, Anthony LaPaglia, Elizabeth Bracco.

Trouble in Mind
US, 1985 – 112 mins
Alan Rudolph

Rudolph began his career with minor low-budget horror flicks
Premonition (1972) and *Nightmare Circus* (1973) before establishing an
association with Altman that would prove instructive in terms of his own
working practices and sensibilities. After serving as Altman's assistant
director and co-authoring *Buffalo Bill and the Indians* (1976), Rudolph
directed the highly personal and idiosyncratic *Welcome to L.A.* (1977).
A kaleidoscopic, largely free-form satire about the lives of various LA
denizens, the film displays an elegant visual style, slightly offbeat
characters and locations and sense of doomed romanticism (all evident
in *Trouble in Mind*) that were to become Rudolphian hallmarks.
However, the commercial failure of *Welcome to L.A.* necessitated Rudolph's
signing up for a number of impersonal and largely inferior studio projects
that did little but allow the director the opportunity to try out different
genres and squirrel away finance for the pictures he wished to make; it's a
pattern Rudolph has, frustratingly, been forced to follow ever since.

The film was made hot on the heels of 1984's *Choose Me*, Rudolph's
most commercially successful though wholly independent feature.
Trouble in Mind takes place in the mythical, dangerous and retro-futurist
Rain City. Fresh out of jail for the slaying of a mobster, former cop Hawk
(Kristofferson) returns to a familiar haunt, a neon-lit café run by old
flame Wanda (Bujold). He soon finds himself falling under the spell of a
young mother, Georgia (Singer), whose reckless, feckless husband Coop
(Carradine) is slowly sinking into a life of crime and extravagance.
To protect her after a scheme involving Coop and his partner Solo (Joe
Morton) goes disastrously wrong, Hawk must confront his old adversary
Hilly Blue (Divine, impressive in a rare straight role), a wealthy and
extremely powerful crime lord.

Featuring many of Rudolph's regular performers, most notably Bujold
and Altman alumnus Carradine (who, in a display of the film's inherent

Coop (Keith Carradine), seen here with Hawk (Kris Kristofferson), has another bad hair day in *Trouble in Mind*

humour and sense of the absurd, sports increasingly outlandish hairstyles and clothing as his criminal activities increase), *Trouble in Mind* is a characteristically eccentric, ambiguous and decidedly offbeat delight. Rudolph's talent for invoking atmosphere is well complemented by a suitably moody, melancholy and eclectic collaborative score from regular composer Mark Isham, here ably assisted by chanteuse Marianne Faithfull. The film borrows freely from melodrama, the Western, film noir (Rudolph's regular source of inspiration) and even sci-fi/fantasy (Rain City, actually Seattle, Washington, seems to be set some time in the future during what looks like a state of martial law). The various influences merge and react to dazzling and often dreamlike effect.

Similarly disparate, the film's imaginative and at times distinctly surreal production design and *mise en scène* (particularly evident in Hilly Blue's opulent home) positively revels in stylistic excess.

Perhaps, though, the minimalist, achingly lonely paintings of Edward Hopper ultimately win out as the most pronounced influence on the film

– which is fitting given that *Trouble in Mind* is an elegiac meditation on regret, love and longing. It is certainly among the most visually striking of Rudolph's intermittently independent works, with Toyomichi Kurita's cinematography winning an Independent Spirit Award. The film offers confirmation that Rudolph's esoteric talents are not best suited to the commercial demands of mainstream production.

Dir: Alan Rudolph; **Prod**: Carolyn Pfeifer, David Blocker; **Scr**: Alan Rudolph; **DOP**: Toyomichi Kurita; **Editor**: Tom Walls, Sally Coryn Allen; **Score**: Mark Isham; **Main Cast**: Kris Kristofferson, Keith Carradine, Lori Singer, Genevieve Bujold.

Two-Lane Blacktop
US, 1971 – 101 mins
Monte Hellman

Like Paul Bartel, Hellman is a product of the Roger Corman stable.
Early Hellman pictures configure to the low-budget genre knock-offs with
which Corman made his name. Hellman's starkly original Westerns *Ride
in the Whirlwind* and *The Shooting* (both 1966, but not released until
two years later), however, though made at Corman's behest and shot
back-to-back in the Utah desert for a combined $150,000, display a less
commercial and more cryptic, European sensibility than the earlier films.
Two-Lane Blacktop offered an advance on Hellman's wilfully esoteric
approach and withdrawn visual style, and considered man's abject futility
and mythical search for identity in an existentialist landscape of the kind
more commonly found in the films of Antonioni and the literature of
Sartre and Camus.

Greenlit by Universal boss Lew Wasserman along with Hopper's *The
Last Movie* (1971) and Peter Fonda's *The Hired Hand* (1971), the $850,000
project was seen as an opportunity to capitalise on the chord that *Easy
Rider* (1969) had struck with America's youth market. The omens were
initially good; *Esquire* was so impressed by the Wurlitzer/Corry screenplay
that it made the film its April 1971 cover, printed the script in its entirety
and proclaimed the film, which they had yet to see, the movie of the year.
However, after viewing a film that was even more determinedly oblique
and intransigent than the director's Westerns, *Esquire* awarded themselves
a prize for over-hyping. The film was accorded a few positive
endorsements by critics who admired director-editor Hellman's ability to
capture the contemporary mood of alienation without resorting to the
visual clichés of drugs, sex and violence, but it was largely marginalised by
reviewers and the public, who were left cold by what J. Hoberman termed
'absurdly inert' characters (Hoberman, 2000b).

Opaque, with little investment in character or plot consequentiality,
the film centres on two young car enthusiasts, The Driver (singer Taylor)

and The Mechanic (Beach Boy Wilson), who trek across the American Southwest in their finely tuned '55 Chevy, occasionally competing in drag races to maintain the car's upkeep. Barely speaking, except when a discussion of the car necessitates it, the duo experience friction after allowing a girl (Bird) to enter their circle. At a gas station, the trio encounter GTO (Oates), a middle-aged braggart who travels the highways in his Pontiac picking up hitchhikers and listening to loud music; in one of the more lucid moments, he divulges that his job and family have 'fallen apart'. A challenge is suggested, a race to Washington DC, in which the victor will claim the loser's car. A mesmeric duel unfolds over the two-lane blacktops of Oklahoma, but gradually the race fizzles out as the nomadic participants lose interest.

Two-Lane Blacktop's self-destructive final image is of the film jamming in the projector and igniting, a 'closure' that highlights Hellman's disregard for convention, while acting as a metaphor for his subsequent career: unable to assimilate into the system, Hellman returned to the fringes with the relentlessly bleak *Cockfighter* (1974). Excising all possible tension, Hellman revels in the abstract, creating a stunningly and languorously shot parable about desolation and inertia. The film has itself subsequently attained a mythic status (Malick and Wenders took note) and is now commonly regarded as the quintessential road movie.

Dir: Monte Hellman; **Prod**: Michael Laughlin; **Scr**: Rudolph Wurlitzer, Will Corry; **DOP**: Jack Deerson; **Editor**: Monte Hellman; **Score**: Billy James; **Main Cast**: James Taylor, Warren Oates, Laurie Bird, Dennis Wilson.

The Unbelievable Truth
US, 1989 – 90 mins
Hal Hartley

Hartley's feature debut, following three well-received shorts, was made while working for a TV company specialising in public service announcements. It is an early expression of the thematic and formal concerns that have remained throughout the director's subsequent career. It also reveals the then thirty-year-old to be a tyrant of economy (both textural and in terms of working within the tight confines of a seemingly prohibitively low budget) and a master chronicler of the minutiae of suburban life.

Made for just $75,000 and financed by Jerome Brownstein, Hartley's sympathetic boss, it boasts no stars, though all the actors involved went on to form part of Hartley's regular repertory company. The film has a highly idiosyncratic and elliptical structure coupled with a non-naturalistic ambience and an at times endearingly goofy affection for European art movies – particularly those of Godard. In a video interview, the director cites Howard Hawks and Preston Sturges as other influences (Anipare and Wood, 1997). Moreover, in what was to become a defining motif in later works such as *Trust* (1990) and *Simple Men* (1992), the film displays a winning reliance upon the writer-director's immaculately constructed, highly comic and tersely delivered dialogue. Hartley has been compared to the playwright Harold Pinter for his epigrammatic aphorisms and interest in patterns of speech and repetition. Here, Hartley reaffirms the independent film-maker's mantra: talk is cheap.

In terms of narrative, it's a characteristic study of the journey towards selfhood and knowledge. Here the journey is made by Audry (Shelly), a politically committed, bookish intellectual whose dreams of attending college are dented by her fear of impending apocalypse and the lucrative modelling career that seems to be unfolding. Also making the pilgrimage is Josh (Burke), a sombre slaughterman returning from prison to his home town of Lindenhurst, where he takes a job as a mechanic in a

Trouble and desire: Audry (Adrienne Shelly) and Josh (Robert Burke) discuss the mechanics of love in *The Unbelievable Truth*

garage run by Audry's father. A shared appreciation of George Washington ensures that romance ensues between the enigmatic pair, but in a small town ruled by idle tittle-tattle and prejudice, misconception haunts their every action and conspires to keep them apart.

Quizzical in spirit and in terms of the playful approach to *mise en scène* and structure (jump-cuts, overlapping dialogue and gently comic intertitles such as 'Meanwhile', 'A month, maybe two months later' recur), *The Unbelievable Truth* also reveals Hartley's often undervalued eye for crisp compositions. The film may have been made on the cheap, but cinematographer Michael Spiller makes sure that it doesn't look it. Another defining feature is the absence of establishing shots, a format Hartley has declared his disinterest in, with many scenes often beginning as if interrupted mid-flow. Light-hearted it may appear (a fondness for outlandish, almost cartoonish physical humour such as staccato slaps and punches is revealed), but the concerns are unmistakably serious: the corrupting nature of money, the division between ambition and achievement and between truth and hearsay, the fraught nature of relationships, and the decay of the American family.

A Grand Jury Prize nominee at 1990's Sundance, *The Unbelievable Truth* was a seminal work in terms of American independent cinema in the immediate aftermath of *sex, lies and videotape* (1989). Though freely borrowing from melodrama and the Western (a genre Hartley studied), it largely eschews and positively defies convention, existing in a world all of its and Hartley's very own.

Dir: Hal Hartley; **Prod**: Bruce Weiss, Hal Hartley; **Scr**: Hal Hartley; **DOP**: Michael Spiller; **Editor**: Hal Hartley; **Score**: Jim Coleman, Phillip Reed, Wild Blue Yonder, The Brothers Kendall; **Main Cast**: Adrienne Shelly, Robert Burke, Christopher Cooke, Julia McNeal.

Variety
Germany/UK/US, 1983 – 100 mins
Bette Gordon

Originating from a short story by Gordon, an experimental film-maker and leading light in New York's post-punk scene, *Variety* attracted heightened interest due to its Kathy Acker credit. Acker was invited to add a number of key discussions about men and the pivotal sex monologues delivered by the film's female protagonist, Christine, played by Sandy McLeod. McLeod later became a script supervisor on John Sayles' films, including *City of Hope* (1991). The film was independently produced by Variety Pictures, Channel Four and Germany's Zweites Deutsches Fernsehen, with further financial assistance from the New York State Council on the Arts.

Variety begins with struggling writer Christine accepting a lowly job selling tickets at the Variety, a New York sex cinema. Alienated from her boyfriend Mark (Patton), a journalist investigating a story about union links with the Mob, Christine becomes increasingly drawn to the images on screen and to entertaining strangers with graphic, monotone descriptions of hardcore sex. Christine also begins to obsess over Louis (Richard Davidson), a powerful and affluent regular at the Variety whose shady activities suggest Mafia links. Segueing into thriller territory (with allusions also to film noir), the film concludes unresolved with Christine waiting on a darkened street corner, seemingly on the cusp of being drawn into Louis' nefarious world.

Made at the height of feminist debates on pornography, *Variety* is regarded as a feminist work, a perception Gordon refutes: 'My life, my sexual identity is as a feminist, but my films don't fit easily into that category' (quoted in Jenkins, 1984, p. 138). Moreover, though various pornographic discourses appear (soundtracks, images from men's magazines and Christine's aforementioned monologues), *Variety* is not specifically about women and pornography at all. It is more an examination of how Christine deals with sexuality, which she does in a way that women are seldom shown doing. Gordon deliberately sets out to raise eyebrows by 'saying things about my own sexuality that won't be popular, in talking about things that contradict the positive view of women that you are supposed to show' (ibid.), and compares her approach to Fassbinder's attempts to force the audience to question prescribed notions of race, class and sexuality.

Asserting that Christine re-makes herself and takes charge of her own actions, Gordon is also at pains to make clear the patriarchal culture that surrounds her central character. This is most evident in a montage sequence in which Christine recalls various men shaking hands, the circle of handshakes symbolising patriarchy and the unwritten bond between men that women have to break into. This was replicated by the director's own experiences making the film, when she frequented porn emporiums to find that men would move away from her, 'unable to deal with a real woman, only a woman on the page' (ibid.).

As befits a film set in a sex cinema, *Variety* intelligently reflects an interest in the act of looking. Christine's initial objectification in the opening swimming pool section is commented upon through use of dissecting close-ups. *Variety* is a technically accomplished work featuring the cinematography of Tom DiCillo and John Foster; the equally classy jazz and blues score is courtesy of John Lurie. Closer inspection of the credits yields similar riches and further establishes the film's independent pedigree: Christine Vachon is a production assistant, and among the cast are Steve Buscemi's writing partner Mark Boone Junior, photographer Nan Goldin and John Waters' regular and ubiquitous figure on the New York underground scene, Cookie Mueller.

Dir: Bette Gordon; **Prod**: Renee Shafansky; **Scr**: Kathy Acker; **DOP**: Tom DiCillo, John Foster; **Editor**: Ila von Hasperg; **Score**: John Lurie; **Main Cast**: Sandy McLeod, Luis Guzmán, Will Patton, Nan Goldin.

Wanda
US, 1970 – 100 mins
Barbara Loden

A remarkable directorial outing from Loden, the actor wife of director
Elia Kazan, *Wanda* is a relatively little-known classic of American
independent/underground cinema. The film's reputation rests largely on
its impressive past showings at international film festivals such as London
and Venice, where it won the Prix FIPRESCI (the European Film Academy
Critics' Award) as best first feature.

The film, written by Loden, also stars her in a poignant if miniaturist
and utterly convincing performance as the meandering, emotionally
confused and half-destitute Wanda of the title. The film opens with her
rising from her grubby bed to impassively attend the divorce proceedings
that will see her ejected from the lives of her family. Having all too easily
relinquished her sense of security and permanence, she subsequently
drifts through drab, semi-industrial American townships and from one
dead end and unfulfilling sexual relationship to the next.
Wanda eventually takes up with a hapless, volatile crook (the superb
Higgins) who coerces her into acting as his getaway driver in a poorly
conceived bank robbery. Characteristically, but perhaps fortuitously,
Wanda botches her involvement by getting lost in a traffic jam on the
way to the bank. Back on the road again, Wanda winds up in yet
another run-down backwater bar where, disconnected from her fellow
revellers, she embarks on yet another meaningless affair with a stranger.

Wanda was shot in real, largely unremarkable and down-at-heel
locations with available (i.e. limited) resources on poor-quality 16mm
stock that was subsequently blown up to 35mm. It is unassuming,
understated and at times unapologetically rough and ready in style, and
draws on influences as diverse as Italian neo-realism (Fellini's *Nights of
Cabiria*, 1956, is frequently cited as an inspiration), the documentaries of
Shirley Clarke, and the cinéma vérité approach adopted by John
Cassavetes. Loden also used untrained actors to authentically capture the

semi-articulate nature of everyday speech. The film portrays America as a sad and shabby environment of aimless losers. Perhaps as importantly, *Wanda* also achieves a kind of transgressive objectivity through its ambiguous recording of Wanda's total and at times infuriating passivity, with Loden signalling her central character's abject powerlessness and the ultimate oppression of women like her without immediate recourse to heavy-handed politicising.

Others took a different view. Writing in *Jump-Cut*, Chris Kleinhans criticised the film for never revealing Wanda's consciousness of her oppression, describing the viewing experience as ultimately depressing and unnecessarily nihilistic (Kleinhans, 1974, p. 14). Similarly, the film was also targeted for unsympathetically portraying Wanda as little more than a confused and vapid mess, whose subservient nature makes her a conduit for male desire. *Wanda*, however, has grown in reputation in the years since its release and remains an uncompromising, fascinating and socially salient work. Tragically, it was to be Loden's sole directorial effort; she died from cancer in 1980.

Dir: Barbara Loden; **Prod**: Harry Shuster; **Scr**: Barbara Loden; **DOP**: Nicholas Proferes; **Editor**: Nicholas Proferes; **Score**: Uncredited; **Main Cast**: Barbara Loden, Michael Higgins, Charles Dosinan, Frank Jourdano.

Welcome to the Dollhouse
US, 1995 – 88 mins
Todd Solondz

Such was the impact of *Welcome to the Dollhouse* on the independent landscape that it was mistakenly believed to be New Jersey-born Solondz's debut feature. In fact, he'd made his first feature six years earlier, the studio-produced *Fear, Anxiety and Depression* (1989). That film was re-cut against Solondz's wishes. The incident caused him to turn his back on the business to teach English as a second language to Russian immigrants, an experience that informed his third film, the remarkable and hugely controversial *Happiness* (1998).

Self-penned and self-produced, *Dollhouse* marked a triumphant return to film-making for Solondz, a move achieved entirely on his own terms and capped by the Grand Jury Prize at Sundance. The film stakes out the terrain he has continued to make his own: the depiction of suburbia as a peripheral, excruciating hell in which gawky, adolescent teenagers interminably suffer the physical and verbal taunts of their equally maladjusted parents and peers.

At times unbearably cruel with extremely violent, callous overtones, the film is also an uncannily authentic and perceptive account of outsiderism and the desire to belong as depicted through the eyes of dorky Dawn Wiener (the astonishing Matarazzo), an eleven-year-old New Jersey seventh-grader reviled and hated by her classmates. Dawn's home life is little better; her mother makes it patently clear that her affections lie with her pampered, prissy ballerina-wannabe sister Missy, while her computer nerd brother refuses to let her anywhere near the high-school heart-throb with whom he has formed an uneasy musical alliance. In fact, the only friendship Dawn enjoys is with her equally ostracised, runty neighbour Ralphy, with whom she forms a 'Special Persons' club. An altercation with local thug Brandon (Sexton Jr) brings fresh complications when he threatens to rape her after school – but at least that would involve physical contact, put an end to the 'lesbo' rumours and perhaps precipitate the much-sought onset of puberty.

Solondz directs with the judicious precision and formal economy that goes hand-in-hand with working in the independent sector. The approach of Solondz and his production designer Susan Block (the *mise en scène* alone signals a clarion call for help) also perfectly captures the details of thoroughly unremarkable, suburban life. Sharply satirical and written with a darkly comic attention to detail, the film invites an autobiographical reading: the anguish of the agonisingly painful, lonely youth of its 'geeky', bespectacled author.

As with his subsequent work, Solondz refuses to pull his punches, tackling issues such as abuse, petty crime, sexual confusion and pre-teen sex with candour, directness and a staunchly unsentimental tone far removed from mainstream treatments of juvenile disaffection. At times, the film seems to wilfully exacerbate the barbaric inhumanity on show (a charge levelled at Solondz with increasing regularity), but the ultimately insightful *Dollhouse* also offers moments of extreme tenderness that reveal the hidden depths of this very darkest of black comedies.

Dir: Todd Solondz; **Prod**: Ted Skillman, Todd Solondz; **Scr**: Todd Solondz; **DOP**: Randy Drummond; **Editor**: Alan Oxman; **Score**: Jil Wisoff; **Main Cast**: Heather Matarazzo, Victoria Davis, Christina Vidal, Brendan Sexton Jr.

The Woodsman
US, 2004 – 84 mins
Nicole Kassell

Tackling the taboo subject of child abuse with intelligence and sensitivity, Nicole Kassell's sober and sombre account of a man struggling to control his impulses towards molesting young girls contrasts sharply with the hysteria frequently found in films of this nature. There are exceptions, Michael Cuesta's *L.I.E* (2001), for example, but *The Woodsman* is relatively unique in choosing to focus on the abuser rather than the victim. Another brave choice is refusing to give its protagonist his own history of child abuse, thus making any motions towards empathy all the more hard won.

With a twelve-year prison sentence reaching an end, convicted paedophile Walter (Bacon) faces an uncertain process of re-acclimatisation. Attempting to keep his previous indiscretions sheltered, Walter pieces together his shattered life by finding a job and an apartment. Possessing a natural talent for woodcraft, the ex-con finds employment at a lumberyard and a home, in a cruel twist of irony, in a building overlooking an elementary school. Though his brother-in-law (Bratt) seems willing to stay in touch, Walter is refused all other contact by his family members and lives an isolated, monastic existence. With Sgt Lucas (Def) keeping a watchful eye over his every move, Walter makes faltering strides towards romance with a no-nonsense co-worker, Vicki (Sedgwick, Bacon's real-life spouse), who comes to terms with his past. But with neighbours making nervous glances in his direction and colleagues speculating on the source of his unease, Walter begins to find a familiar temptation on his road towards redemption.

Working from potent source material – a stage play by Steven Fechter elegantly transposed to the screen by Kassell and the playwright – *The Woodsman*'s heart and soul is an astonishing and courageous central performance from Kevin Bacon. The film's executive producer, Bacon has performed similar roles before, most luridly in Barry Levinson's

Sleepers (1996), but here is a model of understatement and restraint, capturing Walter's shame, self-loathing and crippling inwardness. Perhaps most remarkable is Bacon's playing of a scene where he tentatively bonds with a young child, an initially innocent encounter in which the actor's haunted eyes betray the flickering of a desire he is unable to suppress.

Shot in muted browns and greens in and around Philadelphia, there is a brief concession to colour in the fleeting glimpses of red, a reference to Nicolas Roeg's masterful *Don't Look Now* (1973), acknowledged by Kassell as an influence, especially in regard to the editing of the first sex scene between Walter and Vicki. The sole error of judgment is arguably its positioning of Walter in contrast to the far more sinister Candy (Kevin Rice), another serial offender who entices young boys into his car and then sodomises them; that apart, this is pretty much impeccable.

Dir: Nicole Kassell; **Prod**: Lee Daniels; **Scr**: Nicole Kassell, Steven Fechter; **DOP**: Xavier Pérez Grobet; **Editor**: Lisa Fruchtman, Brian A. Kates; **Score**: Nathan Larson; **Main Cast**: Kevin Bacon, Kyra Sedgwick, Mos Def, Benjamin Bratt.

Zoo
US, 2007 – 76 mins
Robinson Devor

Inspired by the events that led up to and preceded a much-publicised 2005 incident in the US, Robinson Devor's controversial *Zoo* explores the provocative issue of zoophilia and inter-species intercourse. A subject seldom explored on screen and one that is apt to inspire revulsion in many, this is undeniably difficult and uncomfortable viewing made slightly more palatable by the director's artistic aesthetic and thoughtful tone.

The small American town of Enumclaw is located in western Washington State. It was here, in July 2005, that a man was delivered anonymously to the local emergency room, suffering with a perforated colon. He later died from massive internal bleeding, and a subsequent investigation led to a nearby farm, where police discovered a number of videotapes, including several showing the dead man having sex with an Arabian stallion. It turned out that the man, known by the moniker 'Mr Hands' (real name K. Kenneth Pinyan), a forty-five-year-old Boeing engineer, had been part of a group that gathered together to perform and record similar acts. While many of the members of this group were identified and a media outcry ensued, no charges were filed because bestiality wasn't illegal in Washington at the time.

Distinctly non-sensationalist in its approach, one of the most striking aspects of *Zoo* is its ambiguity and meshing of fiction and documentary elements. Devor, making his first foray into narrative non-fiction, incorporates interviews with those who were directly and indirectly affected – friends of the deceased, animal advocates, law enforcement members, horse rescuers, urban and rural community members, and government officials – with impressionistic imagery to augment the interviews of those who do not wish to be seen on camera. Reminiscent of Errol Morris, it is these dramatic re-enactments that give the film its beguiling poetry and undeniable beauty.

Artistic but provocative, one of the reconstruction sequences in Robinson Devor's controversial *Zoo*

Claiming to reveal the mysteries and untold depths of a secret way of life and the enormous gulf between what we appear to be and who we really are, Devor, a native of Seattle, offers a momentarily captivating – in part due to the astonishing cinematography and use of the lush Pacific Northwest locations, and atmospheric, trance-like soundtrack – but ultimately frustrating work. Strangely sympathetic and non-judgmental in its humanising of the secret community who indulge their darkest fantasies, the film drew criticism from Jenny Edwards, the animal welfare campaigner who appears in the film, for omitting notable details that would have given both a more accurate picture of those involved and of the social, cultural or moral implications of the acts themselves. There is also something of a void, in that the film fails to engage more fully with the suffering of Pinyan's family.

Dir: Robinson Devor; **Prod**: Peggy Case, Alexis Ferris; **Scr**: Charles Maude; **DOP**: Sean Kirby; **Editor**: Joe Shapiro; **Score**: Paul Matthew Moore; **Main Cast**: Coyote Jenny Edwards, John Paulsen, John Edwards.

Bibliography

Alexander, Karen, Review of *Daughters of the Dust*, in Hillier, 2001.

Allon, Yoram, Del Cullen and Hannah Patterson (eds), *The Wallflower Critical Guide to Contemporary North American Directors* (London: Wallflower, 2000).

Anderson, Melissa, 'The Vagaries of Verities: On Shirley Clarke's *Portrait of Jason*', *Film Comment*, vol. 35, no. 6, November/December 1999.

Andrew, Geoff, *Stranger Than Paradise: Maverick Film-makers in Recent American Cinema* (London: Prion Books, 1998).

Armstrong, Dan, 'Wiseman's *Model* and Documentary Project: Toward a Radical Film Practice, *Film Quarterly*, vol. 37, no. 2, Winter 1984, quoted in an uncredited interview with Susan Seidelman, *New York Times*, 26 December 1982.

Atkinson, Mike, 'That's Entertainment', *Sight & Sound*, vol. 17, no. 4, April 2007.

Barrowclough, Susan, Review of *Born in Flames*, *Monthly Film Bulletin*, vol. 51, no. 601, February 1984.

Biskind, Peter, *Easy Riders, Raging Bulls* (New York: Simon & Schuster, 1998).

Boorman, John and Walter Donohue (eds), *The Director's Cut: The Best of Projections* (London: Faber & Faber, 2006).

Burn, Gordon, 'Rising Below Vulgarity', *Sight & Sound*, vol. 6, no. 12, December 1996.

Carney, Ray (ed.), *Cassavetes on Cassavetes* (London: Faber & Faber, 2001a).

Carney, Ray, *Shadows* (London: BFI Publishing, 2001b).

Cheshire, Ellen and John Ashbrook, *Joel and Ethan Coen* (Harpenden: Pocket Essentials, 2000).

Combs, Richard, Review of *Killer of Sheep*, *Monthly Film Bulletin*, vol. 49, no. 581, June 1977.

Cook, Pam (ed.), *The Cinema Book* (London: BFI Publishing, 1987).

DiCillo, Tom, *Living in Oblivion and Eating Crow: A Film-maker's Diary* (London: Faber & Faber, 1995).

Don't Look Back, Review (author uncredited), *Monthly Film Bulletin*, vol. 36, no. 428, September 1969.

Draper, Ellen, Review of *Sherman's March*, *Film Quarterly*, vol. 40, no. 3, Spring 1987.

Ebert, Roger, Review of *Boyz N the Hood*, *Chicago Sun-Times*, 12 July 1991.

Ebert, Roger, Review of *Hoop Dreams*, *Chicago Sun-Times*, 21 October 1994.

Felperin, Leslie, Review of *High Art*, *Sight & Sound*, vol. 9, no. 4, April 1999.

Field, Simon, Review of *Impostors*, *Monthly Film Bulletin*, vol. 49, no. 577, February 1982.

Fuchs, Christian, *Bad Blood: An Illustrated Guide to Psycho Cinema* (London: Creation Books, 1996).

Fuller, Graham, 'Finding the Essential', Hal Hartley interview in Hal Hartley, *Simple Men and Trust* (London: Faber & Faber, 1992).

Gidal, Peter, quoted on *Lonesome Cowboys*, *Millennium Film Journal*, no. 4/5, Summer/Autumn 1979.

Giles, Jane, 'Auteur of the OTT', *Guardian*, 16 February 1995.

Goodeve, Thyrza, Review of *Tongues Untied*, *Cinéaste*, vol. 18, no. 1, 1990.

Hillier, Jim (ed.), *American Independent Cinema: A Sight and Sound Reader* (London: BFI Publishing, 2001).

Hoberman, J., 'The Wrong Man', *Village Voice*, 30 August 1988.

Hoberman, J., 'Blood, Sweat and Tears', *Village Voice*, 5–11 July 2000a.

Hoberman, J., Review of *Two-Lane Blacktop* (re-release), *Village Voice*, 27 September–3 October 2000b.

Hoberman, J., Review of *Donnie Darko*, *Village Voice*, 24–30 October 2001 <www.villagevoice.com/issues/0143/hoberman.php>.

hooks, bel, 'Dreams of Conquest', *Sight & Sound*, vol. 5, no. 4, April 1995.

Jenkins, David, 'Independents' Day', *Time Out*, 23–9 October 2008.

Jenkins, Steve, Review of *Variety*, *Monthly Film Bulletin*, vol. 54, no. 604, May 1984.

Journal of the University Film and Video Association, vol. XXXV, no. 2, Spring 1983 (author uncredited).

Kemp, Philip, Review of *Clean, Shaven*, *Sight & Sound*, vol. 5, no. 2, February 1995.

Kemp, Philip, 'Mr Pink, Mr Indie, Mr Shh', *Sight & Sound*, vol. 11, no. 8, August 2001.

Kempley, Rita, Review of *Metropolitan*, *Washington Post*, 14 September 1990.

Keogh, Peter, 'Home and Away' (Jim Jarmusch interview), in Hillier, 2001.

Keyssar, Helene, *Robert Altman's America* (Oxford: Oxford University Press, 1991).

King, Stephen, Review of *The Evil Dead*, *Twilight Magazine*, November 1982.

Kleinhans, Chuck, 'Seeing through Cinéma Vérité', *Jump-Cut*, no. 1, May–June 1974.

Leigh, Danny, 'The Beat Up Kid', in Hillier, 2001.

Maher, Kevin, 'A dark beauty masks the cruel beauty of this film', *The Times*, 29 May 2008.

Millennium Film Journal, no. 4/5, Summer/Autumn 1979.

Mottram, James, *The Sundance Kids* (London: Faber & Faber, 2006).

Newman, Kim (ed.), *The BFI Companion to Horror* (London: Cassell, 1996).

Patterson, Richard, 'How to Make a Successful Feature for $22,315.92', *American Cinematographer*, vol. 64, no. 2, February 1983.

Pierson, John, *Spike, Mike, Slackers & Dykes: A Guided Tour across a Decade of Independent American Cinema* (London: Faber & Faber, 1996).

Pym, John, Review of *Angel City*, *Monthly Film Bulletin*, vol. 45, no. 528, January 1978.

Rayns, Tony, 'Chinese Boxes', *Monthly Film Bulletin*, vol. 49, no. 577, February 1985.

Renan, Sheldon, *An Introduction to the American Underground Film* (New York: E. P. Dutton, 1967).

Rich, B. Ruby, 'What's New Pussycat', *Village Voice*, 17 January 1995.

Rosen, Dan, with Peter Hamilton, *Off Hollywood: The Making and Marketing of Independent Films* (New York: Grove Press, 1990).

Rothman, William, *Documentary Film Classics* (Cambridge: Cambridge University Press, 1997).

Sarris, Andrew, 'The Village Voice', 21 September 1967, in Thompson and Gutman, 2001, p. 88.

Sarris, Andrew, *The American Cinema* (New York: Da Capo Press, 1968).

Sayles, John, *Thinking in Pictures: The Making of the Movie* Matewan (Boston, MA: Houghton Mifflin, 1987).

Smith, Gavin (ed.), *Sayles on Sayles* (London: Faber & Faber, 1998).

Soderbergh, Steven, *Getting Away with It, Or: The Further Adventures of the Luckiest Bastard You Ever Saw* (London: Faber & Faber, 1999).

Sweet, Louise, Review of *Sherman's March*, *Monthly Film Bulletin*, vol. 55, no. 654, July 1988.

Tartaglia, Jerry, 'The Gay Sensibility in American Avant-garde Film', *Millennium Film Journal*, no. 4/5, Summer/Autumn 1979.

Taubin, Amy, 'Girl n the Hood', in Hillier, 2001.

Thomas, Kevin, Review of *Heavy*, *Los Angeles Times*, 28 June 1996.

Thompson, Cliff, 'The Devil Beat His Wife: Small Moments and Big Statements in the Films of Charles Burnett', *Cinéaste*, vol. 13, no. 1, 1983.

Thompson, David and Ian Christie (eds), *Scorsese on Scorsese* (London: Faber & Faber, 1989).

Thompson, Elizabeth and David Gutman (eds), *The Dylan Companion* (New York: Delta Books, 1991).

Thomson, David, *Rosebud: The Story of Orson Welles* (London: Little Brown, 1996).

Thomson, David, *The New Biographical Dictionary of Film* (London: Little Brown, 2002 [4th edn]).

Winter, Jessica, *The Rough Guide to American Independent Film* (London: Rough Guides Ltd, 2006).

Wood, Jason, *Projections: The Directors* (London: Faber & Faber, 2006).

Zavarzadeh, Mas'ud, Review of *Smithereens*, *Film Quarterly*, vol. 37, no. 2, Winter 1984.

Video Materials

Anipare, Eileen and Jason Wood, *Trouble and Desire: An Interview with Hal Hartley*, 1997.

Rodley, Chris and Paul Joyce, *Made in the USA*, Lucida Productions (for Channel Four), 1994.

Websites

<www.thestickingplace.com>.

Index

Page numbers in **bold** indicate a film's main entry; those in *italic* denote illustrations.